D0221355

Trade Union Gospel

AMERICAN CIVILIZATION

A series edited by Allen F. Davis

Trade Union Gospel

CHRISTIANITY AND LABOR IN INDUSTRIAL PHILADELPHIA, 1865–1915

KEN FONES-WOLF

TEMPLE UNIVERSITY PRESS

Philadelphia

Temple University Press, Philadelphia 19122

Published 1989
Printed in the United States of America

The paper used in this publication meets the minimum requirements of American National Standard for Information Sciences—Permanence of Paper for Printed Library Materials, ANSI Z39.48-1984

Library of Congress Cataloging-in-Publication Data
Fones-Wolf, Ken.
Trade union gospel : Christianity and labor in industrial Philadelphia, 1865–1915 / Ken Fones-Wolf.
p. cm. — (American civilization)
Revision of the author's thesis (Ph.D.)—Temple University.
Bibliography: p.
Includes index.
ISBN 0-87722-652-0
1. Trade-unions and Christianity—Pennsylvania—Philadelphia—History. 2. Labor movement—Religious aspects—Christianity—History. 3. Church and labor—Pennsylvania—Philadelphia—History. 4. Labor movement—Pennsylvania—Philadelphia—History. I. Title. II. Series.
HD6519.P5F66 1989
331.88'09748'11—dc20 89-4622
CIP

Contents

Preface

THIS book began as an effort to explain the timing and significance of the Labor Forward Movement, the American Federation of Labor's attempt to use evangelicalism to organize workers in the years just prior to World War I. Nearly a decade ago, when Elizabeth Fones-Wolf and I uncovered this overlooked trade-union revival, there was little mention of it in the secondary literature. The movement struck us as an oddity, an anachronism that defied the conventional wisdom about religion and the labor movement. Our first coauthored investigation was really more of a survey than an analysis. Over the past six years as I have worked on this (aided by Elizabeth's insights and sound judgments), working-class religious sentiments received a good deal more scrutiny in the scholarly literature, but still not of the sort that leads to an understanding of the Labor Forward Movement.

The inadequacies of the scholarly literature prompted me to move far beyond the years of the trade-union revival for this study. Now convinced that Christianity was not of marginal importance to organized labor, I wanted to know what its true relevance was. Finding evidence that working-class religious sentiments were not formed in isolation from the dominant religious culture led me to wonder how churches and trade unions interacted over time. Specific questions quickly mounted: Why, in the Progressive Era, was organized labor's relationship to religion quite different from that which Herbert Gutman had described in the Gilded Age? Did working-class Christianity influence churches in the same way as did the beliefs of employers?

How did trade unionists interpret the messages of church leaders and what were the political results of labor's connections to Christianity? Throughout my research, I was guided by the suggestion of British historian Eileen Yeo, who has warned that scholars "have taken too little account of Christianity, not as the possession of any one social group, but as contested territory."

To begin to answer many of these questions, I felt it necessary to investigate a much longer time period than the years 1912–1916 that immediately surrounded the Labor Forward Movement. To understand the origins of the trade-union revival, I had to grasp something of the historical relationship of Christianity and the labor movement. But the Labor Forward Movement was also a string of *local* revivals. In addition to chronological breadth, I decided that the depth one can get through a local study was required. Consequently, my analysis of the timing and significance of the Labor Forward Movement came from an intense investigation of Philadelphia, the city with perhaps the longest union revival and a long string of important revival crusades. In the end, however, Philadelphia's Labor Forward Movement was only a small part of the study.

The real subject of this book, the social history of religion and the labor movement in Philadelphia from 1865 to 1915, suggests the variety of ways that Christianity mediated between the elite and working-class versions of American society. Religion and voluntary associations helped people accommodate themselves to, and at times resist, social change. Christianity provided a value system that helped contain industrial strife, but more through a process of negotiation than one of deception. Workers obtained many concessions, including the acceptance of trade unions as legitimate American institutions. If labor failed to build an idealized class-conscious movement, unionists could nevertheless point to many achievements. To accomplish anything, labor had to build a broad alliance; the embrace of Christian values, which were central to American culture, allowed unions to gather support from a much wider cross-section of the American people.

I have incurred many debts while completing this book. First and foremost, my debts are to archivists and librarians who have accumulated, made available, and helped me find relevant sources. The libraries and archives I visited during my research include: Paley Library and the Urban Archives Center, Temple University; the Historical Society of Pennsylvania; the Philadelphia Free Library; the Manuscripts Division and the general collections at the Library of Congress; the U.S. Department of Labor Library; the State Historical Society of Wisconsin; the Samuel Gompers Papers and McKeldin Library, University of Maryland; the Presbyterian Historical Society in Philadelphia; the Lutheran Seminary library in Mt. Airy (Philadelphia); the Jewish Archives Center in Philadelphia (now part of the Balch Institute for Ethnic Studies); the headquarters of the Philadelphia Council, AFL-CIO; and the University of Massachusetts at Amherst Library. Although I met excellent librarians and archivists at all of those institutions, several deserve special mention. Fred Miller of Temple's Urban Archives Center has compiled perhaps the premier urban archives in the country. Furthermore, he hired me to work there, a factor that did much to give this study its Philadelphia perspective. Fred Heuser of the Presbyterian Historical Society, Harry Miller and Jim Danky of the State Historical Society of Wisconsin, David Myers, formerly of the Library of Congress, and Charlotte Brown, formerly of the University of Maryland, were all extremely helpful.

This study began as a dissertation at Temple University. There, my advisor, Allen F. Davis, gently prodded me to improve my writing, expand my perspectives, and get it done. Morris J. Vogel urged me to clarify my ideas and helped me avoid facile generalizations about Philadelphia and urban history. Herbert Ershkowitz and Mike Harris facilitated my path through graduate school requirements and were generally supportive. Diane Koenker, now at the University of Illinois, taught me European labor history and exposed me to important works. The late Fred Zimring shared research and his own unique insights. Several fellow graduate students and friends offered useful advice and important encouragement. These include Lisa Waciega, Marc Gallicchio, Kathryn Meyer, and Karen Schoenewaldt. All of these mentors and friends deserve more thanks than they know.

Many scholars have been generous with their time and support. Stuart Kaufman, Jim Gilbert, Leslie Rowland, Joe Reidy, Ira Berlin, Craig Donegan, Pete Hoefer, and David Grimsted at the University of Maryland first expressed an interest in the Labor Forward Movement. Michael Frisch and Daniel Walkowitz pushed an earlier effort by Liz and myself to its limits. David Montgomery, Patricia Cooper, Brian Greenberg, and Ron Story critiqued several parts and products of my work surrounding religion and the labor movement. Bruce Laurie, Milton Cantor, and Walter Licht each gave most insightful readings of the entire manuscript. More recently, discussions of parts of this work with Gerald Friedman and Robert Weir at the University of Massachusetts, Bruce C. Nelson of Northern Illinois University, Sherri Broder at Boston College, and Sally Deutsch at MIT have sharpened some aspects of my thinking. The people at Temple University Press—Janet Francendese, David Bartlett, Terri Kettering, and Karen Schoenewaldt—have been models of patience, perception, and assistance. They have also been excellent people with whom to work.

Three people deserve special mention. Nick Salvatore of Cornell University has been an enthusiastic advocate of this work for some time while nevertheless serving as a perceptive critic. Elliott Shore has been a most patient but insistent friend as well as being an excellent sounding board for my ideas. He often kept me going on this project when my interest flagged. Finally, Elizabeth Fones-Wolf has been important to me in every way. Her own abilities as a historian made this work better at every stage; everything else about her made it fun and worthwhile.

This book is dedicated to my children, Colin and Kasey, to whom religion and labor have, until now, been foreign countries. I hope their generation does better.

Material that appeared earlier in Ken Fones-Wolf, "Employer Unity and the Crisis of the Craftsmen," *Pennsylvania Magazine of History and Biography* 107 (July 1983): 449–55, and in Ken Fones-Wolf, "Mass Strikes, Corporate Strategies: The Baldwin Locomotive Works and the Philadelphia General Strike of 1910," *Pennsylvania Magazine of History and Biography* 110

(July 1986): 447–57, is used by permission of the Historical Society of Pennsylvania.

Material that appeared earlier in Ken Fones-Wolf, "Religion and Trade Union Politics in the U.S., 1880–1920," *International Labor and Working Class History* no. 34 (Fall 1988): 39–55, is used by permission of the editors of *ILWCH.*

Material in Elizabeth and Kenneth Fones-Wolf, "Trade Union Evangelism: Religion and the AFL in the Labor Forward Movement, 1912–1916," in Michael H. Frisch and Daniel J. Walkowitz, eds., *Working Class America: Essays on Labor, Community, and American Society* (Urbana: University of Illinois Press, 1983), ch. 6, is used by permission of the University of Illinois Press.

Material that appeared earlier in Kenneth Fones-Wolf, "Revivalism and Craft Unionism in the Progressive Era: The Syracuse and Auburn Labor Forward Movements of 1913," *New York History* 63 (Oct. 1982): 389–416, is used by permission of the New York Historical Association.

Material that appeared earlier in Ken Fones-Wolf, "Contention and Christianity: Religion and the Labor Movement in Philadelphia, 1890–1920," in Vincent Mosco and Janet Wasko, eds., *Critical Communications Review: Popular Culture and Media Events* (Norwood, N.J.: Ablex Publishing Corporation, 1985), ch. 3, is used by permission of the Ablex Publishing Corporation.

Introduction

BETWEEN 1912 and 1916, trade unionists in more than 150 cities and towns across the United States launched organizing drives drawing on the sentiments, tactics, and even the name utilized by a Protestant revival crusade, the Men and Religion Forward Movement. Prominent labor activists of both Protestant and Catholic backgrounds supported labor's evangelism, which itself represented the American Federation of Labor's most ambitious effort to expand its power and improve its public stature in the Progressive Era. Even so unlikely a proponent as Samuel Gompers, a Jewish immigrant, testified to the importance of establishing the AFL's links to Christianity; he asserted that a campaign of trade-union revivals would "give a tremendous impetus" to the organization of workers and "carry an incalculable chain of influences and results" for the labor movement.[1]

Little in the scholarly literature on American trade unionism helps explain the timing or importance of the Labor Forward Movement. Rarely have historians seen Christianity as a positive force for working-class movements. Indeed, even the earliest theorists on the role of religion in a modern, class-differentiated society—Karl Marx, Max Weber, Emile Durkheim—posited Christianity as a bulwark of capitalism. To these early theorists, religious values either were part of an ideological superstructure that reflected and contributed to the existing capitalist mode of production, or were "social facts," the moral rules a society creates to "shape individual consciousness and behavior."[2] In either case, Christianity contributed mightily to legitimating the status quo.

Recent historians of labor–capital conflict in the United States have contributed to and expanded the insights of Marx, Weber, and Durkheim, but have not challenged their basic assumptions. Paul Johnson, for instance, in his study of religious revivals in Rochester, New York, argues forcefully for the role of Christianity in establishing the moral authority of the middle class and in creating a mood of internalized restraint—developments that proved beneficial to the emerging system of capitalist wage labor. More importantly, Johnson asserts that the revivals won converts from the working class, thus establishing a new consensus of values.[3] Similarly, most other scholars argue that religion was firmly on the side of capitalist development. From the early mill villages to the twentieth-century steel and metal-working cities of Pittsburgh, Pennsylvania and Worcester, Massachusetts, religion promoted such values as temperance and hard work, which were central to capitalist labor discipline and reinforced harmonious but deferential relationships between employers and workers. In American society, according to the conventional wisdom, the free moral agency of evangelical Protestantism facilitated the efforts of employers to deal harshly with those refusing to bend to the rules of the new industrial order.[4]

A second related theme in the literature on religion and organized labor concerns the ways that diverse religious beliefs blocked the development of a unified working-class movement. Worker loyalties to denomination, persuasion, or creed heightened ethnic, gender, and nationalistic differences among wage earners. Irish, German, and Polish Catholics competed with German and Anglo-American Protestants in the labor market and eventually in the streets for the precarious security of job and neighborhood.[5] Pietistic working women interested in gender equality and domesticity contested the union leadership of chauvinistic men who held meetings in saloons and ignored female interests.[6] Moreover, one of the most persistent charges leveled against working-class radicalism by both middle-class and working-class political liberals (whether Protestant or Catholic) had to do with the irreligion of socialism and anarchism.[7]

In the confusion that characterized the new industrial society, workers often allied with employers of their same religion rather than with workers of different faiths with whom they shared the same occupation or class. Churches of various sorts frequently nourished a cultural perspective that pitted temperate, industrious wage earners against their rowdy, indulgent counterparts in the political arena. Issues of alcohol use and Sabbath observance at times overshadowed economic concerns on election day. Finally, religious affiliation both mirrored and reinforced the status hierarchies based on skill and wage differentials within the working class: Protestant craft workers often identified more closely with the middle class than with the poorer, Catholic, or non-churchgoing unskilled workers.[8] Religion, then, frequently cut across divisions based on ethnicity, leisure pursuits, gender, job opportunities, and political perspectives in a highly complex fashion but with remarkably static results. Whatever other purposes religion had, in industrial America it contributed greatly to the fragmentation of the working class.

The late Herbert Gutman provided the principal counterpoint to the dominant interpretations of the relationship between religion and the rise of modern labor movements. Two decades ago, Gutman awakened historians to the importance of Protestantism as a source of critique and empowerment for working-class movements. Traditional Christian values actually "heightened rather than obliterated the moral dilemmas of a new social order." For late nineteenth-century wage earners, Protestantism was a bridge to preindustrial American reform. It offered a premillennial idiom for predicting the doom of a "hell-born" system of capitalist wage labor. Protestant perfectionism also provided labor activists with a postmillennial justification of trade unionism as exemplary of Christ's true teachings. For Gilded-Age workers, the Christian morality of trade unionism was nothing less than "a protest against the mammonizing interpretation of religious truth"; the suffering of Jesus paralleled the trials of contemporary labor activists; "the Holy Writ" substantiated basic trade-union logic—"in unity there is strength."[9]

In Gutman's hands, Christianity took on a greater complexity. Religion ceased to be the property of capitalism alone. Instead, the values and sentiments of Protestantism became areas of contention between employers and workers.[10] Labor activists utilized their own reading of Scripture and their own popular interpretation of Jesus' teachings to criticize industrial capitalism. Organized labor's connection to Christian morality, then, became a "legitimizing notion" for its activities, broadening the range of political discourse.

As brilliant as Gutman's reformulation of religion's interaction with the labor movement was, it left several stones unturned. First, just what was the political effect of labor's Protestant rhetoric? Gutman suggested that working-class religious expression had little connection to the social gospel of middle- and upper-class critics of industrialism. They were parallel rather than interactive developments, he argued, implying that for all of the succor workers might draw from Protestantism, the Progressive-Era labor reform inspired by middle-class social Christianity owed nothing to trade unionism.[11] Secondly, evangelical Protestantism was the outlook of a transitional group of labor leaders, according to Gutman. Christian inspiration did not "grow with or into modern society." By 1900, labor's religious idiom had disappeared, sacrificed to a secularized urban industrial order.[12]

Another factor compounded the inability of Gutman's work to account for the timing and significance of the Labor Forward Movement—the role of Catholicism. Gutman argued for the transformative power of Protestantism for Gilded-Age wage earners, but after 1900 the urban working class was increasingly Catholic. The frequent episodes of nativistic politics and Catholic–Protestant hostility in American history made it seem unlikely that a predominately Catholic labor movement would turn to Protestant-inspired mechanisms to revitalize a sagging trade-union movement. Consequently, labor historians, when they mention the importance of religion at all in the Progressive Era, focus principally on Catholicism.[13]

The tremendous energy that the AFL and local labor activists expended on the Labor Forward Movement, however, suggests the need to rethink the role of Christianity in the early twentieth-century American labor movement. Such a rethinking must begin with the premise that religion was truly a contested terrain. Christianity promoted progressive change as well as conservative inaction. Religious sentiments, as historian William G. McLoughlin has noted, periodically revitalized American culture with awakenings "to overcome jarring disjunctions between norms and experience, old beliefs and new realities, dying patterns and emerging patterns of new behavior." These awakenings, moreover, typically resulted in constructive personal and social action.[14] Progressive-Era reform movements, to which trade-union evangelism was inextricably linked, exemplified one of these cultural awakenings, one that transformed the laissez-faire political economy of early industrial capitalism into a liberal program of legislation and government intervention intended to stabilize the new industrial order. And Social-Gospel Christianity played a major role in creating the atmosphere for constructive social action.[15]

A second premise crucial to reformulating the relationship of religion and labor concerns the importance and autonomy of working-class religious beliefs. If religious awakenings were related to social change, individual convictions cannot be reduced simply to a category of secular, social analysis. The religious beliefs of wage earners did not conform automatically to their political and economic interests. In addition, workers who followed the conservative evangelicalism of a Dwight L. Moody or a Billy Sunday were not victims of false consciousness. In most cases, religious beliefs preceded political commitments. Furthermore, working-class followers of Moody and Sunday subjected their messages to a critical scrutiny.

Related to the first two premises is the notion that religion was a dynamic force, not a fixed system of doctrine. Mainstream churches and clergy were capable of altering their social views when they confronted other social forces and realities—in this case, class. The middle-class Social Gospel, I argue, emerged as much from interaction with working-class activists who employed sophisticated criticisms of those churches that supported an inequitable and unjust social order as it did from theological developments and the advent of Darwinian science. Middle-class women and men with sincere religious convictions displayed a remarkable ability to cooperate with popular social movements when their interests overlapped. To cite one example, Russell Conwell—no friend of organized labor—convened trade-union meetings in his Baptist Temple when the bakers and barbers sought support for a Sabbath day of rest.[16]

Just as it is important to acknowledge the dynamic character of religion, so is it necessary to recognize that there are various types of religious expression. Without resorting to the rigidity or the dichotomies of church and sect to analyze religious experience, I believe that labor activists expressed Christian sentiments in different ways than did middle- and upper-class Christians.[17] Among the characteristics of labor's religiosity were a greater reliance on direct Scriptural inspiration, a limiting of social contacts to the fellowship of believers, a lack of concern for such traditional gauges of religiosity as church attendance or participation in church voluntary associations, and a belief that religion should lead to an alternative social and political order. Although it coincided with more popular or sect-like religious behavior, however, the two were not inextricably and unalterably linked. Rather, organized labor's popular Christianity was on a continuum of religious expression, with church and sect representing the extremes.[18] Furthermore, because of the dominant religious culture's dynamism, the popular religion of labor activists also moved considerably along that continuum.

A final premise pertains to the importance of the dominant Protestant religious culture in late nineteenth- and early twentieth-century America. Despite the labor movement's growing Catholicism, trade unionists felt that building widespread support for organized labor's social, political, and economic goals rested on their ability to tap connections to mainstream churches and religious leaders. And for labor prior to the first world war, Protestant churches offered far more legitimacy and political influence than did Catholic churches.[19] Consequently, Irish-Catholic trade unionists were the staunchest defenders of interaction with Protestant ministers. Catholic labor leaders and Protestant clergy shared the podium at public events, exchanged fraternal delegates, and spoke approvingly of one another's goals.

The dominant religious culture, however, also framed the boundaries of legitimate political debate and action. Labor's quest for support in American society meant that it had to adhere to certain cultural rules as defined in large part by Protestant churches. Most Protestants disapproved of boycotts, violent strikes, rowdy behavior, drunkenness, and radical politics. Those trade unionists wishing to win the churches' approbation then had to reject those practices and distance themselves from large parts of the working class still attracted to those practices. Craft unionism in particular thus placed the agenda of reform, with all of its cultural rules, above a program of class solidarity.

These premises are critical to understanding the interaction of organized labor and Christianity in the half-century following the Civil War. The culmination of this interaction in the Labor Forward Movement was not an aberration, but the result of considerable flexibility on the part of Christian activists and trade unionists, a flexibility that speaks to the inadequacy of earlier explanations of religion's impact on modern labor movements.

Guided by the premises outlined here, this study explores the interaction of Christianity and trade unionism in Philadelphia from 1865 to 1915. It would be convenient if I could paraphrase the now-famous article by Sam Bass Warner, Jr., and state that "all the world was Philadelphia."[20] Such is unfortunately not the case. Nevertheless, studying one specific city enabled me to examine relationships between churches and labor organizations, between Catholic and Protestant workers, and between religious sentiments and social conditions in ways and over a period of time that a national study would have precluded. The fact that Philadelphia was home to such an impressive array of religious and labor figures of national importance—Russell Conwell, Samuel Zane Batten, Edwin Heyl Delk, Frank Feeney, Denis Hayes, Harry Parker, Thomas Phillips—will suggest that a local study can have wider applications and contribute to more general conclusions. Where I have found the local situation to touch on broader national trends and substantiate claims I make for Philadelphia, I have indicated.

The Philadelphia example confirms that, indeed, Christianity was not merely the possession of one social group, but rather was a dynamic social force capable of complementing a wide spectrum of political and class positions. Far from imposing a single way of understanding the moral rules of the new system of capitalist wage labor, Christianity itself underwent transformations in the fifty years following the Civil War. The autonomous power Philadelphians invested in religion meant that neither labor nor capital could expect the churches to consistently support their objectives. Instead, each side made claims upon Christianity for justification and legitimacy. By representing a set of ideal aspirations commonly accepted by most Philadelphians, religion both mediated social tensions and served as an arena for class conflict throughout the period. But if Christianity was not merely the domain of capital, it did impose limits within which conflict could legitimately occur.

Trade Union Gospel

1

Work and Workers in Industrial Philadelphia

WHEN Edwin Cooke and George Collins entered factories to take their first jobs in the 1870s, they were carrying on family traditions that could be traced back for generations. Cooke, who later migrated to Philadelphia, went into a Kidderminster, England, carpet mill as had his father and grandfather. Beginning as a creeler, he expected to work his way up to a loom and become a skilled weaver, like his forebears. Collins was a fourth-generation shoemaker, a skilled laster who had "no desire but to be a good laster and to make a good living at lasting." In contrast to Cooke and Collins, the experiences of Edward Keenan and Lucinda Hall were quite different. Like many of their Philadelphia contemporaries, Keenan broke with the dominant occupations of his Irish ancestors for the opportunity to learn a trade in the rapidly expanding machine tool industry. Hall likewise benefited from industrialization, joining the growing numbers of daughters of Kensington immigrants who comprised the power-loom carpet industry in the 1870s. Both escaped the unskilled, low-paying trades in which women and Irish immigrants had formerly been concentrated.[1]

In important ways, each of these young people was crossing a chasm that would divide their working lives from those of their parents. Unlike his forefathers, Collins found it progressively difficult to maintain the high wages and artisan working conditions of a laster in an industry increasingly dominated by the new machinery of the late nineteenth century. By 1900 he had moved several times, merely postponing his eventual decline to the steady but lower wages of a Philadelphia shoe factory employee. Cooke also entered an industry increasingly shaped by technology. By 1886, after he had migrated to Philadelphia and had become a weaver, the power loom had replaced the handloom of his father's era. Competing for many of these machine-tending jobs however, were women like Hall, for whom weaving was an advancement. Keenan, like Hall, also benefited from the expansion of machinery in the Gilded Age. He earned high wages, enjoyed steady employment, and continued to have a good deal of autonomy in his work. Yet he too witnessed the negative discipline of modern industry. In many larger shops machinists learned how to work only one machine, producing standardized parts. The resultant loss of job autonomy and the threat of replacement by less-skilled, lower-paid workers was always present.[2]

For these four people and many like them, the last quarter of the nineteenth century was a time of challenge. Philadelphia's industrial base, mirroring that of the nation generally, developed unevenly: certain industries declined and were replaced by others, that experienced dynamic growth. Mechanization intruded into the lives of many workers, yet other occupations remained untouched by technology or new power sources. While the scale of production increased dramatically, more than a third of Philadelphia's workforce labored in small shops until the end of the century. Despite the persistance of certain pre-industrial traditions, new trends were being established. Larger, more capital-intensive firms attained superior positions in the labor market and expanded rapidly. These new, concentrated establishments divided the tasks of labor and reduced skill levels, thus wresting control of production from their workers. Industrial giants, like Stetson's hats, Wanamaker's garment business, Baldwin Locomotives, Cramp's Shipyard, and Dobson's textile mills, became an ominous presence in Philadelphia's industrial landscape in metalworking, textiles, and clothing.[3]

In the tremendous industrial diversity of Gilded-Age Philadelphia, workers scrambled for the best opportunities. Children of craftsmen in declining industries either sought new occupations or formed organizations to resist the transformation of their inherited trades. Concurrently, children of unskilled, poorly paid factory workers often secured formal and informal apprenticeships in burgeoning new trades and industries. This shift upward, which allowed the children of many native and immigrant workers a chance to improve their lot, nevertheless robbed artisans of the possibility of bequeathing stable prosperous crafts. Between industries and within industries, dynamic change significantly altered the conditions and status of both skilled and unskilled workers.[4]

The Economy and Local Industry

In April 1872, local statistician Lorin Blodget reported on the census of industrial employment, wages, and social conditions in the city to the Philadelphia Social Science Association. The city seemed primed for sustained economic growth and prosperity. According to Blodget, the skill and intelligence of the workforce, the good wages in a diversity of industries, and the development of machinery and power sources appeared to offer boundless opportunities for expansion.[5] He could not have guessed that within two years the city would be caught in a major national depression, one result of the violent fluctuations in the American economy that would mold the next quarter century. Continued severe downturns in the economy wreaked havoc on wage earners. Long bouts of unemployment, frequent wage reductions, and new discipline in the workplace displaced and impoverished thousands. The few private relief agencies struggled under the weight of unprecedented numbers of needy people, and the city's elite lived in dread of social agitators.[6]

The instability of the worker's world was, in part, the result of the onset of a period of worldwide economic stagnation. Ironically, the previous period of economic growth in America, stretching from the 1840s to the 1870s, generated the crisis that enveloped the next two decades. The unchecked industrial expansion prior to the 1870s provoked intense competition, which resulted in a decline in both prices and profit margins. Furthermore, growth had occurred through the tapping of new sources of labor, particularly women and immigrants, rather than from altering production methods to intensify labor productivity. The resulting long-wave stagnation in the economy brought sharp depressions in 1873–79, 1882–85, and 1893–97. Between 1883 and 1897, businesses failed at a rate unequalled even in the depression of the 1930s.[7]

Within this general stagnation, some industries did worse than others. In consumer industries like clothing and shoemaking, competition was especially intense: To survive, firms often slashed wages and increased their size, in many cases forcing competitors out of business. Small-scale production persisted in these industries, but increasingly the older artisanal settings became little more than sweatshops, with wages often below the level of semiskilled labor in other trades.

Industries concentrating on producer goods, like machine tools, chemicals, and fuel, were less affected by economic stagnation. Already highly capitalized with large-scale organization by 1880, firms in these industries averted the intense competition and falling prices that characterized consumer industries. The rise of industries like electrical equipment, chemicals, and machinery, which would be the backbone of American economic expansion for succeeding generations, enabled some to view this era as a second industrial revolution. The large scale and expensive machinery encouraged these industries to pay good wages even to unskilled machine tenders rather than have highly priced capital equipment damaged by carelessness or lie idle.[8]

Throughout the Gilded Age, employers experimented with new ways to organize production and reduce costs. One method, an increasingly large scale of enterprise, facilitated greater control over raw materials, product marketing, and the pace and division of labor. Exemplified in Philadelphia by Dobson's textile mills, Cramp's shipyards, and the Baldwin Locomotive Works, these larger factories captured local and regional labor markets by recruiting new workers, thus forcing labor into competition as employers reduced wages. The 1870s and 1880s witnessed the beginnings of the consolidation of capital that would greatly accelerate during the merger movement of the 1890s. The number of publicly traded industrial securities grew dramatically in the 1880s, as the path to success through a small or undercapitalized family enterprise became increasingly difficult.[9]

Another route to expansion in the late nineteenth century was reliance on new mass production techniques that utilized technological and managerial innovations. Continuous process machines and the reorganization of the factory sharply reduced the number of workers required to produce a specific unit of output. Growing industries tended to become both capital intensive and management intensive: Since the introduction of machinery by itself could increase production only incrementally, efficient factory design and the development of managerial practices were necessary to take full advantage of dynamic technological change and achieve unprecedented rates of productivity.[10]

Some industries were better suited than others to adapt the new technology. In mechanical industries like clothing, textiles, leather, and wood products, machinery replaced the manual operations in sewing, weaving, or cutting. But beyond this initial introduction of machinery and reorganization of the factory into specialized units, the possibilities of accelerating production were limited. Some machines increased speed, but they were still labor intensive.

Truly significant advances occurred in metalmaking, distilling, and refining, where production processes required the application of heat and involved chemicals rather than machines. Here, "improved technology, a more intensified use of energy, and improved organization greatly expanded the speed of throughput," eliminating many workers from the production process. Finally, the metalworking industries initiated improvements in both mechanical and chemical processes, which put them at the forefront of the most significant changes in both machine tools and the application of modern scientific factory management techniques. In the Nicetown section of Philadelphia, for example, the large number of metalworking firms—Midvale Steel, the Niles Bement

Company, and William Sellers's precision instrument factory—pioneered workplace discipline and reorganization.[11]

Both through concentration and the use of mass-production techniques, then, employers attempted to gain greater control over their workforces. The increase in management personnel far outstripped that in production, and the segmentation and reorganization of the factory enabled employers to enforce a stricter discipline. But this innovation was largely confined to firms at the cutting edge of the transformation of industry and labor during the last quarter of the nineteenth century. More typically, factory concentration and mechanization produced neither immediate economies of scale nor secure firms dominating their own industries. Manufacturers hoped to stay competitive by reducing labor costs, but were thwarted by worker resistance, the lack of capital, the slow spread of technology, and insufficient managerial expertise.[12] Well into the 1910s many workers retained control of their labor and resisted attempts to reduce production costs, even as market competition slashed prices.

Ironically, Philadelphia's earlier development actually impeded its expansion into the new dynamic industries. Between 1869 and 1899 the city's percentage of value added by manufacture dropped in relation to the national figure. Philadelphia's early concentration and growth in industries that could not take advantage of the full potential of mass production techniques worsened its relative position. Despite technological improvements and increased scales of production, these powerful textile, clothing, and shoe firms, typified by Dobson's, Strawbridge and Clothier, and Mundell, increased their profits not by significantly lowering the cost of production per unit, but by employing more and more low-paid workers.[13]

Philadelphia maintained its reputation for small shop production and family-owned, as opposed to corporate, enterprise. The city's industrial giants—Stetson's hats, Cramp's Shipyards, and Disston's saw works—were all family businesses, and textile capitalism, which was Philadelphia's largest industrial sector, was largely a family affair. Many of the potential pioneers in large-scale production did not have the experience or knowledge to manage unwieldy work forces, allocate resources, or rearrange production methods. Consequently, Philadelphia remained hospitable to small-scale, flexible production methods long after the degradation of self-regulating craftsmanship elsewhere.[14] From the numerous small firms that maintained a tenacious hold in segments of the city's economy to the immense Baldwin works in the Spring Garden section of the city, old production methods died slowly. Baldwin's continued its traditional methods of inside contracting, whereby expert workers assembled crews, bid on jobs, organized production, and distributed profits.[15]

The earning potential for workers varied greatly in this transitional economy. Dynamic urban industries like metalworking offered higher annual earnings than consumer industries like shoes. Such traditional crafts as printing and construction fell in between. There was likewise tremendous variation within a given industry, a worker's wages often determined by the size of the firm and its strength in the market. In many industries, the larger the firm, the higher the average salary. Contrary to the usual assumption, the adaptation of some trades to the factory system actually allowed workers to prosper because the use of steam power still demanded much hand technology. Large-scale production included many skilled workers who exerted artisan-like control within the factory setting and commanded wages reflecting the prosperity of the company. Even more striking is the fact that unskilled workers in large factories and rapidly growing industries often garnered wages nearly as high as those in older crafts and small workshops. While a substantial differential remained between the earnings of skilled and unskilled workers within industries, the degraded state of many crafts reduced these now-nominal artisans to the status of sweated workers.[16]

Although the decline of certain trades like butchering, tailoring, and cabinetmaking was the bane of the ethnic groups controlling those crafts, the transition in the economy profited others. In Philadelphia, second-generation German-Americans left the furniture industry, which their fathers had controlled, as conditions declined. Many attempted to enter the expanding machinist craft, but met stiff competition from the Irish-American sons of laborers in metalworking plants. Similarly, Irish sons no longer favored the textile industry, but instead parlayed experience on a construction site into an informal building trades apprenticeship. In such shifting, the children of many occupationally limited ethnic workers may have benefited from abandoning the dying artisanal crafts.[17]

In nearly all industries, only a few earned enough to maintain an adequate standard of living and still have money to survive difficult times. Such a tenuous existence was especially challenged during the severe economic slumps that plagued the last quarter of the century. For example, the average male annual wage in 1900 for all Philadelphia was $532, yet twenty years earlier, a sound estimate of the adequate standard of living for a family of five ran over $600. Skilled building trades workers reported a wide range of annual earnings to the state secretary of internal affairs, with many earning over $700, but significant numbers earning less than $500.[18]

An 1887 investigation by the state labor bureau offered clues on how workers sustained their families under such conditions. Of forty-four workers questioned, seventeen lived in households where there was more than one wage earner. Indeed, one textile worker who made only $360 lived in a family of six, where three others combined their incomes to total $1,315. Similarly, a file worker who made $500 lived with a sister who made $360; together they were able to purchase a home. Other families, especially young ones, lived a marginal existence until children were of working age. An English-born weaver with a wife and three young children reduced his family's living expenses to $561 in 1886; despite privation he was still ten dollars short for the year.[19]

Yet Philadelphia's industrial base was particularly well suited to the family economy. By 1900, one of every four industrial workers was a woman; by 1914 the ratio was over three of every ten. The low wages of the daughters and young sons who flocked into the clothing and textile industries were often just enough to push families over the subsistence level. Surprisingly, a 1915 investigation of an Italian garment district in center city found that over 14 percent of the families made enough to purchase their home. Significantly, the five homeowners responding to the state labor bureau investigation in 1887 all reported earnings from other family members.[20]

Taking in boarders provided another source of family income. A study of family budgets in Kensington revealed that significant numbers of households augmented their earnings by renting space and providing meals for a nonfamily member. Consequently, despite the heavy concentration of Philadelphia's industrial workers in low-wage occupations, many wage-earning families had a total income somewhat above the standard. This was especially true for unskilled workers and immigrants who filled the lower rungs of the occupational ladder but who had a far higher percentage of multiple-income families and boarders.[21]

Philadelphia publicists bragged of the city's lower cost of living and uncrowded conditions. Henry B. Gombers, a steam fitter, claimed that workers in his trade earned a dollar less per day than they would in some cities, but lived better. "We have instances where Philadelphia men have been sent to New York [where they received $3.75 a day, but] complained of not having as much money in their pockets as they did in Philadelphia," Gombers told the 1900 U.S. Industrial Commission. As far as housing was concerned, there was a great measure of truth in these assertions. In both 1893 and 1909, housing rents in Philadelphia were nearly a dollar less per week than those in New York and Chicago, and substantially lower than Boston, Cincinnati, or St. Louis. Philadelphia's reputation as the "city of homes" owed much to its horizontal rather than vertical development, which also allowed a lower incidence of tenements and overcrowded districts. The number of occupants per Philadelphia dwelling was one-third that of New York's average and 25 to 40 percent less than Boston.[22]

The advantages of a lower cost of living and the opportunities in the family economy, however, could not offset the poverty of most Philadelphia wage earners. Figures on persons per dwelling seriously underestimate the lack of decent living conditions. In some districts entire families lived in one-room apartments where plumbing and sanitary conditions were woefully inadequate. Philadelphia's mortality rate was higher than any major city except Boston, and more than one of every four children died in infancy. Many of the homes about which Philadelphians bragged were two- or three-room alley dwellings with little access to clean air and light. Nearly 15 percent of the population in 1880 received some assistance from public and voluntary relief agencies, although this considerably underrepresents the actual number of people in need.[23]

The tenuous financial status of Philadelphia wage earners was exacerbated by the unstable economy. Major economic slumps brought persistent agitation for public works projects. Even those who through stringent economy were able to put aside some savings frequently had them wiped out by periods of unemployment that could last six months or longer. In 1915, Kensington settlement worker Robert Bradford noted the effects of an almost chronic state of unemployment in his district: "If it is not one industry, it is another. If one mill escapes, another is hit. The fear of unemployment and part time employment hangs, a permanent pall, over Kensington."[24]

Thus, the condition of Philadelphia's working class remained insecure into the twentieth century. In the aggregate, falling prices and slowly rising wages led to a positive improvement in real wages and earnings. But the uneven process of economic development tended to benefit some industries at the expense of others, and occupational differentials within industries widened. Consequently, the elite of the working class, often called the "labor aristocracy," profited far more than most wage earners.[25] Certain other factors in the city economy—the family economy, lower housing costs, less crowded conditions—somewhat eased the precarious existence of the rest. Still, the vast majority of marginally stable working-class families were barely removed from disaster. A death in the family, injury, the loss of a job, a downturn in the economy—all common occurrences in an industrial city—could plunge a household into dire circumstances.[26] The quest for some sort of financial security was the driving force of Philadelphia's working class.

The aggregate picture actually reveals little about the new

industrial conditions causing so much turmoil among Philadelphia's workers. The fragile status of the working class was not new to the late nineteenth century. At a much earlier date, most city dwellers had joined the wage-earning class and had become inextricably linked to the fluctuations of business cycles. What made the turn of the century so unsettling to workers was change at the workplace. In the effort to survive the competition of a dynamic industrial society, capitalists subjected their employees to a discipline and control unheard of a generation earlier. Besides the technological change that made traditional skills obsolete, workers faced speed-ups in output that taxed the limits of human endurance. New corporate structures and bureaucratized production reduced the older, more intimate contact between master and journeyman to the impersonal relationships of the cash nexus. The interplay of market forces, new technologies, and corporate strength overwhelmed many traditional artisans.

Varieties of Work Experiences

It was in this atmosphere that young men like Edwin Cooke and George Collins witnessed the disappearance of the world of their fathers. Their workplace experiences forged new perspectives on the progress of capitalist society from the traditions and culture of the skilled worker. While some clung to the autonomy crucial to their traditional notions of citizenship and "manhood," others fought a losing battle against a seemingly faceless enemy that threatened their status and stability. Whatever their perspective, nearly all workers witnessed the changes overtaking the wage earner. A brief survey of several types of work experience offers insight into the forces shaping and impeding working-class mobilization.

Degraded Crafts

When Philadelphia cabinetmakers struck for an eight-hour workday in June of 1872, they were attempting to preserve their craft independence. One cabinetmaker complained that "the workingman was treated as a commodity, which was contrary to man's being a human being." Strike leader William Derrick pointed to the "un-American arrogance" of employers who ignored the recent Pennsylvania eight-hour law. He told Kensington workers that everyone, including employers, should be "law-abiding citizens." The craftsmen, principally of German origin, claimed that a shorter workday would allow them to fulfill their family responsibilities and the duties of citizenship, which included cultural and educational improvement. So enmeshed were they in traditional artisan thought that rather than take their tools, which they still owned, out of the shop, they left them on the bench to reserve their places.[27]

By late June, however, the cabinetmakers engaged in a very different sort of rhetoric. Led by members of the German branch of the International Workingmen's Association, they asserted their opposition to a system of exploitation that extracted "surplus labor" from workers. An eight-hour league, formed by strikers, marched from shop to shop encouraging other workers to "down their tools." The craftsmen turned on their ethnic press, which supported the largely German employers, and a riot broke out at a German picnic, prompting the arrest of several strikers who fought with furniture manufacturers and their sympathizers. Employers countered by threatening to throw the tools of their workers into the street.[28]

Furniture making, as this struggle shows, was in the process of change. Between 1850 and 1880, small artisan shops, which produced higher-priced furniture for local consumption, were giving way to factory production. Nearly 45 percent of craftsmen in 1880 worked in factories where steam or water power increased production, enabling manufacturers to expand their markets. Although Philadelphia never became a large producer of furniture (the number of workers in the industry remained at about 3,000), the transformation of the workplace accelerated over the next generation. By 1900, three of every four furniture workers labored in a factory of over fifty employees, each using the employer's tools and machinery. Wages, which had outstripped most trades in 1850 but had dropped to the city average by 1880, continued their downward trend.[29]

The work experience of most furniture workers in 1910 was radically different from that of 1880. The U.S. Commissioner of Labor found seventeen separate jobs in factory production, many of them unskilled, compared to the four skilled jobs characterizing hand production. Even furniture made by hand showed the influence of the factory; employers divided tasks and local shops survived by paying factory wages to skilled artisans.[30] Worsening conditions caused the Germans who led the 1872 eight-hour strike to discourage their children from entering the trade, and furniture production became increasingly the domain of new, less-skilled immigrants.[31] German artisan traditions, forged in workshops and neighborhoods, had placed such craftsmen in the forefront of the working-class movement in the 1870s; by 1900, new factory workers in the stagnant industry had little leverage and even less of a culture with which to fight.

Employers in other Philadelphia industries followed the strategies of furniture manufacturers. Especially in light consumer trades like shoemaking, hatting, and clothing, employers concentrated production, subdivided tasks, and enlarged their workforces without making significant investments in machinery. Manufacturers could not completely abolish skilled labor in such settings, but earning potential and autonomy in the degraded crafts were increasingly limited by national markets and factory production.

Labor unions unsuccessfully fought the decline of these crafts. Hatting and clothing manufacturers in particular exploited new ethnic groups or gender divisions to solidify their control of production. In Philadelphia, John Stetson's immense hat establishment not only divided production into simple tasks, but parcelled each task to specific ethnic groups to foster competition among workers. Similarly, garment factories employed German and Irish men in relatively well-paid fabric cutting positions and used Italians, Jews, and women for lower-paying assembly work. By 1900, employers could count on status, ethnic, and gender hierarchies to block the mobilization of workers in degraded crafts. Former artisans frequently blamed new immigrants as much as their employers for their declining position. Both United Hatters leader Edward Moore and Garment Workers leader Tunie Symonds attempted to rebuild their craft unions by banning immigrants from the trade. But unions could not repel such overriding forces as industry concentration, subdivided labor, and national markets.[32]

Industrial Labor

The gradual decline of craftsmanship in the light consumer goods industries invoked fierce resistance on the part of many former artisans. Yet, in many industries of the late nineteenth and early twentieth centuries, craft traditions were either nonexistent or easily destroyed. Steel production, sugar and petroleum refining, brewing, and chemical manufacturing so completely mechanized and reorganized production that the necessary level of human skill was reduced to a minimum. In steel, for instance, such technological breakthroughs as the Bessemer converter and the ability to make a steel with the quality of iron in an open-hearth furnace, allowed for the "integration of every process from the blast furnace to the loading platform."[33] Former skilled workers in iron production, such as puddlers and rollers, were replaced by less-skilled workers at vastly reduced wages.

The impulse for economy provided the driving logic for these industries to initiate continuous production. Steelmakers concentrated production into ever larger factories with tremendous capital investments in equipment, which they were reluctant to see lie idle. Steel producers even began demanding twelve-hour workshifts seven days a week to obtain maximum output from their machinery and their workers. In general, workers in sugar and petroleum refining, brewing, and chemical manufacturing toiled long hours in the harshest of industrial settings.[34]

The elimination of skills and the demanding conditions of work made these technologically advanced industries less desirable employment options. By 1915, new immigrants and blacks were disproportionately concentrated in chemicals, steel, and refining, where they were also excluded from the higher rungs of the occupational ladders that these industries developed to create the illusion of potential career progression. Blacks in steelmaking, for example, toiled almost exclusively as unskilled labor or at the blast furnace, a place white workers sought to avoid at all costs.[35]

Work in distilling, refining, and metalmaking was not without rewards. Annual earnings often rivalled or surpassed those in degraded crafts, particularly since the work was steadier. Meanwhile, these industries provided industrial jobs desired by new immigrants and blacks who were often excluded from better employment opportunities by either racism or lack of skill.[36] But by and large, with the exception of brewery workers, wage earners in steelmaking, refining, and chemicals had little contact with a labor movement devoted to skilled, white male workers. Their employers, empowered by nativism, racism, a surplus of unskilled labor, and tremendous resources, dictated the terms and conditions of their employment.

Philadelphia was not a major center of either steelmaking, refining, or distilling, but the combined industries comprised a significant number of workers, particularly after 1900. Moreover, the experiences of labor in these industries paralleled that of the large numbers of unskilled factory workers in metalworking, papermaking, woodworking, food production, textiles, and glassmaking, among others. For many such workers, industrialization exacted a heavy toll in the harsh and often unrewarding conditions of factory labor. Yet technological change was creating a whole new category of "skilled laborers," suggesting that proficiency acquired on expensive machinery, even where tremendous skill was not required, became a valued commodity.[37] Although unions welcomed few semiskilled workers before the 1930s, machine tenders began to have some bargaining power as factory managers sought to reduce turnover and maintain a trained workforce.

Factory Craftsmen

Industrial concentration and technological change did not entirely eliminate the need for skilled labor. Throughout the fifty years following the Civil War, craft workers maintained a vital role and a relatively stable percentage (about 15 percent) of the workforce.[38] Some were in industrial sectors untransformed by technology, such as construction, which comprised 5 to 7 percent of city workers. A much larger group learned and plied highly valued skills in a factory setting, working in conjunction with machinery and new sources of power.

No sector provided more opportunities for skilled labor than metalworking. Machinists, molders, patternmakers, and coremakers became, on the basis of earnings alone, the true aristocracy of labor. Metal trades workers controlled their crafts through strict apprenticeship rules and high initiation fees and dues. During the nineteenth century, comprehensive machinists planned a job, set up their machine, and determined their production level. Unlike craft workers in many other industries, metal workers also enjoyed the bounty of dynamic industrial growth. Between 1880 and 1900, the number of machinists in Philadelphia rose from 5,000 to more than 15,000. Moreover, the machine tool industry was less affected by economic recessions, affording workers relatively steady employment at good wages. In 1914, when the average industrial wage in Philadelphia was $550, metal workers averaged well over $700.[39]

The combination of earning power, security, and independence, one would think, would probably shape a conservative, individualistic outlook. Indeed, where manufacturing relied on inside contracting and preserved the traditional craft autonomy of skilled team leaders, such was the case. Inside contractors not only made extraordinarily high salaries, but also hired their own crews, giving them the opportunity to exert considerable influence in their families and communities.[40] At Baldwin Locomotives, for example, metal craftsmen proved difficult to organize because a small group of workers held tremendous power.

Baldwin's was, however, an exception to the industry norm due to its commanding position in the market. In the more highly competitive sectors of the machine tool industry, employers pioneered the transformation of the workplace to gain greater control of production and reduce labor costs. Applying the theories of Frederick W. Taylor, Philadelphia metal manufacturers inaugurated many of the changes that stripped skilled workers of their control in the machine tool industry. High-speed tool steels, standardized parts, machinery specialization, and managerial reorganization converged to constrain the autonomy, independence, and wages of skilled metal workers.[41]

Dynamic change and workplace confrontation meant that even relatively prosperous metal trades workers frequently adopted a radical political stance. Machinists developed a socialist faction that pushed to establish independent labor politics in the city. Even moderate members were among the most militant trade unionists in the city. When metal manufacturers led an attack on machinists and molders after the turn of the century, the devotion to militancy and autonomy of these moderate workers led them to advocate socialism. In 1910, even the cautious metal workers at the Baldwin Locomotive Works joined the citywide general strike.[42]

Factory artisans existed in many industries outside of metalworking. The specialty goods emphasis of Philadelphia's textile industry enabled large numbers of expert upholstery and carpet weavers to survive craft degradation. In addition, machine fixers and card cutters earned substantially higher wages than their coworkers.[43] In the clothing industry, fabric cutters maintained much of their autonomy and significant wage differentials between themselves and other garment workers. Similarly, the increased mechanization of printing could not circumvent the highly valued skills of compositors and pressmen who asserted jurisdiction over new machinery. Some publishing actually created more skilled labor by utilizing the new crafts of photoengraving and lithography.[44]

In more subtle ways, the craft elites were also removed from the bulk of the working class regardless of the new disciplines they were witnessing in the factory. Higher annual earnings frequently enabled skilled workers to move to "better" neighborhoods; more disposable income allowed them to join clubs and voluntary organizations beyond the reach of their coworkers; and control over entry to the craft provided them with a legacy to pass on to their kin and friends. In Kensington, for instance, the tight community and family networks in the textile industry sustained the Scottish, English, and Irish domination of the trades well into the twentieth century.[45]

The employing class apparently hoped its attempts to control production would give a uniform shape to the working class. The evidence, however, suggests that such a homogenization did not occur.[46] At the workplace, wage earners experienced dynamic industrial growth in a myriad of ways. Degraded craftsmen, factory laborers, and factory artisans obviously held different perspectives on industrialization. So too did public employees, clerks, transportation workers and construction workers. Only a minority of workers had unions strong enough to shield them from the employer's arbitrary discipline. For others, mainly blacks, new immigrants, and women, unions were just as often an enemy that limited their opportunities. By 1900, two labor markets had emerged: one of native-born or old-stock immigrant male workers in primary sector jobs characterized by higher earnings and steady work, and increasingly influenced by union protection or limited entrance; and a secondary market typified by low wages, casual work, and wage earners excluded from labor unions. The composition of the two sectors, however, was at times antagonistic but often in flux, fostering in organized labor a protective rather than an inclusive outlook.

Working-class Cultures

If workplace experiences projected a variety of viewpoints on the industrial city, the community, ethnic, and kin networks of wage earners further refracted working-class perspectives. No single working-class culture appeared with the rise of industrial capitalism. Instead, much of the routine was residual, a product of older customs and past ways of life. Persistent in some workers were the roughest aspects of working-class behavior, which displayed an open hostility to Victorian culture in the same way that the "lower orders" had jostled the patrician elite in the eighteenth century.[47] Others were adherents to an earlier deferential evangelicalism encouraging full support of the dominant free-labor politics and Victorian morality of the day. Residual cultures, however, could take on new meanings for workers trapped in a rapidly changing society where ascendant values clashed with vestiges of a moral economy. Fearing the loss of their autonomy at work and their independence in the community, workers refashioned their associational connections, organizational abilities, and financial means into a subculture of opposition which gauged capitalist social relationships against standards forged from Christianity and republican egalitarianism.[48] In these time-worn values were the elements of an emerging critique.

Rough Defiance

The various strains of working-class culture—residual and emergent, rough and respectable—overlapped in working-class communities. Indeed, they overlapped in many individuals. A sober worker attending a lecture one night might well spend the following night in a saloon. But if the makeup of working-class culture was complex, the leadership was not; craftsmen dominated, primarily by having more time and money than their less-skilled coworkers.

Only in the roughest aspects of working-class culture did the very poor and casual laborers compete with skilled workers in shaping a class culture. In flaunting the strict Sabbath, attending illegal cockfights, or patronizing the saloon, the laboring poor demonstrated contempt for the well-to-do. Neither ethnicity, gender, race, nor occupational level barred participation. Particularly on holidays and festive occasions, wage earners celebrated with an abandon that caused considerable anguish among the middle class. During Christmas, mumming, masking, and drinking characterized week-long rowdiness. On the Fourth of July, workers mixed drinking with fireworks, which eventually prompted "safe and sane" campaigns by city officials. Other holidays, like Halloween and election night, provided occasions for neighborhood gangs to harrass the local middle-class citizens.[49]

Rough working-class culture also had a more regular presence. In the Ramcat section of Southwest Philadelphia, the working-class Irish adopted a defiant attitude toward the neighboring wealthy of Rittenhouse Square, which often took the form of petty vice and crime. In the predominately black Seventh Ward, as many as one-sixth of the population, including many women, could be seen entering saloons on any Saturday night. Even more tenaciously, working-class rowdiness was a constant irritant on

Sundays when horse races, prize fighting, and drunken parties interrupted the quiet Sabbath.[50]

Future Communist Party leader William Z. Foster, who grew up at Seventeenth and Kater Streets in South Philadelphia, remembered vividly the culture of the laboring poor. His neighborhood, populated by poor blacks, immigrants, and laborers, was dotted with saloons, bawdy houses, and pool halls. Gangs controlled the streets and youths graduated from drinking, craps shooting, and petty thievery to "gangsterism." Similar conditions in the slum near the Third Presbyterian Church prompted Reverend Hugh O. Gibbon to declare that the people were "in a wretched condition." The neighborhood around his church was "crowded with houses of prostitution, speakeasies, and gamblers on the streets every day."[51]

While the rougher strains of working-class culture found their clearest articulation among the steadily increasing numbers of Catholic immigrants in the poorest sections of the city, more affluent craft workers also took part. Skilled textile workers in Kensington refused to give up their lunch-time drinking and often joined with casual laborers in the roughest of working-class pastimes, the street fighting and gang warfare revolving around ethnic, racial, and religious differences. This conflict peaked in the 1840s, but periodic economic downturns renewed hostilities as various groups tried to stake out particular occupations or neighborhoods. Major depressions in the 1870s, 1880s, and 1890s led to vicious outbreaks of Orange and Green riots in Irish neighborhoods and the revival of nativism. Also, white ethnic groups engaged in "murderous brawls" with blacks to prevent their participation in elections and certain occupations.[52]

The streets in Philadelphia's working-class neighborhoods served as conduits for rough culture. There, parades, demonstrations, and riots exploited the "interpersonal interaction of the corner or dooryard." Women relied on this interaction for child-watching, lending, sharing, and even afternoon trips to the pub. In densely packed neighborhoods like Kensington or Southwark, large crowds mobilized quickly to repel ethnic or racial intruders, thwart police or charity investigators, or merely take advantage of spontaneous festivities. The grid pattern of Philadelphia streets proved especially congenial for block parties sponsored by working-class social clubs, which settlement worker Mary Simkhovitch recalled as "prone to debauchery."[53]

Saloons provided the other main entry into rough working-class culture. An elaborate saloon culture emerged in the nineteenth century, transcending ethnic, neighborhood, and occupational diversity. It was characterized by a democratic spirit and rituals of treating, which demonstrated resistance to the individualistic values of industrial America. Saloons offered a wide range of services—check cashing, free food, clean water, and meeting places—in addition to entertainment such as prize fighting. Clerics and reformers recognized the power of the saloon's sociable atmosphere, and regarded saloons as formidable opponents of Victorian respectability.[54]

For all their defiance of bourgeois morality, however, the devotees of saloon culture, street life, and rough behavior did little to create a working-class political presence. At times class hostilities surfaced, as when the Law and Order Society attempted to enforce state blue laws in working-class neighborhoods or when gangs trashed streetcars during strikes. But far from sustaining political opposition to the wealthy, the largely immigrant industrial proletariat made up the backbone of the entrenched Republican machine, at times supported by the Catholic Church in their resistance to Protestant reformers. In return for assistance in keeping police or repressive elites out of their communities, working-class roughs helped Republican bosses "mobilize the slum vote" despite the ethnic, racial, and gender antagonisms dividing them.[55] Many casual laborers sought insulation from, not power against, the disciplines of industrial capitalism. They were estranged from politics and conservative in their loyalties, equally contemptuous of middle-class reformers and disciplined working-class activists.

Respectable Deference

Significant numbers of wage earners, typically those in a better financial position, were imbued with a commitment to respectability and self-help ideology. The aspirations of these largely well-paid skilled workers surfaced in fraternal orders, building and loan societies, church associations, and respectable leisure activities. Many of these pursuits predated the rise of industrial capitalism and thus were part of a residual deferential culture built upon mutual, but unequal, relationships between employer and worker. Others, like building and loan societies, were part of an emergent culture that blended with Victorian concepts of self-help. In either case, the outlook of many wage earners owed much to the Protestant morality and republican citizenship that informed the dominant culture. For them, respectability offered both a means to distance themselves from common laborers and the chance to assert their rights to full and equal participation as citizens of the republic.[56]

A key element in working-class respectability was home ownership. Philadelphia's development scattered industrial establishments widely throughout the city, while a post–Civil War construction boom filled neighborhoods with inexpensive row houses. In Germantown, Manayunk, Kensington, and even the outer edges of the built-up city, high percentages of working-class residents worked close to homes that could be purchased by people with modest means. Family strategies facilitated home buying, and plentiful employment opportunities for women and children meant that even many semi-skilled and unskilled immigrant families acquired houses.[57]

The large number of building and loan associations in Philadelphia testify to the importance of home ownership. In 1875, there were 692 associations in the city handling over 36,000 mortgages, more than half of which belonged to wage earners. Ethnic associations, like the Irish Shamrock, Parnell, and Michael Davitt building and loans, or the German Goethe and Humboldt associations, demonstrated the appeal of home ownership as a form of immigrant self-help; the Davitt association held over $164,000 in assets in 1893. Through an association, a worker could buy a Kensington row house costing $1,000 for only about $12 a month.[58]

For the half-century following the Civil War, manufacturers and publicists trumpeted the benefits of home ownership to encourage a stable and conservative working class. In the 1870s, the Philadelphia Social Science Association argued that "workmen have learned that organized labor is of little lasting benefit without organized and systematic saving." Thirty years later, such diverse observers as newspaper editor Addison Burk and the Marxist Friedrich Sorge attributed the low incidence of strike activity in the city to the influence of building and loans. "The demagogue is without influence in a meeting of building association men who have acquired properties by their thrift," Burk claimed.[59]

Home ownership, however, appealed to union as well as anti-union workers. In 1913, a Kensington textile union leader told a government commission, "I am a good citizen. I own property," asserting a republican faith in the virtuous independence flowing from home ownership, a faith that at times became a powerful working-class force. Home ownership could also free workers from the burden of rent during strikes or provide collateral for loans as well as add to family income in the form of room-letting. Various labor newspapers in the city recommended fair real-estate developers and working-class building and loan societies, which taught "that it pays to help as well as prey upon their fellows."[60] But in large part, both by reducing the ability to move to other jobs during strikes and by discouraging militancy during the mortgage period, building and loan associations encouraged in workers attitudes and behavior conforming to the existing social norms.

In the mixed class composition of Philadelphia's neighborhoods, earlier forms of associational life persisted and bolstered cross-class mutuality. Workers and employers participated as equals in such fraternal orders as the Moose, Odd Fellows, Elks, Masons, and Red Men, besides the equally numerous ethnic associations. Fraternal orders fostered feelings of interdependence between the classes, especially through elaborate secret rituals, oaths, and financial aid. The orders offered death and sickness insurance and assisted members at times of trouble. For example, the city's Odd Fellows lodges banded together to assist 911 families of members who were unemployed during the depression of 1873–74.[61]

Many orders built club houses and sponsored activities to increase cross-class social intercourse. The Masonic Home in North Philadelphia provided a dining room, billiard tables, showers, and meeting rooms, and the 20,000-member Loyal Order of Moose dedicated a building in 1915 which housed military drill teams, a minstrel troupe, and a ladies auxiliary. Parades, pageants, and civic activities attracted thousands of members, many of whom were skilled workers, for public affirmation of the dominant culture.[62] At least twelve of the twenty-nine members of the Philadelphia Masons' Monument committee were working class; the five citywide officers of the Moose included a jeweler, a boilermaker, and a finisher; and twenty-one of the fifty-two men comprising the Odd Fellows' Temple committee were wage earners.[63] Some groups (such as Foresters and Moose) had higher working-class concentrations while others, like the Masons, contained more of the city's elite, but classes overlapped in nearly every case.

Participation in fraternal orders was bound to an ethic that mitigated conflict. While older ethnic organizations routinely had engaged in pitched battles and intense rivalries, by the 1880s, fraternal orders adopted a more sober, respectable image. The Masons' home held religious services every Sunday and the Odd Fellows asserted that men's "lives are linked together in common trials and responsibilities, . . . Capital and labor, the rich and the poor, the mighty and the lowly, will all stand shoulder to shoulder in this mission for humanity." The expressed mutuality of interests, bolstered by advocacy of religious spirit, self-discipline, industriousness, and temperance in all things, made fraternal orders "bulwarks of the status quo."[64] The sheer devotion of time, energy, and money to a lodge often diminished interest in labor reform. Samuel Gompers, for one, had to choose between running an Odd Fellows lodge or becoming a trade-union activist, and Adolph Strasser argued that the competition from fraternal order benevolent features detracted from organized labor's strength in Pennsylvania.[65]

At times, fraternalism's political message was more ambiguous, even blending with working-class opposition. Lodges frequently hosted union meetings and most unionists remained active in both types of organizations. In one Labor Day parade, when the Painters Union passed Odd Fellows Hall its band played, "Hail, Hail, the Gang's all Here."[66] But more often, the success of the fraternal order outweighed the commitment to union solidarity, impeding class-based loyalties. Musicians Local 77, for instance, debated the problems of getting fraternal orders to use union waiters, bartenders, and musicians. Likewise, the Printers Union railed against lodges using non-union print shops.[67]

Political organizations complicated these loyalties even further. William Z. Foster recalled the heated disputes generated by political clubs in his impoverished neighborhood. In addition, political organizations handed out many jobs important to an insecure working class. Black activist W. E. B. Du Bois lamented the Republican machine's ability to win the city's black vote through jobs and appointments. Wool merchant Theodore Justice's Germantown club hired unemployed textile workers to spread his party's message during the 1893 depression. But especially in areas where more prosperous workers mixed with clerks and businessmen, such as in North Philadelphia, clubs like the "S" Company of the Republican Invincibles attracted large numbers to the rituals of politics. The Invincibles combined a blend of protectionism and free-labor ideology with parades, uniforms, and baseball games to enlist many craftsmen for the 1888 Benjamin Harrison campaign.[68]

Fraternal orders and political clubs were only two of the potential voluntary organizations attracting respectable wage earners. For recreation, the elite of the working class turned to cycle clubs, rowing clubs, turnvereins, and drill teams, depending upon athletic interest, ethnicity, or religion. Others joined ethnic, occupational, or neighborhood singing societies, musical groups, or social clubs for concerts, balls, picnics, or parades that had less formality but no less regularity in punctuating the year. Finally, there were theaters, lectures, libraries, and parks which drew a steady flow of respectable working-class citizens striving for self-improvement. But all of these activities also included people from outside the working class, blurring differences between businessmen, clerks, employers, and workers.[69]

Skilled, white males of Protestant backgrounds dominated this cultural perspective within the working class, but it was not as overwhelmingly male as the rougher aspects of working-class culture. Particularly since respectability was closely linked to religion and voluntary church associations, women played a larger role. In fact, many of the social and athletic clubs that attracted wage earners traced their origins back to churches, and many had female auxiliaries or addressed the recreational needs of the entire family. More importantly, the primary vehicles for social reform and self-help—temperance, educational and benevolent organizations—were more often than not linked to churches where women had influence equal to or greater than men. In part, because the plethora of church-related activities afforded women an outlet for public activity and female companionship and encouraged ideals of domesticity that empowered women, females formed a central part of respectable working-class culture.[70]

Religious sentiments also frequently rationalized deferential aspects of respectability. Many employers, for instance, shared weddings, christenings, funerals, and religious holidays with their workers, hoping to imbue them with their own lifestyle and outlook. Manufacturers also dominated public religious institutions. At the Eighteenth Street Methodist Church in Southwest Philadelphia, nearly three-fourths of the congregation was working class, but contributions from several local manufacturers in the congregation underwrote church operations. Similarly, wage earners comprised about 40 percent of the Germantown YMCA's membership, but contributed only a small fraction of its resources; Sunday schools, financed in large part by the elite, enrolled more than 260,000 city children in 1904; and many well-to-do Philadelphians sponsored church Workingmen's Clubs, with libraries, lounges, game rooms, and lectures. These organizations—the most pervasive in Philadelphia's landscape—routinely emphasized the mutual, but unequal, interdependence of employers and workers.[71]

Respectability slowly spread beyond the white, Protestant working class. Although native-born and old-immigrant workers dominated the better-paying trades that enabled them to enjoy a respectable lifestyle, by 1880 Irish and German Catholics comprised a growing portion of the labor aristocracy, particularly in the building and metal trades. They infused some different elements into the mix of deferential respectability, but for the most part mirrored facets of the dominant Protestant culture. Indeed, Philadelphia Catholics established parallel voluntary organizations and activities, including temperance associations, young men's clubs, female benevolent associations, and even revivals to both rival and utilize appealing aspects of Protestantism. Even in the home, respectable Catholics increasingly replicated the Sabbath routines, family-centered religion, and domestic architecture of their Protestant counterparts.[72]

In Victorian Philadelphia, then, a semibourgeois lifestyle penetrated growing numbers of working-class homes. Particularly since the city was not strictly segregated by class, many working-class families intermingled with manufacturers, clerks, and shopkeepers in ways that encouraged both deference to and a penchant for respectability. In the fraternal order, political club, building and loan association, lyceum, or church, wage earners strove for self-improvement and acceptance. Many still expected to become master craftsmen or owners of small businesses or had aspirations of mobility for their children. Others were permanent wage earners who accepted the free-labor ideals of harmonious labor–capital relations so pervasive among northern Protestants. In either case, respectable workers, whether Protestant or Catholic, were typically set off from their working-class peers both by their earnings and by their choice of lifestyle.

A Labor-Movement Subculture

Since much of working-class culture militated against class-based organization and opposition, the attempts of workers to create political and economic force necessitated construction of their own subculture. This did not mean rejecting all the activities and institutions in which either rough or respectable workers participated; rather it meant that workers needed to meet these needs in a different context: recreation, self-improvement, and fraternalism had to be given a class-specific institutional framework. Merged with the traditional ideals of republicanism and Christianity, they formed the basis of a working-class moral economy, emphasizing collective self-reliance and mutuality in place of individual self-help.

Working-class organizations placed a particular emphasis on sociability. By the 1870s, labor unions began to take over the organization of parades on patriotic holidays, partly to legitimate themselves through links to republican traditions, but principally to encourage union-oriented recreation. Craft unions dominated Washington's birthday and Fourth of July celebrations with huge parades that featured workers marching in the uniform of their craft and floats publicizing labor's messages. At the city's bicentennial, skilled workers comprised the largest contingent and even hired union bands to parade with them.[73]

Holiday parades frequently ended in picnics offering games, dancing, athletic events, refreshments, and speeches. One Labor Day celebration culminated at Rising Sun Park where several bands provided music from 1:00 p.m. to 9:30 p.m. Over 1,100 union members bought tickets for the 1907 picnic at Washington Grove Park featuring a baseball game between the crack Painters Union team and an all-star team, as well as the election of "the most popular union man in Philadelphia"—the venerable old cigarmaker, I. W. Bisbing.[74] Picnic speakers were selected for their ability to stir and unify the diverse audience. The 1879 Fourth of July celebration hosted Irish, German, and socialist speakers in addition to Congressman Hendrick B. Wright, a revered friend of labor.[75]

A specific craft-oriented sociability complemented the larger celebrations. Bookbinders Local 161, for instance, held annual banquets at Odd Fellows Hall where comedy, singing, magic shows, and refreshments entertained members and their families. Unions also used events to attract new members; the Leather Workers kicked off an organizing drive with a big smoker featuring Irish comedian James Murray, a song and dance team, and the Rounder Trio. Others unions planned annual expeditions to Atlantic City or boat excursions to local sites. Anniversary balls often mixed ethnic locals of the same craft or raised contributions from workers in other trades.[76]

More than a simple desire for sociability motivated union-oriented leisure; these activities stemmed from a working-class subculture that demanded both individual commitment and group solidarity. That they appear removed from the arena of industrial conflict does not obscure their significance in providing a cultural continuity to labor consciousness. Unions competed with many other associations for the loyalties of wage earners; it was important to maintain the commitment of members through sociability rather than wait to test solidarity in the crucible of a strike.

Union sociability undoubtedly was dominated by males, but enabled circumscribed participation from women and children. Within German labor organizations, ladies auxiliaries attached women to union or socialist causes, and the daughters of Kensington weavers absorbed so much of their fathers' labor culture that they rapidly created their own unions when they moved into power-loom weaving in the 1870s. Moreover, women assumed major labor-oriented roles in their households. Organized into women's label leagues or cooperatives, female consumers both championed the patronage of union-made goods and organized family budgets to maintain respectability. Because union men largely accepted the Victorian domestic ideal, however, women were not treated as equals despite their importance in maintaining the working-class household and its respectability.[77]

Unions also attempted to expand their appeal among families through benefit systems. These were crucial for marginally stable households where the loss of a primary male wage through sickness or death frequently meant disaster. Cigarmakers, clothing cutters, iron workers, and bricklayers were among the many crafts that established benefit funds by the 1880s. While attempting to supplant the benefits offered by fraternal orders, they typically imposed a similar morality. Glass Bottle Blowers president Denis Hayes, for instance, stated that his union fund "discourages intemperance and will not tolerate neglect of work or any [mis]conduct on the part of our members."[78] Thus even class-based mutual aid had a moralistic character.

The free borrowing from Victorian respectability is further demonstrated by labor's use of secret oaths and religiously influenced rituals. These not only pervaded cross-class fraternal orders, but also the Noble and Holy Order of the Knights of

Labor and many other Philadelphia unions that relied on "occult arts" to unite men for mutual assistance and collective advancement. The most well known of the rituals of solidarity, the *Adelphon Kruptos* of the Knights, was specifically religious. The ceremony of the Order actually opened with a responsive reading of the Twenty-ninth Psalm.[79]

Sociability allowed a labor subculture to compete for the allegiance of workers, but unions also recognized the need for educating workers to a new political economy. Education, in fact, was another component of the Victorian ideal of self-help. One Philadelphia machinist wrote of an almost universal desire for a shorter workweek to enable more time for developing "mental culture." Labor groups hoped to turn this desire to new purposes. Cigarmakers Local 100 and the Socialist Labor Party set up central reading rooms, making available the major works in political economy. The local labor newspaper, *The Trades*, which sold inexpensive books on mechanics, history, and the classics of poetry and literature, also published the "Tracts on Socialism" of Detroit labor leader Judson Grennell.[80]

Labor movement reading rooms and lyceums routinely sponsored all sorts of events to spread the labor gospel. In Victorian Philadelphia, workers' groups hosted debates and lectures by such movement luminaries as British leader Ben Tillett, George Jacob Holyoake, an advocate of cooperatives, and Uriah S. Stephens, founder of the Knights of Labor. Cultural events often followed these gatherings, including performances by the "Arbeiter Maennerchor," theatrical entertainments, and an "Edelweiss Zither" concert.[81] Labor groups also fought for worker access to parks, exhibits, and museums. In 1877, workers lobbied successfully to have the Centennial Exhibit open on Sundays; in 1893, the United Labor League pressured the city for free admission to the Zoological Park; and a year later it prevented the city's licensing of a private company to construct railroads through Fairmount Park.[82] The concern over access to intellectual and cultural resources demonstrates labor's dedication to a regimen of self-improvement typifying respectable working-class culture, but labor increasingly expressed this seemingly bourgeois attitude in a new oppositional context.

Educational and cultural programs blended with political and economic organizations attacking the status quo. Greenback Labor clubs sprouted up in many working-class neighborhoods in the 1870s, "keeping alive the spirit of reform" during hard times. A decade later, Socialist Labor Party branches maintained a political presence in many Philadelphia wards. Although they rarely challenged entrenched parties, political clubs mobilized workers and prepared literature in crises like the 1877 railroad strikes or the Philadelphia general strike of 1910.[83] Cooperative stores and shops reinforced labor movement ideas of mutuality. The Sovereigns of Industry in the 1870s and the Knights of Labor a decade later created neighborhood cooperatives to help working-class families meet weekly expenses. Workers also sought alternatives to industrial capitalism in cooperative production, particularly when they were displaced by a strike or a depression. Groups of union molders, printers, shoemakers, and boxmakers set up factories in the city between 1865 and 1895. While cooperatives attracted some support from middle-class spokesmen applauding self-help, labor's cooperativists stressed a somewhat different "commonwealth ethic" emphasizing collective opposition to capitalism and the regulation of the trade.[84]

The labor press publicized the subculture by covering union events and serving as a forum for discussion. In 1902, the *New Era*, organ of the Philadelphia United Labor League, carried debates centering on political versus economic action; a quarter-century earlier, *The People* encouraged readers to argue whether cooperation or unionism was the key to maintaining the republic. Furthermore, the labor press printed the classics of political economy, from Marx to Laurence Gronlund to Henry George, despite their high cost because they viewed this medium as critical to sustaining an oppositional culture.[85]

Obviously, educating people to a new political culture was a long, tedious process, especially in a society where workers participated in such a vibrant associational life. One member of the Knights of Labor wrote to *The Trades* in 1880 that:

> every individual member of the Order is not educated up to the comprehension of its highest teachings. It is true that the fleshpots of the

Republican Pharoahs and the gin mills of the Democratic Egyptians cause many now, as they did in the days of Moses, to look back from the desert of their martyrdom, but these exceptions are not proportionately as large as was Judas Iscariot among the Apostles or Benedict Arnold among the Patriots of the Revolution, and it is as burning and crying a shame, humiliation and injustice to hold up those exceptions as exemplifications of the spirit and intelligence of the workingmen of America as it would be to exhibit the apostates we have quoted as representatives of Christianity and Republicanism.[86]

This letter described the foundation of labor's values and ideals in the Gilded Age. Philadelphia workers, like those in other urban industrial centers, were deeply committed to a blend of traditional Christian morality and the republican principles of the American revolution. Both components had undergone a transformation in the minds of many during the nineteenth century, becoming more closely wedded to self-advancement and the right of property.[87] The promise of republicanism that so attracted workers emphasized the values of a small-scale, self-reliant, egalitarian society. Labor movement spokespersons felt that corporate capitalism threatened to undermine the political and economic independence of American citizens. Wage earners were becoming dependent "wage slaves"; the republic was "in danger from monarchical tendencies" that corrupted politics and skirted the rule of law. Thus, in the 1870s, labor announced a declaration of independence demanding a new social order "in place of that which takes from us the whole results of our labor and transfers them to other classes." Again, in 1891, Philadelphia shoemaker Thomas Phillips wrote a new constitution asserting that "a true Republic is a sovereignty of justice, based upon a recognition of rights, in contradistinction to a sovereignty of power."[88] Many workers felt that justice could not coexist with capitalism.

In much the same way, the labor movement felt that inequality had no place in a Christian country. In Gilded-Age America, the dominant culture had become increasingly acquisitive and individualistic. Protestantism bolstered the virtues of capitalist society by embracing the rising industrialist and equating the failure to improve one's condition with individual sin and depravity. Philadelphia's Russell Conwell was among the best known of these "Gospel of Wealth" spokesmen. But workers also saw another side to the familiar gospels and Biblical prophesies. There, they found cataclysmic premillennial predictions of doom for the "present system of labor" that was "evil-born" and wars "against the heaven-born creation, the system instituted by God for the good of man." There they also discovered a postmillennial justification for labor and social activism. *The People* reminded workers in 1875 that "he loves, and serves his Lord best, who loves and serves his fellow man."[89]

Selected aspects of millennial Protestantism therefore provided workers with a heritage of political and ethical standards useful in attacking the acquisitive individualism of industrial capitalism. The values offered hope to working-class organizations confronting the dominant economic and political systems. Iron Workers leader John Jarrett argued that his union took up "the golden rule" and "kept on preaching in that way" because our "object is really to extend and bring into actual operation Christian influences and Christian principles as taught by the Christian religion in our organization." He added that at an 1883 Philadelphia labor convention, "seven-eighths of those present . . . were men who were connected with Christian churches."[90] Similarly, the Workingmen's Cooperative Printing Company reminded trade-union families that "a family without a Bible is an un-American and un-Christian institution."[91] Working-class movements thus aspired to legitimacy through the traditional values contained in republican and Christian mutuality, but adapted their messages to new purposes.

Respectability, however, was also divisive, threatening many potential adherents who were still devoted to the rough pastimes of saloons and street life, where wage earners with little hope of prospering sought refuge from a heartless economy. More importantly, trade-union respectability could seem tame and conservative. One Philadelphia iron worker proposed the following type of union:

> One for mutual improvement and assistance in the way of procuring employment, for sick and death benefits, building and loan associations, for buying food, coal, clothing and other necessaries of life, and for placing

pure men in legislative halls, but for the purpose of antagonizing our employers, "*never*."[92]

This worker betrays something of the ambiguity emerging from the juxtaposition of uneven economic development and the varieties of working-class culture.

This overview focuses on the distinctive trends of working-class culture, but they were also, in fact, complex and sometimes contradictory. The same issue of *The Workingman* that urged labor movement households to have a family Bible also recommended Steve Nash's saloon. Nash, according to the paper, was "one of the most earnest men in the city in his advocacy of labor's rights. He always has in stock an abundance of Greenback Labor literature, which he presses upon his customers more earnestly than he does his drinks." Similarly, Tobias Hall, a property owner and thirty-year veteran of Kensington's textile mills, personifies some of these opposing elements. Claiming to be a respectable citizen, he was a staunch union member—rising to the presidency of the Upholstery Weavers—and a dedicated socialist. But he also confessed to having been arrested in a barroom dispute, and he probably participated in the lunchtime drinking for which the weavers were famous. In 1914, as he warned a congressional commission: "If you make my life a nightmare and won't permit me through some channel which you control to live, I will not be a law-abiding citizen very long. The animal will predominate then and I will fight back."[93] The rough and respectable, the residual and emergent—all were evident in one man, who certainly did not see these tendencies as mutually exclusive.

Arenas of Conflict

This then was the setting in which Philadelphia's labor movement struggled for power. Between the Civil War and World War I, the city's working class was continually reshaped both at work and in the neighborhood. Rapid but uneven economic transformation impeded the development of a unified working-class experience and precluded the assumption of a predictable industrial future. In addition the lives and livelihoods of Philadelphia wage earners became entangled with those of new immigrants and migrants, creating an incredible ethnic, racial, and cultural diversity in working-class communities. This heterogeneity was a substantial obstacle to trade unionists hoping to simultaneously build broad alliances and protect narrow privileges, to exert power against employers and maintain their favored status among wage earners.

In Philadelphia, as throughout much of the country, the largest portion of the labor movement seized upon a strategy that emphasized its connection to the ascendant ideal of Victorian respectability. Such a strategy sought the support of Christian churches, yet ultimately made churches, which were central to Victorian culture, arenas of class conflict: Support from churches could legitimate organized labor to non-working-class audiences, send messages to potential union members, and exclude undesirables from both the labor movement and society in general. At the same time, employers used the churches to convey messages that condemned unions as un-American and un-Christian organizations. Outside of the churches, however, workers attempting to create a more explicity class-based labor movement criticized religion as a barrier to worker solidarity, and stressed its moderating force and its antipathy to nonevangelical cultures.[94] The contested terrain of religion, then, sheds light upon the competing visions of capital and labor as well as the crucial interaction of class and culture in American society. Labor conflict seldom occurred in churches, but rarely did it occur without the intrusion of religion.

2

Christian Capitalists, Victorian Morality

IN a speech that he was to give over ten thousand times, Russell H. Conwell told Gilded-Age Philadelphians that "the number of poor who are to be sympathized with is very small. To sympathize with a man whom God has punished for his sins, thus to help him when God would still continue a just punishment, is to do wrong, no doubt about it." On the other hand, "ninety-eight out of one hundred of the rich men of America are honest. That is why they are rich," Conwell concluded.[1] It seems inconceivable to us that in a society where large numbers of urban working-class people were on the edge of poverty that Conwell's brand of religion, associated with a harsh emphasis on personal piety and individual failings, could attain any significant following among Philadelphia's industrial workers.

There was, however, another side to Conwell. While he preached the wrongfulness of sympathy, his own Baptist Temple developed "a wider system of ministries" than could "be found anywhere else in America." The Temple supported kindergartens, gymnasium classes, clubs, popular lectures, a library, a dispensary, a savings bank, a soup kitchen, a hospital, and an evening school for the poor, in large part financed by Conwell's donations from his success on the lecture circuit. Even the Temple was said to appeal to the "masses." The main auditorium reminded people of a music hall or theater, especially with the crimson, velvet-covered plush opera seats. Far from being the socially complacent force described by most historians, Gilded-Age Christianity exemplified here by Conwell, sponsored widespread social benevolence.[2]

A dualistic thrust characterized religion in the post-Civil War era. Christians denounced personal depravity, blamed poverty on the lack of individual initiative, and felt generally pessimistic about the ability to improve human society. Yet a resurgence of premillennialist holiness in the 1870s spurred a massive effort to offer both benevolence and individual Christian redemption in the church, the factory, the home, and the neighborhood. The key theme uniting a network of institutional churches, voluntary associations, and benevolent organizations was the Victorian ideal of self-help. Armed with this concept and backed by leading merchants and manufacturers, the clergy confronted urban, industrial unrest with the broadest aspirations for expanding the seemingly related interests of religion and capitalism.

Saving the souls of individuals, however, did not erase poverty or lessen the political conflict engendered by the unequal distribution of wealth and power. Nor did religious benevolence simply sanction capitalist labor discipline. The values of Christianity could not be made to conform so easily to the wishes of employers. Instead, the aspirations of Philadelphia religious leaders frequently thrust them into the middle of the conflict between Christian capitalists and the very working people that clergymen hoped to attract to their churches.

Christian Capitalists

Religion emerged from the Civil War as strong as it had been before. A reform spirit encouraged by religious revivals in the 1840s and 1850s had enlisted the northern working class in the free soil and antislavery crusades, cementing opposition to the "slave power." The victorious war experience seemed to vindicate the righteousness of the free-labor cause, especially for the elite-dominated Protestant organizations that ministered to the suffering Union soldiers. The upper classes viewed their religious obligations as a "heaven-sent opportunity" to guide the national instincts. Through scientifically organized charities like the Sanitary Commission, they demonstrated the value of bureaucracy and rigid rules in benevolent work.[3] As discipline and hard work, not humanitarianism, became the keystone of Christian philanthropy, Protestant elites believed they could utilize private benevolence to achieve greater social order. Religious organizations benefited greatly from this approach, as the business and propertied classes demonstrated their desire for social stability with massive contributions. Between 1860 and 1870, the value of church property doubled, and in 1872 alone, Protestant congregations raised fifty million dollars for their missions.[4]

Philadelphia Protestants joined in the postwar exuberance. Late in 1865, a group of Presbyterians in the old Northern Liberties section of the city organized three new churches in three years to meet the needs of the city's working classes. With the backing of locomotive builder Matthias Baldwin and lawyer Henry J. Williams, Presbyterians helped establish the well-endowed Oxford Church with over 800 in its congregation and 900 in its Sabbath School, the Eighteenth Street Methodist Church with 550 members, and the Hermon Presbyterian Church with a seating capacity for 400. Even denominations like the Baptists, which were thought to have followings of more modest means, raised considerable sums for Gilded-Age expansion, helped by local manufacturers like John B. Stetson and John P. Crozer.[5]

Protestant self-assurance, however, faced new challenges in the 1870s. Like their counterparts elsewhere, Philadelphia's Protestants witnessed the failure of Reconstruction, scandals that smeared local and national politics, mounting numbers of non-Protestant immigrants, and the severe depression of 1873 to 1879 that shattered their optimism. Moreover, periodic national downturns and economic stagnation typified the succeeding two decades, during which unprecedented rates of immigration continually recomposed the working class, giving it an alien and, to Protestants, a threatening character.[6]

These dramatic social changes elicited an array of responses from the Gilded-Age Christian elite. Protestant evangelicals answered with a resurgence of an intensely personalistic perfectionist revivalism. Perfectionist Christians believed that conversion was not the end but the beginning of a redeemed life. First, the convert should strive toward personal sanctification and then to reform and perfect society. Thus armed, the National Camp Meeting Association for the Promotion of Holiness ventured beyond its small-town roots into major industrial cities like Philadelphia. Helped here by such leading local capitalists as Jay Cooke, John Wanamaker, and George Stuart, Bible evangelist Dwight L. Moody and his religious song leader Ira Sankey held an extensive Philadelphia revival in 1875. Moody's faith in individual redemption led him to scorn the social reforms being advocated by immigrant and working-class leaders, such as the eight-hour workday, greenbackism, and cooperatives. As he asserted, "Either these people are to be evangelized or the leaven of communism and infidelity will assume such enormous proportions that it will break out in a reign of terror such as this country has never known."[7]

Other Christians, driven by a similar ideal of free moral agency, nevertheless responded to social change with greater sympathy for working-class hardship. Beginning in the 1870s, merchants and manufacturers financed an impressive network of benevolent institutions. They, too, denounced indiscriminate charity and public works, but financed private welfare agencies where they could instill capitalism's values and "standard of business efficiency" into Christian charity. Although some of these agencies in later years actually provided the foundations for the spread of Social-Gospel ideas, in Gilded-Age Philadelphia branches of the Home Missionary Society, the Society for Organizing Charity, and the Female Society for the Relief and Employment of the Poor dispensed aid with stern self-righteousness.[8]

Individual churches, typically helped by wealthy benefactors, also expanded their services to meet new social needs. Philadelphia clergy and lay leaders sought to surround their congregants with church-sponsored activities, seeking widespread participation in a Christian culture. The First Baptist Church, for instance, offered a number of auxiliary organizations, including boys and girls guilds, a Dorcas Society that raised over $2,000 for charity, a Young People's Society of Christian Endeavor, a Baptist Boys' Brigade, and a Men's League for Social Service. St. Timothy's Episcopal Church in working-class Roxborough went even further. Its congregation swelled through the 110 members of its St. Mary's Guild that taught girls to sew, its 65-member St. Anna's Guild for mothers, the 125 members of the Workingmen's Club, and its gymnasiums. Among its services, St. Timothy's provided a hospital, a temporary relief fund, a library, sports teams, a savings bank, and a building and loan association. Moreover, most of these activities spurred Catholic imitators, particularly as some of Philadelphia's Irish and German Catholics rose to middle-class affluence.[9] The *Catholic Standard* even exhorted lay leaders to keep up with the Protestants.

Christian institutions, well before the influence of the Social-Gospel idea of a "religion for humanity," provided much-needed assistance for the city's poor. Benevolence, for Philadelphia's Protestant elite, was a way of life. In the 1880s, saw manufacturer Henry Disston and ship builder Charles Cramp sponsored Beacon Presbyterian Church, which ministered to over 1,500 people through an aid society, a dispensary, and a working people's institute. Matthias Baldwin contributed to several churches with social ministries in North Philadelphia, and hat manufacturer John B. Stetson did the same for the Baptists. The Eisenlohr Brothers, prosperous cigar manufacturers, were generous donors to Lutheran social service.[10] But perhaps no thriving capitalist put forth the effort of John Wanamaker. The wealthy dry goods merchant and department store magnate almost singlehandedly built the Bethany Presbyterian Church, which by the 1890s was ministering to over 12,000 people each week. Besides standard church-sponsored services, Bethany provided a savings bank, a hospital, an employment bureau, and even a night school that provided commercial training for young men and women.[11]

For Philadelphia's Christian capitalists, however, charity was divorced from social reform. Throughout the Gilded Age, they scorned labor unions and social legislation as irresponsible. Following evangelist Dwight Moody's lead, they viewed Bible holiness and individual self-help as the cure for labor strife. Of course, such a message resonated for many Philadelphia manufacturers. Baldwin, Wanamaker, and Disston, as well as traction magnate Peter Widener and publishing executives Francis Ayer and Cyrus Curtis came from humble backgrounds. Similarly, mayors Morton McMichael (son of an Irish-Protestant groundskeeper), William Stokely (a former confectioner), and Samuel King (a brushmaker) emerged from careers in manual trades. Through hard work, self-help, and attention to Christian piety, they had risen to financial and political prominence. Many others enjoyed a more modest security.[12] The religion of men like King, Wanamaker, and Baldwin taught that people were free moral agents, capable of choosing paths of virtue or degradation. The duty of Christians was not to offer indiscriminate comfort through social reform, but rather the opportunity for individual redemption.[13]

The individualistic aspect of redemption was delineated most clearly in the social uses of benevolence at the workplace. This was not a new practice; many antebellum employers exhibited some religiously inspired paternalism.[14] It was more the extent and formality of welfare work that differentiated postbellum capitalism and attracted strong ministerial support for Christian self-help in the factory. For example, Henry Disston started a company-controlled building and loan association, sponsored free beds in local hospitals, funded a library, and doled out pensions to old or disabled employees. Similar programs undertaken by the Pennsylvania Railroad Company, the United Gas Improvement Company, and Cramp's Shipyards, among others, made Philadelphia an oasis of early welfare capitalism.[15]

Corporate welfare schemes varied widely. Some were limited to a safety program, a benevolent plan, or a savings bank; others established a medical care plan or improved factory heating, lighting, restrooms, and ventilation. Wanamaker's department store strove to foster employee camaraderie through a military band, a bugle and drum corps, and a two-week summer camp of athletics "under military regulations," while Stetson's hat factory encouraged morale through a baseball team with "far more than a neighborhood reputation." Basketball courts, gymnastic equipment, and baseball fields often supplemented more basic welfare services like pension plans, inexpensive lunch rooms, or free vocational education classes.[16]

Christianity, particularly evangelical Protestantism, played a major role in factory welfare activities. Many employers felt a responsibility to provide opportunities for the spiritual as well as material redemption of their employees. Cramp's Shipyard donated a building to the "Cramp Good Fellowship Association" which held noontime religious meetings twice a week and a weekly Bible class. Henry Disston likewise complemented the good financial benefits he offered loyal employees by building several churches near his factory.[17] Other companies of more limited means tried to foster a "family feeling" between employer and employees. One Kensington mill owner stopped work for a holiday and "provided refreshments and music that there should be dancing. He was surprised to see how well dressed [the] girls were when they came, and their admirable manners; . . . he was very proud of that demonstration of the comfort and conditions of the employees." Carpet manufacturer John Gay led his workers in prayer meetings, and Midvale Steel president Charles J. Harrah stated that "while at home I am an Episcopalian, at the works I am an Irish Catholic or colored Baptist because in religion I agree with my men."[18]

The benevolence of Christian capitalists, although genuine enough, had its own earthly rewards. At the Stetson factory, there were "more than a thousand operatives, and none of them, by the way, is a member of a trade union," asserted the Philadelphia *Record*. Charles Cramp testified to the U.S. Industrial Commission that welfare work had stifled labor organizing.[19] Metal manufacturer George Cresson argued simply: "I think that if a man is treated right he will stay with you, if not, he will not." But the more evangelical employers attributed a greater importance to the positive side of better labor relations. Frank Leake, who headed the Star and Crescent textile mills, stated that Philadelphia experienced less labor strife than most portions of the country because of Christian benevolence. "Most disputes were settled in a family way," he noted.[20]

Christian-inspired factory welfare practices, however, were no guarantee of harmonious labor–capital relations; many workers were suspicious of their employers' motives. The International Association of Machinists, for instance, accused Cramp's Shipyard of using its welfare plan as a front for company spies who rooted out union organizers. Moreover, manufacturers themselves openly boasted of Philadelphia's generally lower wage scale. Workers feared that benefit systems "meant either lower wages for them, or that they were to suffer in some way if the organization should flourish," according to the state secretary of internal affairs. In addition, company-run welfare plans were often suspended without notice during bad times or periods of labor agitation.[21]

Workers also questioned the alleged "fairness" of Christian capitalists. The Maislal brothers, who engaged in noon prayer meetings with their workers, hired police to treat these same employees roughly during a strike. Frank Leake tried to settle disputes in a family way, "but where they could not be settled in that way we took the strong hand." The fact that many of these paternalistic employers received praise from ministers was not lost on trade unions. In 1901, as the United Labor League bitterly commented: "Donations to church funds by the men who grow rich off the toil of children appears to blunt the moral perceptions of the clergymen."[22]

Throughout the Gilded Age a few of the largest Philadelphia employers operated smoothly despite criticism, but most had far less ability to shape a morally upright, self-disciplined workforce. Several corporate executives bristled at the antagonism engendered by their welfare plans and others found that paternalistic efforts did not have the desired effect. Baldwin Locomotive Works president Alba Johnson, whose workforce was one-half immigrant stock, had established a lounging room and a clean, well-equipped lunch room in addition to subsidized noon-time meals. But Johnson "found that the better class of employees would have nothing to do with it, but preferred to go to the boarding houses that they had been accustomed to go to or the lunch houses. The class of men who patronized it constantly deteriorated until it became a nuisance and we closed it up."[23]

Increasingly, then, employers found that the factory environment alone was insufficient as an arena of redemption. Instead, establishing and shaping community institutions was a necessary complement to factory facilities offering self-help to workers. The creation of a modern industrial workforce—"of loyal citizens as well as disciplined operatives"—demanded systematic intervention outside of the factory.[24] Existing charity associations only partly filled that need. Gilded-Age capitalists consequently channeled their energies into an aggressive array of voluntary associations and political causes aimed at penetrating the realms of neighborhood and family where the working class was shielded from capitalist labor discipline. In particular, Victorian Christianity provided much of the rationale and legitimacy for these intrusions, and Christian capitalists expected that religious leaders would applaud their efforts. Instead, they discovered that they had ventured into an arena charged with tension and contradiction. Elite crusades over Sabbath observance, child-saving, and political reform demonstrated that Christianity was not simply a mechanism bolstering the status quo of the dominant culture, but rather a contested terrain where both capital and labor offered competing versions of an ideal economic and social order.

The Uses of the Sabbath

One of the most persistent areas of tension between employers and working-class people in the Gilded Age was the use of the Sabbath. In part, this was a carryover from the early nineteenth century, when the traditional relationships between masters and journeymen and older customs of mixing work and leisure gave way to new capitalist relationships and a more structured work regimen. With journeymen no longer members of the master's household, employers sought new means with which to control their workers' leisure time, especially since a tightened work discipline encouraged workers to place a greater emphasis on celebrating during their leisure, quite frequently in the saloon. Evangelical Sabbatarianism in the antebellum era was one of the responses to the new market relationships of capitalist production that carried over into the personal sphere. In Philadelphia, as elsewhere, however, the local elite and middle classes found it difficult to control rowdy Sabbath activities that often included drinking, gambling, and illegal gaming practices like cockfighting and horse racing.[25]

Philadelphia Protestants stepped up their demand for the enforcement of the state's blue laws after the Civil War. To some degree, this reflected the increased numbers of immigrants in the city for whom a day of rest from a harsh work routine was reason enough for rejoicing. That only a small percentage of these immigrants were Protestant was another cause for concern, especially since the Catholic Church was less concerned about blue laws.[26] But the renewed emphasis on Sabbatarianism also demonstrated the success of workers in reducing their hours of labor, particularly through gaining the half-holiday on Saturday. A worker writing in the local labor paper *The Tocsin* in 1886 remarked that during the wage earners' free Saturday afternoon, the city gave the "appearance of a general holiday." For employers counting on steady attendance at work and routinized production, imposing some limitation on the use of the increasing amounts of leisure time became a major concern.[27]

Employers were not the only people interested in the strict Sabbath. Protestant ministers frequently complained about boisterous celebrations interferring with quiet Sunday services. Similarly, women tended to support blue laws as a means of closing saloons. The Women's Christian Temperance Union and the ladies' auxiliary of the Independent Order of Good Templars actively recruited working-class women to embrace an ideal of domesticity based on the increased power of women within the home. The public militancy of women on the issue of home protection grew into a veritable realm of social activism in behalf of domesticity, temperance, and Sabbatarianism in Philadelphia and other major cities.[28] Finally, workingmen's organizations, striving for a degree of respectability, also occasionally supported Sunday blue laws. Labor newspapers, like *The Workingman* in 1882, criticized the Sabbath drinking and carousing that occurred in public parks in an effort to assert their connection to public morality and religion.[29]

Not surprisingly, Protestants blamed the breakdown of the strict Sabbath for a whole range of social ills. Reverend Frank M. Goodchild pointed to Sunday saloon activity as a major cause of prostitution among Philadelphia's working-class women. Others blamed corruption in the city government on the influence of the liquor dealers and grog-shop proprietors who bribed city officials to ignore their Sunday traffic.[30] Primarily, however, Sabbatarians singled out rising labor strife as the principal evil of the loose enforcement of Sunday blue laws. *The Philadelphia Inquirer* drew attention to the fact that union meetings routinely took place on the Sabbath, and during strikes in 1872, reporters cited Sunday meetings as "almost conclusive evidence" that the strikers were "Communards and demagogues," not representative American workers.[31]

The emergence of well-endowed Sabbatarian organizations in the 1870s and 1880s emphasized the class nature of the issue. The Philadelphia Sabbath Association and the Law and Order Society enlisted wealthy manufacturers and merchants, particularly ones associated with Baptist, Methodist, and Presbyterian churches. These "theocratic businessmen" targeted Irish and German working-class districts, where they engaged in surveillance, notified authorities, and pursued convictions against proprietors of speakeasies and gambling houses. Although the Law and Order Society promised to uncover "the most powerful moneyed and political interest that exists" in the city, its prosecutions were limited almost exclusively to petty proprietors or wage earners.[32] Nevertheless, the most prominent Protestant citizens in the city contributed generously to the movement to restrict working-class leisure on Sunday.

Sabbath agitation in the city, as well as the movement to restrict the liquor trade, tended to peak at times of labor unrest. The German-led eight-hour movement of 1872 coincided with the arrest of a large number of German liquor dealers for infringement of the blue laws. The Philadelphia Sabbath Association made its most determined stand against easing Sunday restriction in 1877, coinciding with the great railroad strikes and, not coincidentally, temperance activist Francis Murphy's well-financed revival.

The first years of the Law and Order Society coincided with the 1883–86 nova of the Knights of Labor.[33] Sabbatarianism enlisted many prominent manufacturers who agreed with Congregationalist minister Samuel Lane Loomis's explanation of the social unrest in Gilded-Age America: "To the mass of the workingmen, Sunday is no more than a holiday, . . . a day for labor meetings, for excursions, for saloons, beer-gardens, base-ball games, and carousals." Conversely, Sabbatarians rarely chastized employers for the evils resulting from Sunday labor. *The Presbyterian* did pause in 1877 to wonder if the breaking of the Sabbath by the railroads had bred the sort of men who resort to violence.[34]

Philadelphia wage earners responded by attacking upper-class Sabbatarianism on several fronts. By far the most prevalent method was through illegal or extra-legal resistance. Despite the extensive efforts of repressive organizations, grog-shops and speakeasies sold liquor openly on Sundays. Immigrant neighborhoods also had those who found ways to skirt the letter of the law; German fraternal clubs and Irish shebeens catered to rowdy Sabbath celebrations. Even when they maintained some decorum, however, the flagrant violation of the law angered Philadelphia's Protestant elite, especially when city officials knowingly ignored blue-law violations. To Sabbatarians, this proved that ward politicians represented unredeemable neighborhood constituencies, and that not only them but the mayor had been corrupted by the liquor interests.[35]

Many working-class opponents of Sabbatarianism organized politically to confront blue laws more directly. Throughout 1877, working-class and immigrant groups lobbied to have the Centennial exhibit open on Sundays. When the mayor finally assented, prominent Sabbatarians John Wanamaker, Edward Biddle, and Isaac Clothier resigned from the permanent exhibition committee. Nevertheless, record numbers of people went to the exhibit on the first Sunday it was open.[36] Workers striving for respectability, like Robert D. Layton, argued that changes had to be made in blue laws because people who worked six days a week needed to be free to cultivate social and intellectual interests on the seventh: "Our libraries are not open on Sunday, and a man cannot go anywhere to enjoy himself mentally." Ironically, working class triumphs against barriers to Sunday leisure elicited responses that were voiced in class terms. When the commissioners of Fairmount Park finally opened its grounds to Sunday athletics in 1919, long-time Sabbath Association leader T. N. Mutchler accused Sunday athletes of radicalism: "They are criminals in the same way the Bolshevists are."[37]

In other cases, workers deflected criticism for their lax Sabbath practices by citing the "elitist" character of the churches. In 1887, "Old Soldier" wrote to *The Tocsin*: "If there are no churches for the masses, of what value to them is the Sabbath, as an educative agency?" Many agreed with sentiments expressed by Boston printer Frank Foster that churches were organized in such a way as to make the worker feel inferior. "It was not the spirit of religion that the workingman objects to," he asserted, but rather the inability "to come up to the social requirements of church membership, in dress and in contributions to the various objects that the church carries along with it." Indeed, even Protestant clergymen began to criticize such church practices as pew rents, which discouraged working-class participation. In 1892, Robert Ogden, a Philadelphia Presbyterian minister, challenged his colleagues with the question, "Should Protestant churches be upholders of caste?" Similarly, working-class criticism caused some ministers to regret the desertion of "downtown" congregations by Protestant churches.[38]

More disturbing to wealthy supporters of blue laws, however, was trade-union use of Sabbatarian arguments to attack capitalist practices. Textile worker Lucinda Hall charged in 1879 that it was "a great blessing that the Sabbath was set apart as a day of rest by the Lord, for if man had his way we would be required to work night and day the year round." Workers frequently pointed to the hypocrisy of Sabbatarians. *The Tocsin* found it strange that the Ministerial Union would advocate a boycott of Sunday newspapers when clergymen called workers criminals for exercising their right to boycott unfair firms. Likewise, labor editor David Pascoe suggested that Philadelphia would be better served if the Law and Order Society would take up the campaign to close barber shops and bakeries, as well as saloons, on Sundays.[39]

Not altogether surprisingly, trade unions eventually enlisted the support of some religious leaders in opposition to employers who forced Sunday labor. In June 1880, the Saturday half-holiday movement obtained backing from many clergymen. In a fierce and protracted battle to close bakeries on Sunday, the largely immigrant bakers' union obtained assistance from such groups as the Presbyterian Ministers' Association, the Christian League of Philadelphia, the Baptist City Mission, the Methodist City Mission Society, and the Philadelphia Sabbath Association. In June 1895, one Sabbath Association leader actually applauded union labels as instruments of "the bond of humanity and brotherhood among all classes of society, [and] the moral right of every man to rest one day in the week."[40]

Devoted Sabbatarians, even ones like T. N. Mutchler who denounced Sabbath breakers as "bolshevists," found themselves thrust into investigating the working conditions of men and women who labored seven days a week. They frequently were appalled by what they uncovered. Around the turn of the century, as steel producers, chemical manufacturers, and gas companies joined breweries, bakeries, and barbershops in routinely demanding a seven-day week for at least some of their workers, Mutchler worked closely with trade unions. When laws forbidding Sunday labor in many trades were passed in the late 1890s, the United Labor League applauded "the efforts of Rev. T. N. Mutchler [for his work] in the interest of the Sabbath as a day of rest for laboring men."[41]

Sabbatarianism, then, gradually changed in character. It remained in many ways decidedly anti-working class and anti-immigrant, a useful tool for employers. Yet Sabbatarians were not merely a vanguard of reaction; most sincerely believed in the cause and followed where it led. Eventually, the complex interplay of moral principles and social realities forced clergymen to reconsider the church's institutional constraints to working-class participation in many ways. Pew rents, the decay of downtown churches, and the services needed by the poor all came under scrutiny. Just as importantly, the moral principles of Sabbatarians enlisted clergymen in broader social campaigns. Through opposition to Sunday labor, even conservative ministers quite frequently came to support improved sanitary conditions, fair wages, and sometimes even the union label. If employers had hoped Sabbatarianism would be an answer to the labor problem, they found it to be a far more problematic force.

Rescuing Young Infidels

Quiet Sundays were only one concern of Philadelphia's middle class. In fact, no issue held more potential for Christian redemption than the fate of working-class children. In January 1886, amid the tremendous upsurge of the Knights of Labor, Elizabeth Biddle told a conference of churchwomen from the Episcopal Diocese of Pennsylvania that children working in Philadelphia mills were in almost total ignorance of Christianity. "There are thousands who do not know the Creed, the Lord's Prayer, or the Ten Commandments, who read no Bible, offer no prayer, keep no day holy, who live without God and die without hope." Under such circumstances, she continued, young infidels were maturing. There was even an incident "recorded of a boy of twelve, who *on that account refused to take an oath on the Bible in a court of justice*."[42]

Like Sabbatarianism, the questionable fate of children agitated Gilded-Age Christians. Protestant groups in particular, from the Society to Protect Children from Cruelty (SPCC) to the Interchurch Child Care Society (ICCS), frequently intervened to remove children from what these associations viewed as unwholesome home environments, usually in working-class and immigrant neighborhoods. In response, Catholics formed rival groups that performed the same role under different auspices. Most often, the cause cited for the removal of children from their parents was drunkenness. But even when poverty was the only offense, the "fundamental principle" of the Home Missionary Society was "to take indigent children out of their environments, especially Catholic and immigrant homes, and secure for them homes in selected (usually Protestant) families, and then by visitation and careful inquiry follow and direct their development."[43]

To better protect children, Protestants banded together in nondenominational associations. The SPCC and ICCS obtained support from nearly every Protestant denomination in the city. Furthermore, much of the financial backing of this child welfare activity came from the same evangelically inclined businessmen who contributed so heavily to Sabbatarianism. They forced child welfare associations to apply the "labor test" as a condition of relief: Home assistance was available only to those families who would sign up at the Employment Register for unskilled or menial jobs. The Charity Organization Society argued that "relief divorced from personal service is like medicine divorced from treatment." Consequently, assistance aimed at keeping families together was severely restricted. Also, while the associations claimed to seek remedies for poverty "without the slightest taint of bigotry or sectarianism," religious training for children removed from their home was closely monitored. This routinely meant Protestant instruction for children no matter what beliefs the parents held.[44]

Wealthy supporters of child welfare activities in Philadelphia had additional motives. An elaborate structure of indenturing children to "Christian" employers was integral in attracting elite support for agencies intruding into working-class home life. The Home Missionary Society, for instance, revealed its intent to place children where they would be "taught lessons of industry, sobriety, virtue and religion, not forgetting the individual capability of the child in branches of useful occupation." Some employers, like the Baldwin Locomotive Works, Cramp's Shipyard, and the Stetson Hat Company, established reputations for utilizing church connections to recruit obedient and deserving poor children for trade training.[45]

The expansion of child welfare work also coincided with many developments in religiously inspired vocational training. Midvale Steel executive Charles J. Harrah advocated vocational training, as opposed to liberal arts education, for poor youths, and the city's Protestant homes, supported by the contributions of manufacturers, routinely began to offer vocational programs for children removed from their natural home. The House of Refuge, the Industrial Home for Girls, and the Church Home for Children, to name just a few, attempted to train indigent children for useful, loyal, lives. Evangelical objectives could thus easily coexist with the promise of preparation for a well-paid trade or skilled craft that otherwise would not be available to the children of Catholic immigrants.[46]

Inimical to Protestant child welfare advocates were trade unions. Religious leaders like Russell Conwell denounced unions for preventing the entry of deserving Protestant children into a trade. Alba Johnson, superintendent of the Baldwin Locomotive Works, echoed Conwell's statements: "We believe that organized labor levels downward. We believe that it deprives the earnest, ambitious boy of a chance to rise out of his position."[47] For Christians committed to the salvation of the individual, this collectivist restriction against entry to a trade was the epitome of evil. The fact that unions also taught workers to be rebellious and frequently held their meetings in saloons was ample proof that Protestant young men and women should avoid them.

One of the prime goals of Protestant-inspired vocational education, then, was the training of skilled and semiskilled workers outside the trade-union environment. Elite backers of industrial education endorsed the sentiments of Russell Conwell and Alba Johnson. Such evangelically inclined employers as Isaiah Williamson and John Wanamaker founded trade schools that frowned on unions. Others, like John B. Stetson, Alba Johnson, Charles Cramp, and Samuel Disston, donated funds to YM and YWCA vocational education programs, hoping that even trade training begun without a specific position towards unionism, would cause workers to lean more toward the employer than the union.[48]

Youths who learned trades outside the rigid union apprenticeship system proved a problem for organized labor. In many cases, as at Stetson's hat factory, they replaced strikers and drove down wages. In the building trades, graduates of Protestant vocational training flooded the labor market as half-trained mechanics, allowing employers to subdivide labor among workers who had learned only one or two skills, instead of being trained as an all-around craftsman. Furthermore, the philanthropic trade schools, by not teaching the entire craft, left the trainee with less flexibility in employment. If trade schools created more loyal workers—and many employers believed they did—in part it was because the graduates had fewer skills to offer in the labor market.[49]

Unions faced a long battle against trade schools and employer-dominated vocational education, but another area of child welfare activity—the slow emergence of protective labor legislation—worked to organized labor's advantage. As *The Trades* charged in 1879, it was immoral to even allow child labor. "Christ sets a holy example" against the practice, argued the local labor paper; He did no work as a child. Furthermore, the paper suggested that child labor was a danger to the republic. "For lack of education we do not know how liberty is being tampered with. . . . We need the discarded principles of 1776 reasserted." Unions proudly pointed to their leadership in the crusades for free public schools and the abolition of child labor. "There is no nobler work than that of freeing children from the miseries of mill and factory life," proclaimed the *New Era*. "And that noble work has been left by the ministers of all churches to the misunderstood and despised labor agitators."[50]

As was the case with blue-law enforcement, working-class spokesmen challenged people concerned with child welfare to live up to their convictions. In 1886, the Knights of Labor began reporting violations of the existing child labor laws to the Society to Protect Children from Cruelty (SPCC). Members of women's organizations, especially ones that spoke out for "home protection," like the Women's Christian Temperance Union (WCTU), found themselves in a strange alliance with a trade union lobby seeking a factory inspection bill in 1889. By the 1890s, the powerful sentiment motivating child welfare activists created a unity of purpose for groups as diverse as the SPCC, the WCTU, the Civic Club, the Consumers' League, the Charity Organization Society, the Public Education Association, and the United Labor League. In January 1895, these groups met at Holy Trinity Parish to denounce the sweating system in the manufacture of garments in Philadelphia. The following week they met at the Baptist Temple at the specific request of Russell Conwell, a staunch conservative on social issues, to promote the union label.[51]

That clergymen like Conwell, who denounced union interference with Protestant-backed trade training, could address these groups on behalf of the union label as a preventative of the sweatshop demonstrates just how complex these issues became. The attacks on the city's working-class culture, which were so often linked, at least in part, to the needs of capitalist production, voiced no single, unified opinion. Indeed, in his 1901 book, *Substitutes for the Saloon*, Raymond Calkins must have shocked many business and temperance leaders when he listed the sixty trade unions in Philadelphia as the single most successful substitute to the saloon.[52]

In another way, however, the complexity of religious opinion in these matters should come as no surprise. E. P. Thompson's discussion of the British elite's use of the "rule of law" as an instrument of class domination noted that such idealized concepts as law and justice posed problems because "they [had to] pretend to absolute validity or they [did] not exist at all." If law—or religion for that matter—"is evidently partial and unjust, then it will mask nothing, legitimize nothing, contribute nothing to any class's hegemony." To be effective in its function as ideology, religion had "to display an independence from gross manipulation and [at least] seem to be just."[53] Thus, workers could utilize the ideals expressed by local Protestant elites to attack aspects of class domination. On such issues as Sabbath observance and child welfare, as we have seen, the working class exploited Protestantism's own logic and criteria of equity to defeat the objectives of evangelical employers.

This counter strategy, however, also posed serious problems for organized labor. Many workers objected to blue-law enforcement under any circumstances. They cared more about their freedom to enjoy a free Sunday than about the workers who were forced to labor. Similarly, families needing children's earnings to survive looked askance at protective legislation. There was abundant testimony about parents involved in tenement-house production, who, in need of extra wages, taught their children to answer "fourteen" whenever asked their age. The emergence of the "family wage" agitation had not yet begun to obviate the family economy that demanded the labor of young children.[54]

While Protestants dominated political and social dialogue in Gilded-Age Philadelphia, the Catholic Church represented an audience more heavily weighted at the lower ends of the social scale. It is true that prominent Catholic laymen established voluntary associations parallel to rival Protestant ones, and the tensions created by class divisions within the Catholic communities were perhaps even sharper. But through the 1880s, Philadelphia's Catholic clergy sided more consistently with the working-class majority of its membership. It seemed at times almost as if religious affiliation and class perspective were intertwined. Moreover, because of the church's greater reliance on ritualistic observances and because of its desire to protect working-class families, Catholic priests typically frowned upon Sabbatarian and child-saving organizations or suggested that they addressed only Protestant concerns.[55]

Consequently, even though workers could bend Christianity's own logic to their advantage, Sabbatarianism and child-saving proved troublesome and divisive to working-class unity. Christian voluntary associations and the cultural transformations they pursued only heightened the religious, cultural, and ethnic tensions already existing among wage earners. Skilled workers striving for respectability, often possessing the financial means for attaining it, quite often sided with businessmen seeking greater restraints on working-class culture. Their opponents were generally unskilled, immigrant, and Catholic laborers—the backbone of the rougher variants of working-class culture.

At the same time, such issues as Sabbatarianism and temperance, or the domestic ideals associated with child-saving, splintered the working class in another way, pitting male conceptions of class formation against female hopes for greater participation in a more equal society. The arguments with which male working-class leaders attacked elite morality substituted "manly" temperance for prohibition, a patriarchal household for middle-class child welfare associations, and male-dominated leisure centers for church attendance. These alternatives no doubt rang hollow for working-class women, who were already excluded more from the cultures of working-class opposition than from the institutions of their social betters.[56] Thus, Victorian religious values neither allowed simple class domination nor eased the emergence of a unified working-class opposition.

Redeeming City Politics

During the eight-hour campaign of 1872, the Philadelphia *Evening Bulletin* editorialized about the wrong direction being taken by immigrant wage earners. "If the workmen of this city will to-day abandon these preposterous strikes and combine for the purpose of purifying our local politics," the paper argued, they could make real progress in bettering their condition. "But there is no hope that they will do so. They never yet have striven to seek through wise methods to advance their own interests, and the folly of their present demonstrations affords no hope that they will display more sagacity in the future."[57] According to Philadelphia's Christian elite, the poverty facing the working class resulted not from the relationships of production and consumption, but rather from a wasteful, corrupt city government doing little to further local commercial and industrial interests. Philadelphia's schools, utilities, and other public institutions lagged behind those of other cities while corrupt contractors and public service monopolies drained the city treasury.

More than Sabbatarianism and the welfare of children, the political reform initiatives of Christian businessmen required the building of a mass movement. Stricter enforcement of blue laws or monitoring and removing children from unwholesome environments were activities that could be (and were) pursued without widespread popular support. Obtaining a political mandate however was another matter. Electoral success meant enlisting at least sections of the working-class—a circumstance that demonstrates the limits of the power of "theocratic businessmen." It was the professional politicians and their machines, not reform-oriented Victorian elites, who mobilized the voters in immigrant and working-class neighborhoods.

Undoubtedly, there was much in late nineteenth-century Philadelphia government with which to be dissatisfied. The three terms of Republican Mayor William Stokely, who was elected as a reform candidate in 1871 before building his own political machine, were clouded by scandal, bribery, and fraud, during which the city incurred huge debts but offered few services. The machine stayed in power largely by controlling ward politicians and their immigrant and working-class constituents. The reform movement, led by Protestant businessmen, regretted that it could not somehow dissuade immigrants and workers from their allegiance to the entrenched powers, despite echoing the republican and Christian rhetoric being used by Gilded-Age labor reformers. But, as historian Leon Fink has noted, the similarities between labor's moralistic political critique and Victorian respectability or contemporary liberalism should not hide the differences: "In both cases, the middle-class and working-class radical variants derived from a set of common assumptions but drew from them different, even opposing, implications."[58]

Elite political reform agitation peaked with the formation of the Committee of 100 in 1880. The committee brought together 100 prominent Philadelphia businessmen for the purpose of ending machine corruption. Centering on the awarding of construction and street cleaning contracts, the licensing of street railway companies, and influence peddling by the notorious Gas Trust, critics of the Stokely machine sought to root out the major sources of graft. In addition, the committee hoped to end the redistribution of the city's revenues among an immigrant working class: The twenty-five city departments, controlled by ward bosses like James McManes, doled out jobs generously in the most impoverished and congested downtown neighborhoods. By contrast, the committee's exclusively Protestant, business-class composition testified to its opposition to Irish wardheelers.[59]

The committee, buoyed by exposés of Stokely's corruption, launched a successful political strategy to usher in reform. In 1881, it chose the self-made businessman Samuel King, a former brushmaker, to head the Democratic Party's ticket in normally Republican Philadelphia. King, a devout Bible reader of old-stock English and German ancestry, rode to power preaching economy in government to skilled, respectable workers concerned with the growing power of Irish politicians. Many such skilled workers may also have remembered Stokely's repression of labor during the 1877 railroad strikes.[60] But reform's appeal was even stronger for Protestant businessmen; the committee's moralistic rhetoric masked its true goal of reducing city expenditures and private taxes, programs designed to help local manufacturers. Prominent local churches, like Grace Episcopal Church, and such local religious publications as *The National Baptist* trumpeted the reform cause as a powerful antidote to Irish and immigrant power.[61]

Other programs emphasized the Protestant elite's assault on the sources of immigrant and working-class autonomy. In 1882, reformers wrote new municipal charter legislation, known as the "Bullitt Bill" after author John C. Bullitt, epitomizing the efforts of the committee to take power away from ward leaders aligned with James McManes, the local boss. McManes's supporters at the state level, however, blocked the bill's passage until 1885, when reformers won the support of rival political boss Matthew Quay, enabling the charter to pass. The new charter centralized administrative power in the hands of the mayor at the expense of ward politicians who represented working-class communities. The reformers also added civil service regulations designed to hamper mayoral patronage to immigrants. Committee leaders felt they could exert greater control over a popularly elected mayor than over councilmen who built power bases in single wards. By placing administrative departments directly under the mayor, the new charter gave elites a larger voice in the granting of contracts and the provision of services.[62]

The second major program of the reform administration, although unsuccessful, targeted the public school. In the 1880s, the Philadelphia schools still had no centralized authority or administration. Ward school boards, responsible to local constituents, tailored public education to meet neighborhood needs. Reformers, through the Public Education Association (PEA), linked their efforts to the Committee of 100, and attempted to remove administrative decision-making from ward-level politicians. Like those changes in the Bullitt Bill, they argued for a centralized school administration, efficient management, professional educators, and a homogenized educational program. Critics of the PEA argued that

> the real object is an effort of the so-called social status people, who have no faith in the wisdom of boilermakers, carpenters, painters—in short the bone and sinew as well as the good common sense element in all our wards—to take a hand in the management of our public schools.[63]

What resulted, in part, was a school system that tracked working-class children into manual training programs and blocked their chances of obtaining a thorough education in a traditional school curriculum. In this case, the ward committees and their supporters rebuffed, at least for a decade, the reformers' efforts to take control of the schools.

To many workers, the moralistic rhetoric of the committee and the religious support for reform seemed shallow. Indeed, the Republican bosses regained the mayoralty in 1884 with the election of William Burns Smith. Despite King's honesty, the Committee of 100 split when Smith—nominally a reformer—won the GOP nomination. In addition, the committee's influence waned, especially among skilled workers involved in growing labor turbulence in the mid-1880s who identified committee leaders as anti-union manufacturers. James Dobson and Sevill Schofield, for example, were committee members associated with anti-unionism in the textile industry, and William Sellers, George Cresson, and Charles Harrah all staunchly opposed labor organizations in the metal trades.[64]

Other factors widened the chasm separating political reform and a working-class agenda. As suburban residents, many reformers championed the diversion of city funds away from older immigrant and working-class wards to new middle-class districts.[65] Also, there was the patronage of Irish contractors, a practice that Pennsylvania governor John Hartranft called "the license to peculate and plunder," but that nevertheless engendered the loyalty of the underemployed. Finally, the machine gave some assistance to labor reform, passing an eight-hour law for municipal contract work and a mechanics' lien law.[66]

To make matters worse for the reformers, their moralistic Christianity was linked to repressive cultural organizations. The list of Committee of 100 members overlapped with the Social Purity Alliance, the Law and Order Society, and the Sabbath Association. Particularly among Catholic immigrants, this link limited reform's appeal.[67] Although the labor movement realized it could utilize Victorian morality in its own critique of capitalistic labor practices, trade unionists rarely welcomed the activities of elite-controlled associations. Consequently, workers rapidly abandoned the reform committee; while Protestant craftsmen more than likely found much to admire in Samuel King, the Catholic, immigrant, and unskilled workers perceived far greater benefits from the Republican machine that did not attack their culture or their ward-based political autonomy.

For a number of reasons, then, the Committee of 100 could not translate its 1881 victory into a lasting movement. When the Republican machine regrouped and returned to power in 1884, it swept the working class. *The Tocsin* stated that no self-respecting worker would support the "snobs" on the Committee of 100.[68] The reduction of city debt, which was King's most significant accomplishment, actually hurt immigrant neighborhoods since it was achieved through the reduction of city payrolls and contracts that had allowed ward leaders to hand out thousands of jobs. In fact, it seems probable that the emergence of a reform party had less to do with ending corruption than with an attempt by corporate capitalists to reduce the financial burden created by the Republican Party's alliance with immigrant and working-class voters.

Given that the Committee of 100 was led by men who were also at the forefront of an assault on wage earners at the workplace, their attempt to centralize political power under elite control took on an ominous significance for workers and immigrants. The reformers' liberal rhetoric must have sounded insincere, especially after 1884 when it competed against a working-class variant rooted in an older ideology of the producing classes. Similarly, the committee's church-like moralism—emphasizing order, protection of property, individualism, and prohibition—flickered against the bright glow of the Knights of Labor's sectarianism, with its voluntaristic temperance, glorification of brotherhood, and espousal of "labor's lordly chivalry."[69]

Tainted with the Morality of Capitalism

Writing from the perspective of the early twentieth-century Social Gospel movement, Baptist clergyman Walter Rauschenbusch characterized Gilded-Age Christianity as "tainted with the money morality of capitalism."[70] Since then, Rauschenbusch's rather harsh judgment has been largely accepted. Pointing in particular to the commanding influence employers exerted over nineteenth-century Protestantism, most historians have portrayed religion as a means of capitalist domination. In part, the local examples of Sabbatarianism, child welfare, and reform politics offered here confirm that view. The voluntary associations established and controlled by Christian capitalists did aim to impose their moral imperatives on an unwilling and uncooperative working class.

Nineteenth-century Christianity, however, was far more complex than Rauschenbusch admitted. The prevailing static and instrumentalist perspectives used to analyze the social role of religion ignore the conflict that could, and often did, result from attempts to employ religion for the purposes of class domination. Furthermore, this view disregards the existence of sincere religious beliefs and the tensions that arose when those beliefs were tested against new realities. As wage earners took up the issues of Sabbatarianism or child welfare and attached them to a working-class agenda, Christian morality became a contested terrain. Similarly, Protestant-led political initiatives were clearly limited by their clash with the needs of immigrants and workers. If Christianity was indeed tainted with capitalism's morality, it was not a permanent dye.

3

A Noble and Holy Order

TESTIFYING to the Senate Committee on Education and Labor in 1883, printer Frank Foster gave voice to organized labor's ambiguous relationship with organized religion. "It is not the spirit of religion that the workingman objects to; he rather strives for that; but it is rather the ecclesiasticism and the dogmatism of some of the church members and the hypocrisy of others," which turned workers from the church.[1] Throughout the Gilded Age, articulate working-class leaders as well as religious observers asserted that trade unionists distrusted ministers and prominent laymen. To many workers, churches were attempting to constrain specific types of Sunday recreation; ministers were more interested in bettering their salaries than in reaching wage earners; religious leaders cared more about order and property than the suffering of humanity. Moreover, organized religion seemed singularly incapable of fostering harmony among the rural-born American Protestants, Irish Catholics, and radical German freethinkers that comprised the working class.

Nevertheless, popular Christianity remained deeply imbedded in the Gilded-Age labor movement. Prominent labor leaders like Uriah Stephens and John Swinton implanted their religious beliefs in their labor organizations. The labor press made liberal use of Biblical imagery and recast parables for trade-union purposes. Speeches and testimony claimed Christian morality for organized labor, not its capitalist foes. As *The Trades*, a Philadelphia labor weekly, asserted in 1879: "Much of the decline in religious sentiment is due to the enforcement of errors in political government." If ministers desired greater working-class participation, they had to understand that "the highest thought of our age is directed [toward] the abolition of the economic system and the establishment of wisdom, truth, and justice on a broad humanitarian basis, recognizing the Brotherhood of Man and the Fatherhood of God."[2]

Labor activists briefly transcended the apparent incompatibility of the working class's suspicion of organized religion and its abiding popular Christianity. In the Noble and Holy Order of the Knights of Labor, German, Irish, British, and American-born workers transferred their practical, mutualistic morality to a labor organization that was part fraternal order, part trade union, and part radical sect. The Knights demanded an intense commitment, preached a universal brotherhood, and promised ultimate deliverance from a system of wage slavery. More importantly, they did so convinced that labor activism was complementary to true Christianity. Although the Knights of Labor's millennialism could not long contain the explosive religious differences of immigrant and native-born workers, the Order nevertheless awakened many Christians to the social side of religion.

Labor Subcultures and Working-class Religion

To many Gilded-Age ministers, working-class religiosity seemed defensive and reactive, and not characterized by a church-based morality. Ironically, while religious commentators complained that the masses were abandoning Christianity, the denominations that appealed to a wage-earning constituency—Baptists, Methodists, Catholics—were actually the fastest-growing churches in the city. In fact, between 1855 and 1875, the number of churches in Philadelphia more than doubled, easily outpacing general population growth. There was only one church for every 1600 people in 1855, but one for every 1250 in 1875. A generation later, more than 260,000 children attended Sunday schools, nearly one-tenth of them in working-class Kensington alone. In the modest new neighborhoods of Southwest Philadelphia, wage earners dominated Baptist, Presbyterian, and Methodist congregations, and it was generally acknowledged that workers comprised a significant portion of Catholic churchgoers.[3]

The anxieties of ministers, which seemed to conflict with this informal census of religious conditions, were largely due to the anti-church pronouncements of labor organizations. When a group of clergymen voiced support for employers opposing a child labor law, the Knights of Labor's national organ, the *Journal of United Labor*, sneered that "Christian ministers have joined hands with them and prostitute the pulpit to the service of capital." More quietly, a Baltimore trade unionist took issue with religious writer Ernest Hamlin Abbott: "If by religion you mean that which is divine, I don't believe there is any such thing." Instead, he believed that Jesus was merely a man "who preached social reforms; and he was so far ahead of his time that his followers attributed to him something divine."[4] Such skepticism and animosity were unsettling for clergymen, and were proof of working-class irreligion.

The attitudes of the clergy revealed more about their social awareness than about the religious attitudes of workers, however. Coexisting with labor's hostility to the church were testaments to varying degrees of Christian faith. Another Baltimore labor leader, estranged from the Catholic Church, told Abbott that the churches needed "to get hold of the young boys. Now, I've got two young boys, and I've made them join the Young Men's Christian Association." Similarly, *The Trades* recommended the early Social-Gospel book, *Day Dawning*: "It is worth reading, especially by the religious mind, who knows that under the false covering of society there are pillars of eternal truth." Then there was John Jarrett, president of the Amalgamated Association of Iron and Steel Workers, who testified to Congress in 1883 that the object of his union was "to bring into actual operation Christian influences and Christian principles as taught by the Christian religion."[5]

Clearly, working-class religiosity was a volatile and complicated force. Many Irish-Catholic trade unionists, because of their religion, opposed more activist state programs despite their appeal to other labor groups. The free-agency evangelicalism of rural-born Protestants made collective action appear alien and further impeded already tenuous alliances with immigrants. Finally, the free-thought radicalism of some German immigrants made any discussion of religion fraught with tension. It is necessary to sketch out the interaction between religion and the different subcultures that composed Philadelphia's working-class movements before we can understand what attracted each to the Noble and Holy Order of the Knights of Labor.

Protestant Labor Reform

The dominant thrust of working-class activism emerging from the Civil War was the labor reform movement. Composed principally of English immigrant and American-born skilled workers, this movement incorporated elements of British labor activism, especially Chartism, although it drew more heavily upon the free-labor ideology of northern wage earners whose aspirations for postbellum society went beyond mere equality before the law. Philadelphia labor reformers of the 1860s and 1870s sought measures from a more activist government in the areas of currency reform, the legalization of trade unionism, and especially a legislated eight-hour workday. The mouthpiece of Philadelphia labor, *Fincher's Trades' Review*, placed these in the context of the sacrifice of wage earners during the war. The paper's masthead read "Eight Hours: A Legal Day's Work for Freemen." Similarly, Fincher's comrade in the Machinists and Blacksmiths Union, Ira Steward, wrote that "the anti-slavery idea was that every man had the right to go and come at will." Wage slavery, like chattel slavery, threatened that right.[6]

There was also among labor reformers a strong theme of Victorian self-help, reflected most strikingly in their allegiance to cooperatives. Here, however, they tied the cooperative ethic to a political economy of producerism, asserting that workers were entitled to the full product of their labor and that labor created all wealth. Cooperatives of all sorts—productive shops, stores, banks, even building and loan societies—thrived in Philadelphia. These institutions of mutuality elevated men and women "morally, socially, physically, and politically," according to the

Union Cooperative Association, "by freeing them from the cankering cares of poverty . . . and blessing [them] with the plenty and happiness which come of sympathy and united action for a good end."[7]

The goals of the labor reform movement attracted many middle-class reformers applauding labor's pursuit of virtue and independence, but such support did not overshadow the working-class dominance of labor reform. The ethics of moralistic mutual aid derived from a blending of republican and Christian values pervasive among many rural-born Americans as well as the numerous British immigrants comprising a significant portion of Philadelphia's wage earners. Indeed, Britain supplied large numbers of immigrants to the city well into the 1880s, and their presence in the labor movement was great. For many of these immigrants, Chartism had introduced them to working-class activism and had sustained the link between traditional political radicalism and dissenting Christianity. The means and ends of Chartism blended well with the republican and Christian values of America's workers. Religious forms like the camp meeting and the Sunday school were utilized for radical ends, while political goals continued to be expressed through a vocabulary of virtue and morality.[8]

Among the important Philadelphia labor leaders emerging from Chartist traditions were John Shedden, James L. Wright, Frederick Turner, and Thomas Phillips. Shedden and Phillips, in particular, mixed evangelical Protestantism with a radical political philosophy. They were ardent Methodists, opponents of slavery, and staunch trade unionists—Shedden a tailor and Phillips a shoemaker. For both men, cooperative production was the ultimate Victorian self-help mechanism, largely because it attached a Christian ethic to the long-range working-class interests of attaining a shorter workday, securing the full product of one's labor, and reclaiming independence from wage slavery. Throughout his career—in the Union Cooperative Association (1860s), Section 26 of the International Workingmen's Association (1871–76), the Co-Operative General Trading and Manufacturing Association (1876–78), the Knights of Labor (1879–87), and the Industrial

Republic (1891)—Phillips fused trade unionism to a "common-wealth ethic" that saw in cooperatives a vision of the working-class millennium.[9]

For many rural-born Americans, the affinity between Christian virtue and republican independence as espoused by radical English immigrants paralleled their own sentiments. Into the 1870s, Americans from the countryside overwhelmed immigrants in cities like Philadelphia, and they continued to pour in thereafter. Among the prominent labor leaders from small-town rural backgrounds were Uriah Stephens (who trained for the Baptist ministry before becoming a tailor and eventually founding the Knights of Labor), and William Sylvis (leader of the Iron Molders and the National Labor Union). Both grew up in the theological orthodoxy of "free agency," which at once both reaffirmed the liberal devotion to upward mobility and clashed with a system of capitalist wage labor that no longer enabled workers to attain "that manly independence, blended with a just appreciation of individual rights."[10]

While the English immigrants were known for their advocacy of cooperatives, rural-born Americans spoke most forcefully for political solutions. Given the widespread suffrage and the rituals of mass political electioneering in nineteenth-century America this is not surprising. But the political goals of labor reformers —the eight-hour workday or the issuing of greenbacks to ease working-class debt—aimed to unshackle workers so that their inherent Christian virtue could check the rampant abuses of individual rights. Uriah Stephens preached that "an accursed slavery, a heaven-denounced tyranny, a degrading atheistical idolatry remains" in America despite civil and religious liberty. Only a political and economic system that allowed workers the time and means to educate themselves to a more holy mission would make America the "city of refuge" of the prophet Isaiah.[11] Legislating a shorter workday was, as they saw it, the first step to a worldly paradise.

The Christianity permeating the outlook of labor reformers, then, was of a practical variety. They sought a religion of brotherhood and mutuality in which labor was granted its rightful place.

In 1879 *The Trades* reprinted a refrain from an unidentified "Labor Song," capturing the religious inspiration of labor reform.

> The Great Almighty Builder,
> Who fashioned out this earth,
> Has stamped His seal of honor
> On labor from her birth.

Consequently, Philadelphia workers were disappointed at the "dominant Beecherism" of the pulpit, typified by Russell Conwell or by Reverend J. B. McCullough who, as editor of the *Philadelphia Methodist*, asserted that the rich were the preacher's "right-hand men."[12]

The radical purposes that evangelical Protestantism served, however, did not minimize the impediments it posed to working-class formation. Dissenting churches in England often fostered a chiliastic fatalism among its congregants. Similarly, the premillennial evangelicalism of Dwight Moody found its strongest adherents among rural-born Americans who, like many urban dwellers, expected the American political system to counter acquisitive individualism. Moody's revival in Philadelphia, despite its social conservatism, attracted thousands of persons from the small towns of the city's hinterlands.[13] For all the ideas of mutualistic aid and brotherhood that labor reformers took from evangelical Protestantism, many of their working-class counterparts learned only the lessons of individualistic self-help or patient suffering.

Similarly, the free agency of English dissent and rural American Protestantism allowed the attribution of individual failings to workers who embraced different cultural traditions. Thus, the Christian ethic of labor reform brought William Sylvis to temperance; those who continued to drink faced his scorn or his sermonizing. Although some evangelical labor leaders, like Thomas Phillips, could applaud the agnostic Tom Paine before a German free-thought society, most had much less tolerance. In the streets of Philadelphia, Protestants and Catholics continued age-old battles, their potential class solidarity often shattered by temperance and modes of Sunday recreation. Even opposition to German radicalism throughout the late nineteenth century carried strong religious overtones. These too, then, were a part of the cultural heritage of Anglo-American Protestant workers.

Irish-American Radicalism

For many Irish Catholics, the path to the labor movement was torturous. In the 1840s, Protestant workers had roamed Irish neighborhoods in mobs, attempting to prevent Catholic workers from obtaining a toe-hold in Philadelphia's labor market. Ongoing nativist hostilities enforced both Irish group cohesion and ethnic identity throughout the 1850s. The Catholic Church, with its entire range of Catholic voluntary and service organizations—schools, hospitals, benevolent societies, and clubs—became the central focus and voice of authority for Philadelphia's Irish. The church at midcentury was ritualistic, fatalistic, and conservative on social and cultural issues. Additionally, the Irish were concentrated in unskilled occupations where trade unions exerted little influence; thus, the prospect for an Irish-American labor presence was dismal.[14]

During the Civil War, however, barriers to Irish involvement in organized labor began to disappear. Many Irish-Americans entered the skilled trades, particularly in construction but also in printing and metalworking, where trade-union membership was a requirement. In addition, the war itself prompted different political and economic attitudes. The rules for drafting soldiers into the Union Army weighed especially heavy on poorer groups like the Irish who could not afford to pay for release from service. In many places, the implementation of the draft resulted in rioting by Irish-Americans; in Philadelphia, it divided Irish Catholics and empowered rowdy working-class groups weakened by a generation of fear, suspicion and economic competition with blacks. Finally, the war inflated prices while the government and employers held down wages, creating hardship and an impression among all workers of unfair and unequal sacrifices.[15]

Out of such wartime experiences emerged a radical Irish nationalism exemplified by the Fenian Brotherhood. Fenianism, led in Philadelphia by printer James Gibbons, was principally a working-class movement, disowned by the small but growing Irish middle class. Nevertheless, the Fenians dislodged segments of Philadelphia's Irish working class from Catholic Church domination. The Diocese denounced the Fenians and began its own weekly, the *Catholic Standard*, in competition with the pro-Fenian *Catholic Herald*.[16] Several Irish-Americans used this split as a means to bridge the chasm separating Irish working-class activism from American labor reform traditions. Noteworthy in this regard was Damon Kilgore, a lawyer and staunch labor reformer who joined Section 26 of the International Workingmen's Association, helped recruit Irish workers to the eight-hour movement, and promoted mutual understanding among Catholic and Protestant wage earners.[17]

Equally important in 1870s was the growing rapprochement between Catholic and Protestant morality. Irish Catholics mirrored Victorian propriety in attitudes toward sex and respectability, and the growing Catholic Total Abstinence Benevolent Unions (CTABU) spread temperance among working-class Irish men. Just listing the Philadelphia branches of the CTABU in the *Catholic Standard* took two whole columns. Even in Sabbath observance practices and Christian domestic architecture, Catholic and Protestant homes became increasingly similar.[18]

In the late 1870s, the American Land League fused the diverse currents of Irish nationalism, a growing class awareness, and Victorian respectability into a mass movement linking Irish home rule and land reform to labor reform in the United States. The *Irish World*, the most prominent organ of the movement, compared American class relations to the English rule of Ireland, castigating both the Democrats and Republicans on social issues. In Philadelphia, Martin Griffin's Irish Catholic Benevolent Union *Journal*, a vocal supporter of the Land League, helped make the city the center of Irish radical activity in the country. To hear such prominent Land League leaders as Charles Stewart Parnell and Michael Davitt, Philadelphians packed the largest halls in the city and thousands more waited outside to catch a glimpse of their heroes. Increasingly, the Land League cause gained favor with the city's trade unionists; concurrently, Irish-Americans like shoemaker Henry Skeffington and iron molder Joseph McIntyre gained access to Philadelphia's labor leadership.[19]

Ironically, radical Irish nationalism also reduced the religious tensions between Protestants and Catholics. Parnell, in fact, was a revered Irish Protestant leader of a predominately Catholic movement. In the United States, the Land League was attracted to the single-tax program of Henry George, whose rhetoric was steeped in the perfectionism of evangelical Protestantism. Other prominent Protestant labor reformers, such as former abolitionists Wendell Phillips and James Redpath, also praised Irish land reform and the American labor movement as parallel struggles for liberty and "the providence of God."[20]

Irish-American radicalism gained some legitimacy within Philadelphia's Catholic Church. Unable to stem radical nationalist sentiments, the Diocese accepted the Land League; its' organ, the *Catholic Standard*, adopted a sympathetic stance toward organized labor. By the 1880s, the paper supported antimonopoly politics as well as strikes by anthracite miners and railroad workers.[21] On the surface, at least, it appeared possible for trade unions to include Irish-Americans as full partners in their struggles.

Beneath the surface, however, problems remained. Irish Catholics were suspicious of several goals of labor reform. Legislation against tenement-house manufacturing, for example, met opposition from Catholics who feared an ostensibly Protestant state's regulation of family matters. Similarly, many poor Irish-Americans viewed child labor legislation as a threat to family subsistence and family income strategies. According to the *Catholic Standard*, Catholics also objected to increased budgets for public schools, humanitarian efforts in prisons, and federal income tax because they promoted Protestant purposes. Even in support for trade union actions, the church discovered opportunities to criticize Protestants. The *Catholic Standard* backed the anthracite miners because they were oppressed Catholics, cheated by the "respectable citizens" who owned the mines.[22] In times of union growth and economic prosperity, the labor movement could submerge these differences, but when employers gained the upper hand, older hostilities quickly reemerged.

German Free-Thinkers and Radicalism

Philadelphia's German workers, in contrast to the Irish, formed trade unions from the onset of large-scale immigration in the 1840s. Many German artisans had gained experience in labor or plebeian democratic organizations in their homeland and had fled after the failed revolution of 1848. In the United States, many of these "forty-eighters" merged their artisan republicanism into the equal rights and free-labor traditions of northern working-class politics. Throughout the 1850s, such German plebeian organizations as the Turnvereins and the Workingmen's Congress generated support for the Republican Party's program of free soil and free labor, eventually assuming "leadership roles in the political and military mobilization" for the Union war effort.[23]

Following the Civil War, Germans took the lead in reviving organized labor, expecting something in return for their heroic wartime sacrifices. In Philadelphia, they established strong unions in the metal, building, clothing, and tobacco industries. They also helped found the National Labor Union (NLU), which galvanized the northern workers' disappointment with the Radical Republicans' lack of support for labor reform, particularly the eight-hour workday. NLU leader William Sylvis no doubt appealed to German radical craft workers when he noted in 1869 that the "late war resulted in the building up of the most infamous monied aristocracy on the face of the earth. This monied power is fast eating up the substance of the people."[24] Throughout the Reconstruction Era, then, aspects of German working-class politics meshed easily with the republican producerism of English immigrant and American-born workers.

Culturally, Philadelphia's German-American working class remained isolated. Aside from the language barrier, religious beliefs played one of the most significant roles in this estrangement. Most German Protestants were Lutherans, members of a ritualistic religion without the perfectionist or evangelical tendencies of the Methodists or Baptists who bolstered American labor reform. The other major religion in the German community was Roman Catholicism. German Catholics, like their Irish counterparts, increasingly appropriated such forms and practices of American

Protestantism as revivalism and lay initiative. But German Catholics differed in several significant ways, particularly in Sabbath practices and support for temperance. The continental Sunday, emphasizing recreation and leisure, was widespread in Philadelphia's German community and Germans refused to abandon the beer garden. Thus, German Protestants adopted neither Victorian morality nor free agency while German Catholics were at odds with their Irish brethren.[25]

Even more alien to Gilded-Age labor reform was radical freethought, which was pervasive among German artisans. As early as 1850, evangelically oriented Philadelphia workers had spurned a call from German free-thinkers for a unity convention.[26] In the 1870s, the Philadelphia press frequently drew attention to the different cultural traditions of German workers. During a strike for the eight-hour workday in 1872, for instance, the *Philadelphia Inquirer* and the *Evening Bulletin* sneered at strike meetings held in beer gardens and the "unusual indulgence in the beverage of 'der Faderland,'" that lead to unruly behavior. Moreover, they appealed explicitly to the popular religion of Protestant workers. Sunday labor meetings were evidence that strikers were not true American workers, but "communards and demagogues," according to the *Evening Bulletin*, which added that the free agency of American Christians would never permit the dictatorial attitudes of foreign labor agitators.[27]

German radicals in Philadelphia, like patternmaker Anton Koeberlein and cigarmaker John Kirchner, widened the chasm separating them from American labor reform traditions. In the early 1870s, doctrinaire German Marxists representing Philadelphia in the International Workingmen's Association expelled feminists, free-love advocates, and other middle-class reformers because their versions of radicalism did not conform to Marxist class consciousness. Only five years later, Philadelphia Germans walked out of labor congresses when the discussion turned to currency or land reform, two issues of vital interest to American, English, and Irish wage earners. Under the ideology of seeking a specifically working-class program, Germans severed connections with other workers whose programs were genuine but different.[28]

The German immigrants of the 1870s—comprised more heavily of industrial workers steeped in European Marxism, anarchism, and radical free-thought—only reinforced radical, rationalist tendencies. They transplanted the debates between politically oriented Lassalleans and economically oriented Marxists into American soil. Although prodigious labor organizers, their uncompromising radicalism and free-thought ideas added a potentially destabilizing force to organized labor in Philadelphia. In 1877, this radical German element acquired a distinct voice with the founding of *Die Tageblatt*, which played a disruptive role in the Knights of Labor.[29]

Divisions of Labor

Other smaller groups added to the complicated religious makeup of Philadelphia's Gilded-Age working class. The threatened importation of Chinese workers in 1870 triggered an outburst of Protestant and Catholic racist hysteria. Until the 1890s, Southern and Eastern Europeans and Jews were an insubstantial portion of the population, although the latter group began to have an impact on unions in the baking and needle trades. Unions, however, made few attempts to direct cultural appeals to such small groups.[30] Blacks, despite sharing the evangelical Protestantism of native-born white workers, were also largely excluded from organized labor. As the black population approached 30,000 in 1880, Afro-Americans became a reserve army of labor, particularly in unskilled occupations like brickmaking, hod carrying, and longshoring. Tragically, racism overshadowed the similarity of religious backgrounds; the opportunity to include blacks in a broader labor movement culture was never seriously pursued.[31]

Despite the various religious perspectives of Philadelphia's working class, Gilded-Age labor leaders found few cultural common denominators more appealing to workers than popular Christianity. In the labor press, wage earners found Biblical prophesy or cataclysmic premillennial predictions of doom for the present "evil born" system of labor that destroyed "the heaven-born creation, the system instituted by God for the good of man." There was also the postmillennial justifications of labor activism. Philadelphia gold beater Frederick Turner asserted that "cooperation is the practical expression of the law of mutual helpfulness. It is an economic and religious principle." Germans in the Socialist Labor Party claimed that socialism was the vision that carried philosophers so high "that they beheld God." And Uriah Stephens built the Knights of Labor on two inseparable truths, "the immutable basis of the Fatherhood of God and the logical principle of the Brotherhood of Man."[32]

Philadelphia labor organizations did not always live up to such lofty principles. The task was made all the more difficult in the Gilded Age because employers and most ministers attempted to array religious opinion against organized labor. Workers countered with a more practical Christianity, with mutuality and brotherhood, and with a Social Gospel that anticipated the more enlightened Christianity of the Progressive Era. Above the denominational fissures dividing the working class, Philadelphia labor activists constructed a radical millenarian sect to deliver what they believed was the true religion that Jesus had preached.

Armies of God

Following the Civil War, dramatic changes overtook Philadelphia's working class. In the textile industry, for instance, female power-loom weavers supplanted the fiercely independent, skilled male hand-loom weavers, upsetting the delicate balance of shop-floor relations. Several technological advancements in shoemaking decimated its proud craft unions. In furniture making, factory concentration and subdivided labor allowed employers to replace German artisans with semiskilled operatives. Philadelphia wage earners in many industries either experienced or witnessed a diminution of the skill needed in manufacturing and the concomitant reduction in wages.[33]

The degradation of some crafts appeared to coincide with a decline in status for honorable labor. State and federal governments shunned the political initiatives of workers either by passing ineffective and unenforceable laws, as was the case with legislation for the eight-hour workday, or by ignoring them altogether as in the case of currency reform. When Germans led a massive citywide eight-hour strike in 1872 to claim by force what legislators had denied them, they were arrested by the police, castigated by the press, and denounced by the clergy. Fistfights and brawls shattered ethnic harmony, as German workers battled German employers. It was becoming increasingly clear that "the workingman was treated as a commodity, which was contrary to man's being a human being," according to strike leader H. B. Van Tronk.[34]

In 1873, the collapse of a long period of economic growth brought on the most severe depression in American history to that time. Literally thousands of Philadelphia workers—perhaps as many as one-third—faced unemployment. Those who continued to work earned 30 to 50 percent less in 1878 than they had in 1873. The Tradesmen's Union of Philadelphia declared to "fellow workmen" that the "sufferings of the working classes are daily increasing. . . . Soon one-third only of the actual number of workingmen will be able to get employment, while the other two-thirds, homeless and hungry, will look out in vain for the better times prophesied by a lying press."[35]

The voluntarism and free agency of the dominant Protestant culture was unequal to the task of coping with such an economic collapse. Private benevolent associations staggered under the weight of an impoverished working class. Soup lines and employment bureaus barely scratched the surface of the unprecedented need. The Philadelphia Conference of the Methodist Episcopal Church, for example, declared that its churches and relief societies were "in embarrassing financial condition."[36]

Yet few Christians were prepared to abandon individual responsibility. Demonstrations of the unemployed met with scorn from the Philadelphia editor of *The National Baptist.* Religious writer Robert Ellis Thompson's "plain lessons" for Philadelphia workers in hard times focused on temperance, thrift, and avoidance of labor agitators.[37] When the pent-up frustrations of the working class erupted in violent outbursts against railroads in 1877, Philadelphia's Presbyterians blamed Catholics who had not learned to internalize obedience to civil and religious authority. Mayor William Stokely, a devout Bible reader, merely mobilized the militia and private paramilitary organizations to effectively repress any local disturbances.[38]

Despite the unsympathetic attitudes of both church and state toward labor's privations, much of Philadelphia's working class clung to the republic and Christianity. Rituals of the dominant political order, such as an 1879 parade honoring Ulysses S. Grant, attracted 40,000 participants and more than 300,000 spectators. *The Trades* warned that conditions were reducing the "independent citizenry" to tramps, beggars, and convicts. It did not call for revolution but rather feared for the republic's future.[39] Christianity actually expanded among workers with apparent disregard for the clergy's callousness. Lutheran church membership grew at a rate 15 percent above that of the general population; Presbyterian congregants topped the city's population growth rate by nearly 20 percent, with its largest expansion in the working-class districts of Kensington, the Northern Liberties, and Southwest Philadelphia.[40]

Nevertheless, the working class's popular Christianity began to take on a slightly more radical, sect-like character. Typically, participation in sects involves a more intense commitment to the fellowship of believers and a greater attachment to religious inspiration and beliefs. Sect-like behavior also connotes less dependence on the more traditional gauges of religiosity, such as church attendance, membership, and participation in voluntary organizations. Finally, sect-like religiosity tends to flourish among the lower classes and those excluded from power and legitimacy within the dominant culture.[41]

In many ways, these characteristics were reflected in the Christianity of a significant portion of Philadelphia's Gilded-Age wage earners. The local labor press and labor speakers testified to the ability of Christian symbols to establish "powerful, pervasive, and long-lasting moods and motivations" in people, characteristics signifying that religion was at the core of the cultural system. In addition, neither the civic religion of the republic nor mainstream Christianity appeared willing to integrate wage earners into the dominant culture. Instead, workers turned to a radical sect capable of promoting and reinforcing distinctive values. Such functions normally lie at the core of religion,[42] but here, the institution that increasingly fulfilled the religious functions of Philadelphia's working class was the Noble and Holy Order of the Knights of Labor.

The Order appeared peculiarly suited to act as a Christian sect. Its national leaders grew up in Anglo-American Christian and fraternal traditions; Philadelphia founders Uriah Stephens (a Baptist and Mason) and James L. Wright (a Scotch-Irish Protestant) likewise honed the Knights from a blend of fraternal and Protestant cultures. Philadelphia Executive Board delegate, Frederick Turner, was an English-born Protestant gold beater who elevated cooperatives to a "religious principle."[43] Its ceremonies and rituals exploited mystical Christian imagery intended to evoke intense commitment, fierce loyalty, emotional responses, and an ardent belief in the Order's values.[44]

In Philadelphia, the Knights of Labor's moralistic fervor enabled it to overcome the diverse radical cultures that comprised the labor movement. The depression of the mid-1870s had sapped trade-union strength, allowing no group a monopoly over labor ideology. Into the void stepped the Knights. In 1879, its local organ, *The Trades*, began to blend Irish, German, English, and American programs into a multi-faceted whole, praising Irish land reform, German Marxism, cooperatives, and trade unions, for their contributions toward the unshackling of the working class. Irish labor reformer Damon Kilgore spoke of the "systematic wrongs" suffered by workers in the four categories of land, labor, money, and law. As Jakob Franz, editor of the German radical weekly *Die Tageblatt*, told a Fourth of July labor picnic, "The emancipation of the working people must be accomplished by themselves. . . . Thus, 'One for all, and all for one!' so help yourselves and only *then* God will help you." Such stringing together of phrases from Marxism, fraternalism, and Christianity demonstrated the rich tapestry of labor-movement culture.[45]

The Knights desired to unite all workers, regardless of skill, gender, race, or religion, into a single union. Consequently, a single issue of *The Trades* praised the Socialist Labor Party and the Greenback Labor Party. It printed a translation from Marx, trumpeted Parnell's visit to Philadelphia, and lauded the advances of trade unionism among weavers and shoeworkers (two trades with large female, unionized contingents). Another issue offered "Labor's Zion" to workers from all religions: "Roman Catholics desire fair pay for labor the same as Protestants. Nothing should divide the promoters of the common good." It recommended that workers begin to overcome ethnic and gender divisions by reading a paper like *Die Tageblatt*, the *Irish World*, or *The Trades*.[46]

Binding the diverse radical cultures together was the millenarian character of the Knights. As printer J. F. Hawkins wrote, "There is a way out of the wilderness . . . into the lights of a Fraternal Federation of Labor, where hearts beat in unison." Similarly, *The Trades* editorialized,

> To-day a mighty organization is silently creeping among the wage workers. It declares that labor is noble and holy. It comes to draw together men of all classes, to bury differences, to increase intelligence, to stimulate desire for knowledge, to cultivate fraternity and to lift up on to a higher plane the great body of the toilers of the land who heretofore have had no visible bond of sympathy.[47]

Like a radical sect, the Knights of Labor's prophetic vision was critical of the mainstream churches. *The Trades* chastized Henry Ward Beecher's "disgraceful" speech upholding corrupt political machines at a rally in New York: "The decline of influence exerted by the so-called Christian church, of which ministers lament so much, is due to such men largely, and the church is allowing itself to become a tool of the money power to oppress labor and hold it in subjection." Also under attack were foreign missionaries who do "not care a straw for the soul of the heathen. . . . War always follows missionaries. They are soldiers in disguise." The religion of capitalism, according to *The Trades*, was "rent, interest and profit." These comprised "the Holy Trinity of the capitalists by which they impoverish the honest toilers all over the world."[48]

In contrast, the Knights offered more just religious values.

They wanted a "cooperative missionary" in every assembly to spread the message of labor's way out of wage slavery. One correspondent, "L. D.," asserted that labor's cause "is truly unselfish, lifting the downtrodden toiler to the position that God intended him to occupy" as "the preparatory condition for the millennium." The widely read *Journal of United Labor*, official organ of the national Order, supplied the postmillennial justification.

Work for some good, be it ever so slowly,
Cherish some flower, be it ever so lowly;
Labor! all labor is noble and holy,
Let thy great deed be thy prayer to thy God.[49]

The Knights' leaders sought scriptural justification for labor's crusade. John Swinton, who studied at the Methodist Williston Seminary in Massachusetts, recommended that clergymen read the "Epistle of James" as a way to awaken a social conscience. The *Journal of United Labor* found a Biblical vindication of the boycott in Matthew 18, verse 15. It advised means to deal with a "trespassing" brother, which the Knights translated into labor terminology: Go to him first and point out his errors (this to be done by the union shop committee), then take wiser counsel (the Knights arbitration committee) to negotiate the dispute. If the problem is still not adjusted, then "let him be unto thee as an heathen man and a publican;" in other words, boycott.[50]

Among other devices, Knights of Labor publications printed hundreds of poems and parables to guide members to the values of "labor's lordly chivalry." For instance, one poem in the *Journal of United Labor* read:

Oh! Workingmen and women,
Who toil for daily bread,
Cheer up, don't be discouraged,
There's better times ahead;
Only be true unto yourselves,
And true to those you love,
True to your homes and firesides,
And true to God above.

Philadelphia labor correspondent Frank Waters constantly reminded trade unionists to "tempt not Providence. God delivered his people from Egyptian bondage and out of the hands of their task-masters ages ago, and He will as surely do it now." Similarly the Bible had a parallel for politicians who attached themselves to labor only to steal votes and divide workers. Waters compared them to Judas, "a faithless sycophant who would steal his brother's birthright, and—for filthy lucre—betray his Lord with a kiss."[51]

The Order came closest to imitating a religious sect, however, with its "Labor Prayer," which began, "Our father, who sits in Scranton, Pa., T. V. Powderly is thy name, may thy principles of justice rule and govern this country; may thy will be done in Congress as it has been with monopoly." This prayer, in essence, deified Powderly, the Grand Master Workman, and suggested the Knights as an alternative focus for working-class religious sentiments. Concluding, the prayer asked, "Lead us not in the way of monopoly, but deliver us from the Republican and Democratic parties, and thine shall be the power and the glory and the honor. Amen."[52]

After challenging clergymen with a labor interpretation of the gospel, the Knights began to win the respect of a few church leaders. In Philadelphia, the Order received plaudits from Presbyterian minister Mason Pressly, who advised "in the name of outraged humanity, let the laboring classes protect themselves; . . . let them combine, and let the people say 'Amen.'" Similarly, in the working-class Southwark district, two Independent Church preachers, S. Carr Woodhead and J. Vannote, developed pro-labor ministries for their congregations. Local Knights also gained qualified support from the Catholic Church due largely to Grand Master Workman Terence Powderly's Catholicism, but the *Catholic Standard*, disliked the Order's secrecy and "quasi-religious" rituals.[53] Although Philadelphia Knights earned little respect from mainstream churches, the limited clergy support they did receive enabled them to assert that truly religious people, as opposed to those who worshipped Mammon, saw the virtue of labor's cause.

As evidenced by the Knights, church attendance or participation in a religious voluntary organization were poor gauges of working-class religiosity. An ardent devotion to the fellowship of believers, a deep religious inspiration, and a commitment to Christian beliefs pervaded the Order's distinctly working-class program. When the Knights began to grow in the early 1880s, other working-class groups that did not share the Order's Christianity accommodated themselves to its popular millenarian characteristics. But when the Knights became a mass political force in 1885–86, debate began over what tactics would bring the millennium and what that millennium would look like. In the crucible of politics, old religious fissures reopened to crumble labor's solidarity.

The Rise and Decline of Labor's Lordly Chivalry

In 1878, the Philadelphia labor movement was small and powerless, decimated by the long depression. Over the ensuing five years, its growth was steady but divided into two camps. One, dominated by German, English, and native-born craft workers, organized independent unions and, in the early 1880s, created the Central Labor Union to coordinate broader cross-craft solidarity. United principally for economic action, the craft unionists were internally divided over politics: the Germans advocated third-party socialist politics while the English and American-born workers pursued reforms within the dominant two-party system.[54] The other major locus of labor-movement growth was in the Knights of Labor. The Order appealed most strongly to the Irish and American-born workers concentrated in industries experiencing the greatest transformations, especially shoes and textiles. In part, the ethnic and trade composition of the Knights in the early 1880s helps explain the Order's political association with the Greenback Labor Party, which promoted currency and land reform and promised assistance to cooperatives—themes which continued to attract Irish and American workers in degraded trades.[55]

Although cultural and skill divisions persisted, the two wings of the labor movement grew symbiotically. In fact, many workers, like printer W. H. Foster and cigarmaker John Kirchner, held membership in both camps. Germans could be found in the Knights, and Irish workers joined independent unions where they existed. Between 1878 and 1883, the number of trade unions more than tripled, and the Knights had 4,500 members in the city. Building trades unions had won a reduction of hours, the printing trades had organized the major newspapers in the city, and craftsmen in the metal trades exerted considerable power at the workplace. Even trades on the margins of industrial capitalism—barbers, brickmakers, and dyers—all pursued affiliation either in the Knights or in independent unions.[56] To most workers, there was little difference.

Through 1883, organized labor was still principally the domain of skilled, white male workers. Truly dramatic growth for Philadelphia's labor movement began in 1884 when the Knights broke through these constraints and launched an effort to organize factory operatives. The Order generated a new following for labor, particularly among those workers receptive to its moralistic appeal and broad vision. Veteran labor leader Thomas Phillips and the dynamic young Irish organizer Henry Skeffington enjoyed unexpected successes in the shoe industry. There, the Christian rhetoric of the Order was an especially affective device for organizing the large numbers of women in the trade. Linking the necessity of labor action to the dominant domestic ideals and home protection values, women flocked to the Knights.[57] By July 1883, the female Garfield Local Assembly 1684 of shoemakers had 924 members led by the charismatic Mary Hanafin. Its active participation and militance in the shoeworkers strike of 1884 helped set the Order on its path of remarkable expansion.[58]

Having proved that operatives (particularly women) in semiskilled factory jobs could be organized, Phillips, Skeffington, and Hanafin turned to the textile industry. By July 1884, more than 600 weavers had joined the Knights. When textile employers attempted to slash wages in November, many women spontaneously left their looms and poured into the streets of Kensington and Manayunk where the factories were concentrated. Cognizant of the special need for propriety in a strike involving women, Skeffington warned weavers to "avoid intoxication" and disorderly behavior, telling them that the "justice of your cause" would carry the day. In a clever twist on the concept of domesticity, Ann-Marie Sheridan commended the strike in domestic terms:

> Then strive for your right, O sisters dear
> And ever remember in your own sphere
> You may aid the cause of all mankind
> And be the true woman that God designed.[59]

For five months, the strong working-class communities of Kensington and Manayunk sustained the largely female strike. Crowds repelled potential strikebreakers while other workers and the shoemakers' cooperative store provided assistance or extended credit. Eventually a compromise settlement in April 1885 brought temporary peace to the industry; by then the weavers had organized twenty-five new local assemblies in the Knights of Labor, nearly half the assemblies created in 1884–85. Although some of the male craft workers in textiles were dissatisfied with the handling of the strike by the Order's national leaders, the partial success of the Irish, German, and English women in the industry injected a new enthusiasm into the Knights.[60]

The organizing achievements among semiskilled female operatives brought the Order's prophetic character to the surface. Frank Waters, writing in the local labor weekly, *The Tocsin*, warned manufacturers "that the sins of the parents shall be visited upon their children to the third and fourth generations." *The Journal of United Labor* viewed labor's growth as "exalting the downcast of earth and placing the human family on a level—the preparatory condition for the millennium." No issue captured that millenarianism better than the eight-hour workday, a cause that also found many adherents among the clergy and middle class. Revived by trade unions in 1884, the Short-Hour League specifically hoped to capitalize on this broad support; it urged "the clergy to open the eyes of the congregations to the condition of the working classes, and the improvement that shorter hours would tend to bring."[61] When several ministers announced their support, *The Tocsin* declared that

> the cry of the oppressed millions has reached Heaven, and the vengeance of the Divine Master will be our deliverance. Methinks I hear the joyful shout of the enslaved multitude with reverential homage to Him who gave them victory, chanting in happy chorus "Jehovah has triumphed, His people are free."[62]

Enlivened by the shoeworkers, weavers, and the eight-hour campaign, Philadelphia's labor movement mushroomed, principally benefitting the Knights. From 1883 to 1885, sixty-six new local assemblies were formed, thirty-five of which were in the shoe and textile industries. In 1886 alone, workers formed 102 assemblies, twelve of which were in shoes and textiles. The growth in 1885–86 encompassed the metal trades, garment workers, and construction workers as well as many factory operatives and unskilled workers in longshoring, brickmaking, and transportation. But the Knights were not alone; printers, cigarmakers, carpenters, and plasterers spearheaded the eight-hour movement in their own craft unions. Throughout 1885 and the spring of 1886, craft unionists held biweekly meetings and massive demonstrations in preparation for an eight-hour strike which commenced on the first of May.[63]

Once organized, workers rapidly turned to testing their power at the workplace. Following the lead of the eight-hour movement, the number of strikers rose from 3,000 in 1885 to more than 10,000 in nearly 300 establishments a year later. Their demands too demonstrated a new aggressiveness. Relatively few were rear guard actions against wage cuts; instead, workers sought shorter hours, higher wages, union recognition, new work rules, or the protection of members from victimization. Unions learned such elements of strike strategy as timing, preparation, discipline, and negotiation, which enabled them to win concessions from employers in a far greater number of their strikes than previously.[64] Beneath the enthusiasm of labor's great uprising, practical men and women solidified advances in labor relations.

Workers also drew on the upsurge to revive the tradition of co-operatives. Cigarmakers Local Assembly 53 planned a cooperative shop to employ some of its 2,500 striking members. Morocco Finishers Local Assembly 1869 raised over $4,000 in February 1885 toward starting its own leather factory. Manufacturers, fearing competition from worker-owned enterprises, slashed prices to undercut the Quaker City Co-operative Carpet Company and a cooperative hat factory. Employers threatened to discharge any woodworkers who became stockholders in the Cooperative Box Company, and enticed lumber dealers into refusing to supply the cooperative.[65] Little information exists on how many working-class lives were touched by cooperatives, but the 16,000-member city building trades council considered cooperative contract estimating and the use of a cooperative lathe and door mill. Thousands of workers bought their groceries at the Knights-sponsored Kensington cooperative market. Certainly employers considered cooperatives a serious threat, both for market competition and for supplying striking workers with an alternative source of employment.[66]

Although labor's great uprising included independent unions, it was the moralistic fervor of the Knights which resulted in a more widespread movement. Besides its greater appeal for women, the Order also attracted large numbers of Afro-American and Irish workers specifically because it made the first attempts to organize these and other unskilled workers. The recruitment of the unskilled, moreover, pushed at the boundaries of labor's vision. Factory operatives and laborers had little hope of sustaining a movement confined to economic objectives and dependent upon trade union methods; they simply did not have the leverage to force employers to accede to their demands. For the less skilled, then, politics became a crucial arena of struggle. Of course, this push from within blended with the Knights' own vision of redeeming America's virtuous republican order. The dramatic growth of the Knights in Philadelphia almost inevitably inspired the dream that an independent labor party would capture a place in the city's political arena.[67]

The results of early political efforts encouraged the Knights.

Despite the last-minute creation of the United Labor Party prior to the 1886 elections, Frederick Herwig's Congressional campaign in the northern wards of the city garnered about 10 percent of the vote. Machinist William Q. Moore, running for the state senate from the same area, captured a similar percentage for the United Labor Party. Workers fared better in state representative contests, electing steelworker Andrew Lee, dyer William Stewart, and weaver John Faunce on the Democratic slate in Kensington and the Northern Liberties, while narrowly losing three contests in the nineteenth ward.[68]

The Knights' foray into politics, however, did not advance labor's interests; instead it appeared to precipitate a decline. Challenged at the workplace, in the neighborhood, and now in politics, manufacturers united. By 1887, employer associations in the textile, shoe, and construction industries were prepared to roll back labor's gains. In textiles and construction, their major initiatives were trade schools aimed at removing trade training from the control of craft unions. The Master Builders' Exchange and the Textile Manufacturers' Association began supplying craftsmen who were not reared in union apprenticeships. In the shoe industry, employers attacked more directly, locking out workers and shutting down production until shoeworkers agreed to new terms. In other industries, lockouts, the use of strikebreakers, and a city government that entered conflicts on behalf of employers sapped the Order's negotiating power.[69]

The Knights were ill-suited to engage in a protracted struggle with determined manufacturers. The Order's national leaders were officially on record as opposed to strikes. When membership swelled in 1886, they even withdrew support from the eight-hour movement, fearing that large numbers of strikers would seek their support. The Order's pyramid-like organization forced local assemblies (typically organized by craft) to defer to district or national assemblies (organized by geography). This tipped the balance of power decisively by placing strike negotiations in the hands of national leaders not necessarily drawn from the trade being struck. During a carpet weavers strike, for example, garment worker James Wright compromised worker demands in order to obtain a quick settlement. The employers, already critical of the intrusion of outsiders, then embarrassed Wright by revoking the agreement and encouraging rank-and-file accusations that the Knights had "sold out" the weavers. In July 1886, the leaders of Philadelphia District Assembly 1 agreed to terms in an ironworkers dispute only to have the workers negotiate a better settlement on their own. Through 1887, brewers, cigarmakers, brickmakers, and printers had similar complaints against the Knights' negotiators.[70]

Political initiatives brought additional handicaps to labor unity. Opportunists, like Democratic congressional nominee Maxwell Stevenson, actively courted Knights support. After the election, however, the tailors assembly discovered that as a lawyer Stevenson had represented garment manufacturers during a strike earlier in the year. Andrew Lee, an ironworker elected to the state legislature with labor's support, abandoned his Local Assembly 116 in 1887 to accept a job as a mill superintendent. William Q. Moore, another labor candidate, also used his prestige to obtain a foreman's job. *The Tocsin* wondered if these men "lost much sleep" because of the changes in "the political complexion" of their legislative districts caused by their shifting allegiances. Labor columnist Frank Waters simply surmised, "I implore all co-laborers to shun the temptation of arch-traducers to malicious mischief, and work out their own emancipation by a peaceful Christian-like perseverance."[71]

Manufacturers also captured the higher ground in political debate, casting the Knights in an increasingly un-American light. The violence associated with the bombing of Haymarket Square in May 1886 severely lessened labor's legitimacy. Meanwhile, employers launched a legal assault on one of the Knights' favorite weapons, the boycott. The Knights, because of their large numbers of members spanning many trades, used boycotts effectively in labor disputes. But in 1886–87, several employers successfully challenged boycotts in the courts, where they were declared illegal conspiracies.[72]

Disappointments at the workplace, in politics, and in the courts unearthed ethnic and religious differences in the working class that had been submerged during labor's expansion. Many workers blamed the Knights' vacillating politics and failure to support labor militancy on the seemingly close connection between the Order and the Catholic Church. The visibility of Irish Catholics in leadership positions—Terence Powderly and John Hayes nationally, Joseph McIntyre, Patrick Lynch, and James McFeeley locally—symbolized the submission of the Order to European monarchism and Popery in the minds of many Protestant workers. Indeed, the Order's emergence from secrecy in 1879 owed much to gaining favor with the Catholic Church, and Powderly steered the Order away from endorsing radical labor politics in 1886, fearing a break with bishops sympathetic to the Knights. From the non-Catholic perspective, these moves demonstrated a fatal lack of manly independence. Obedient Irish Catholics, charged such diverse sources as *The Nation* and *The Tocsin*, could not reclaim the virtuous egalitarianism necessary to redeem the republic.[73]

Similarly, the crusade against the Knights of Labor boycotts, which were so often associated with the Irish, turned many Protestant workers against their Catholic brethren. The apparent illegality attributed to Irish boycotts fired the imagination not only of resurgent nativist groups like the Order of United American Mechanics, but also of Protestant workers attempting to re-establish the legitimacy of organized labor. By 1888, local Knights leader Joseph McIntyre wrote to Powderly about the antipathy of Protestant workers and the resulting decline of the Order.[74]

As alleged Catholic submissiveness created a chasm between Irish and native-born American workers, radical free thought severed another key segment of labor's strength. German workers, particularly the large numbers of recent industrial recruits, bore the brunt of criticism stemming from the violence at Haymarket. With spokesmen like Johann Most and radical military clubs like the Lehr und Wehr Verein, the revolutionary sentiments of radical German immigrants appeared alien to most native-born American workers. Equally foreign to large factions of the Knights of Labor was the concept of German free thought. In the fall of 1886, these differences shattered relations between the Knights and a substantial part of Philadelphia's German-American working class. The German radical weekly, *Die Tageblatt*, replaced its striking printers with members of the anarchist Gutenburg Bund, a union of typographers unaffiliated with either the Knights or the Central Labor Union (CLU). Philadelphia Typographical Union Local 2 sought a CLU boycott against the paper, but other German unions in the CLU blocked the move, leading to the withdrawal of many of the English-language unions.[75]

In December 1886, tensions increased when Wilhelm Gorsuch, a *Tageblatt* editor and former editor of the Chicago anarchist paper, *The Alarm*, obtained admission to the United Labor Party (ULP) meeting. Gorsuch's credentials came from the Friendship Liberal League which was, according to Typographical Union leader David Pascoe, an atheist organization. Furthermore, he disrupted the ULP meeting by demanding socialist candidates and by attempting to have the phrase "Fatherhood of God" stricken from the Party's preamble (a move defeated by a vote of fifty-six to forty). The English-language unions then denounced Gorsuch and other Germans for their adherence to radical politics and atheism. Over the ensuing months, ULP discussion turned as much on religion as politics, with debates rapidly degenerating to name-calling; Pascoe, for instance, called Gorsuch a "bloodthirsty bombthrower."[76]

By early 1887, Philadelphia's labor movement was in disarray. English-born unionists refused to support German union-made products and German workers had withdrawn into their own organization, the United German Trades. When municipal elections came in October, workers were hopelessly divided: English-speaking unions lined up behind William Leeds, the Republican candidate for sheriff, who had supported several labor measures in the state legislature; but Germans threw their support to the Democrats who opposed high-license fees for saloons and Sabbath observance laws.[77]

The Knights of Labor could not overcome the ethnic and religious factionalism of 1886–87. By 1889, the Order had declined from its peak of 80,000 members in the city to only 20,000. Although craft unions siphoned off some of the decline, in the 1890s they lacked the moralistic fervor that had made the Knights such a commanding force. And as the Knights declined, so did organized labor in general. American Federation of Labor president Samuel Gompers complained that the presence of its affiliates in Philadelphia was "so meager as to allow [the AFL] to be snubbed at every opportunity."[78] From the heights of the nineteenth-century labor movement, Philadelphia workers watched their city sink into anti-unionism at the turn of the century.

Sect and Society

For a brief moment, millennial Christianity presented organized labor with an opportunity to push political dialogue toward a greater egalitarianism and democracy. Despite the complex interactions with mainstream religion that further differentiated various labor subcultures, the sect-like character of the Knights of Labor managed to unite workers around the vision of redeeming the republic through the actions of virtuous citizens. That vision was especially powerful because it absorbed so many ideas from American culture while recasting them in a radical democratic framework.[79] For women, the Knights expanded domesticity and home protection to encompass female labor activism; for immigrants, the Knights promised to protect American democratic ideals; for white and black American-born workers, the Knights provided a link to the moral-reform radicalism of abolitionism, and focused its energy on a new form of exploitation.

Like most sects, however, the Knights were ill-suited to exert power in the dominant social and political order. An organization relying on intense commitment to the fellowship of believers was a poor mechanism for containing debate or effecting compromise, two functions necessary for engaging in American politics. As the Order grew to a size capable of influencing political dialogue, it absorbed elements that held differing social, cultural, and political visions. Size, itself, undercut the cultural homogeneity sustaining the Order's sect-like character. These inherent contradictions, exacerbated by powerful enemies, tore the Order apart. Nevertheless, the Knights engaged the dominant culture, particularly through their religiosity. The Order's social Christianity paralleled the beginnings of a similar doctrine in the mainstream churches, both of which helped pave the way for a different sort of working class religion in the early twentieth century.

4

To Lift the Crushing Burdens of the Poor

IN December 1901, as the Philadelphia labor movement regrouped from the long depression of the 1890s, the Central Labor Union hosted Ben Tillett, the British socialist and labor leader. Tillett spoke of the prominent place Philadelphia workers held in the history of trade unionism and expressed dismay at their current weakened and disorganized state. He urged workers to revive their unions and avoid political alliances with the middle class. In particular, he cautioned the local labor movement against placing confidence in the ability of ministers to mediate the widening gulf between labor and capital. "Clergymen preach to us and dine with the rich," Tillett proclaimed. "When they dine with us and preach to the rich, we will have more confidence in them."[1]

Tillett's skepticism aside, Philadelphia's churchmen went through something of a transformation in their attitudes toward organized labor during the 1890s. Theological developments slowly coalesced with a new awareness of human interdependence and the social message of Christianity, increasingly emphasized by working-class critics of mainstream churches. Urban blight, unpredictable economic cycles, and inhuman industrial conditions exposed the seamy side of American progress. Furthermore, to many churchmen, bad housing, long work weeks, low wages, and undernourishment seemed almost impenetrable barriers to the expansion of religion. In response, seminaries introduced the study of sociology, and prominent clergymen began to reconsider the moral virtues of the labor movement. For the first time, the environmental roots of poverty, crime, and irreligion attracted clerical attention equal to that previously spent on the sins and spiritualism of the individual.

Advocates of a Social Gospel, however, faced many doubters like Ben Tillett. Years of religious opposition had made organized labor extremely suspicious of clergymen. Moreover, Christians were far from united; many continued to view trade unions as "despotic and revolutionary in tendency," and balked at collectivist responses to social ills. Few saw the issue as clearly as Social-Gospel leader Charles Stelzle: "The trades union has come to stay," he argued, and it "is simply a question as to whether it will be a good unionism or a bad unionism."[2]

The Social Gospel, then, emerged from new theological trends and a blend of genuine moral indignation at inequality and the fear that organized labor might acquire radical characteristics. In Philadelphia, as in other Northeastern urban centers, clergymen intruded into the arena of class conflict hoping both to win wage earners to Christianity and also to steer unions away from socialism by advocating a Christian form of social justice. These efforts had important ramifications for a local labor movement that was simultaneously pursuing immediate support while holding long-range ideals.

A War on Slums

The Social Gospel did not suddenly appear in the 1890s. A few socially concerned clergymen had established contacts with working class groups as early as the 1870s. In Philadelphia, a core of independently minded ministers provided moral support for the Knights of Labor. Reverends J. Vannote and S. Carr Woodhead in the Southwark section of the city held meetings for workingmen that championed ethical relationships of capital and labor. Woodhead in particular blamed corporations for "the unpardonable ill-treatment of the laboring masses." Another group of ministers led by Alfred H. Love formed a Universal Peace Union and a Board of Arbitration to help mediate local labor disputes. In addition, Mason W. Pressly's United Presbyterian Church broke with "the dominant Beecherism of the pulpit," according to *The Tocsin*.[3]

Philadelphia Social-Gospel clergymen, mirroring the efforts of influential ministers in other cities, attempted to penetrate the barriers between social reform and the church. Episcopalian Bishop Henry Potter of New York helped establish the Church Association for the Advancement of the Interests of Labor in 1887. Baptist leaders Walter Rauschenbusch, Leighton Williams, and Samuel Zane Batten created an informal Social-Gospel group that institutionalized Baptist liberalism in 1892 through the Brotherhood of the Kingdom. Similarly, Congregationalists formed a Committee on Capital and Labor in 1892, headed by Washington Gladden, one of the most prominent spokesmen for the Social Gospel. Even the Evangelical Alliance, once a stronghold for religious conservatism, became an outlet for the discussion of social Christianity once Josiah Strong took over in 1886.[4]

Although some denominations were slower to respond to social turmoil and labor's challenge than were others, workers began to witness a change in the attitudes of ministers. When Knights of Labor leader Terence V. Powderly queried labor activists around the country about the relationship between the Order and the churches in 1887–88, most acknowledged that clergymen generally were becoming more favorably inclined toward the working class.[5]

The changing spirit of Christianity stemmed from several sources. Both evolutionary theory, and a new theological movement that subjected the Bible to a more critical reading based on historical context and the methods of literary criticism, injected a wave of modernist thought into the churches. This higher criticism or New Theology, as it came to be called, bolstered a group of clergy who stressed the immanence of God in the processes of modern culture. Expounded by such prominent ministers as Horace Bushnell, Daniel Coit Gilman, and Theodore Munger, the New Theology injected German rationalism, a progressive view of history, and the need for the "wider study of man" into

American Christianity. Similarly science, particularly evolutionary theory, forced clergymen to adapt religious thought and institutions to cultural relativism. While these developments divided theologians, they gave a tremendous boost to the liberal activism that surfaced in settlement houses, civic reform, and more generally in progressivism.[6]

In other ways, the Social Gospel drew upon the benevolence and institutional forms already established by evangelical Protestants. The early stages of a Social Gospel in the Catholic Church, for instance, were little more than an extension of traditional Catholic social doctrine with newly pietistic and affluent Catholics creating institutions in direct competition with their Protestant counterparts.[7] Among Protestants, many liberals shared the evangelical tendencies of conservative church leaders. They hoped to win converts to the church quite as much as draw attention to social injustice. Urban missions and institutional churches predated the Social Gospel, and newer, more secular forms of voluntary association work, like the settlements, still employed predominately Protestant men and women who hoped to extend Christian influence to the working class. Social Christianity also continued to emphasize morally uplifting measures like temperance and self-help that attracted conservative as well as liberal support.

Until the lines between the Social Gospel and more traditional evangelicalism became more rigid around 1910, conservatives like Russell Conwell and John Wanamaker could move easily in and out of organizations championed by such liberals as Samuel Zane Batten and Clinton R. Woodruff. The Protestant Episcopal City Mission, headed by Social-Gospel clergymen, routinely encouraged conservative support for its labor bureau, which found employment for men during the depression of 1893, by stressing that "we encourage the working class to labor in some way for everything they receive." Despite severe unemployment, relief superintendent Herman Duhring appealed to conservative sentiments by adding that "self-help is the straight gate and the narrow way." Through a wide diversity of programs, people striving to spread the experience of grace frequently found common cause with others forcing the nation to acknowledge poverty.[8]

The blending of liberal, modernist theology with evangelicalism so expanded Christian social work that it has been portrayed, until recently, as a wholly new crusade. The emergence of new religious associations like the Christian League of Philadelphia (established 1895), the Church Unity Society (1886), and the various denominational social unions (1890–1901), all of which organized church men and women for the discussion of social questions, appears to add weight to that argument. This is especially true when considered in tandem with the ostensibly secular associations like the Woman's Civic Betterment Association (1902), the Civic Club (1894), settlements (after 1890), and the numerous improvement associations, all of which relied heavily upon the involvement of Protestant clergy and lay activists.[9]

However, the thriving condition of many older voluntary associations—the Law and Order Society, the Social Purity Alliance, the New Century Club, the Evangelical Alliance, Catholic missions, and the institutional churches—provided the strong base from which the Social Gospel could build, whatever their social or political perspectives. In the 1890s, distinctions between associations stressing social control and those stressing social justice were minimal; for many workers, settlements were indistinguishable from institutional churches. Indeed, Philadelphia's *Catholic Standard* could discern no major differences between the two.[10]

Nevertheless, the liberal thrust of the Social Gospel invigorated Christian activism even as it remained linked to earlier evangelicalism. In 1893, liberal Protestants inaugurated a dramatic campaign to abolish the slums in Philadelphia. Walter Vrooman, a Christian socialist at the far left of the Social-Gospel movement and one of a trio of brothers involved in an array of reform crusades, had come to the city in 1892 from New York's Lower East Side where he had established a Union for Concerted Moral Effort. In December, he enlisted support from settlement workers, housing reformers, and a number of ministers "to help in the moral and intellectual uplifting of the people." Most importantly, he attracted the attention of Frank M. Goodchild, a Baptist minister whose congregation was in a notorious sweatshop district. On February 6, 1893, Goodchild introduced Vrooman to the Baptist Ministerial Conference, which endorsed Vrooman's idea for a Conference of Moral Workers in part because the program was so vague that it appeared to be as much an attack on vice as it was on slums or capitalism.[11]

The Baptist endorsement allowed for the rapid expansion of Vrooman's conference. Goodchild's Spruce Street Baptist Church and Hugh O. Gibbons's Pine Street Presbyterian Church hosted meetings that attracted ministers from the major evangelical denominations, prominent lay reformers like Clinton R. Woodruff and Hannah Fox, and a strong element of Nationalists and Single Taxers. Speakers advocated everything from kindergartens to abolishing the monopoly on land. Especially for the Protestant young men and women connected with the relatively new settlement movement, the variety of reforms—better housing designs, savings banks, public health laws, building and loan associations—offered guidance on some immediate tasks at hand.[12]

Vrooman and the coleader of the conference, settlement worker Charles Caryl, however, tried to recruit beyond the socially aware Protestant middle class. One of their earliest supporters was the North Philadelphia reform rabbi Joseph Krauskopf, a man intent on Americanizing Judaism and improving the condition of Jewish immigrants. Krauskopf quickly assumed a leadership role. Similarly, the conference made special attempts to solicit Catholic approval, which they eventually received from the editor of the *Catholic Times*. The Catholic Church had recently received the papal encyclical, *Rerum Novarum*, which encouraged a degree of prolabor social consciousness. It also attracted several members from the Ethical Culture Society. Despite this unusually broad, nonsectarian alliance, the conference enlisted support from 453 ministers and held almost nightly meetings during March and April in "a general uprising against the almighty dollar."[13]

Even more strikingly, the conference sought the support of the labor movement. At first, Vrooman and Caryl appealed to members of unions as individuals "interested in improving the conditions of life" in principally industrial sections of the city. However, their appeal quickly expanded. The conference tried to recruit entire unions by investigating factory law violations, and by offering to convince local merchants to sell only goods bearing the union label. These efforts met with some enthusiasm. Alexander Wright of the Knights of Labor was a frequent speaker. Fred Fleury, a union printer, stated that there was "no possibility of failure" in this "marriage of the church and organized labor." Even the socialist delegate from the Cigarmakers Union, Harry Parker, commended the work of Vrooman and moved that the United Labor League support the conference.[14]

The reaction of several craft unions, on the other hand, showed the gap between the church and the labor movement in 1893. The Plasterers Union refused to discuss Vrooman's appeal to the United Labor League. The Philadelphia Typographical Union, despite Fleury's involvement, did not have a "very favorable impression" of the conference's ability to achieve its goals. The Typographical Union committee, based on a "realistic" view of the matter, stated that "the movement does not warrant us in advising members of this Union to individually connect themselves" with the conference.[15]

The rapid demise of the conference's broad alliance also demonstrated how little headway the Social Gospel had made on the local level by the 1890s. In late March 1893, the conference began criticizing the sweatshop production of garments and advocating factory and child labor laws, just as Protestants voiced resentment of the growing influence of Jews in the conference. Besides Krauskopf, who was one of the leaders, Felix Adler and Henry Berkowitz became frequent speakers at conference meetings. Berkowitz, a rabbi at Congregation Rodef Shalom, infuriated many clergymen when he linked slum conditions to the oppression of capitalism. "An analysis of the antipathies of castes and classes," argued Berkowitz, "lays bare the vicious character of the crime of class domination."[16]

The mix of anti-Semitic and anti-labor sentiments combined to shatter the conference. On March 25, Vrooman, Caryl, and many of the settlement workers cooperating with the conference gave full support to a strike led by the largely Jewish garment workers against low wages and sweatshop conditions. When the strike became violent, much of the public support for the conference evaporated. Even the *North American*, a newspaper that had trumpeted the value of Vrooman's Christian social work, deserted the crusade.[17] Moreover, the craft unions that had refused to become active in the conference also turned their backs on the Jewish garment workers. Indeed, trade unions, following the decline of the Knights of Labor, had retreated to a defensive, self-protecting incrementalism that largely rejected new Italian and Jewish immigrants as well as working-class solidarity.[18]

The fact that the conference disbanded in May 1893 when Vrooman and Caryl left the city under a cloud of controversy appeared to justify organized labor's lack of confidence in the recent changes in Christian social thought. Most Social-Gospel activists were not yet ready to actively support any form of trade unionism. For its part, the labor movement was largely content with its role as protector of American-born craftsmen. The power of the employer associations that moved against the Knights of Labor in the 1880s had shattered the broad visions of working-class solidarity. Trade unions were in the slow process of regrouping. The Panic of 1893 and the manifestations of social unrest attending the ensuing depression, however, altered the relationship between Christianity and trade unionism in Philadelphia.

Salvation from the Present Iniquity

Shortly after the collapse of the Conference of Moral Workers, the nation suffered a severe economic crisis. A break in the stock market followed on the heels of the sudden failure of the National Cordage Company, which only five months earlier had paid a stock dividend of 100 percent. The summer brought a run on banks and more business failures. By the end of 1893, 642 banks had failed, more than 22,000 miles of railroads were in receivership, and 16,000 business firms had declared bankruptcy. Unemployment levels were estimated at one-fourth of the workforce, stimulating numerous demonstrations for municipal public works. As Philadelphia's United Labor League (ULL) proclaimed, "The present alarming distress and wide-spread disaster which has overwhelmed the industrial population of Philadelphia, calls for some action on our part as wage-earners. A condition, not a theory, confronts us," which relegates "able-bodied men, willing and anxious to work . . . to the ranks of pauperism and crime." The League, with a modest component of socialists, proposed a labor party as "the means that will encompass our salvation from the present iniquity of industrial slavery."[19]

Philadelphia's labor movement was not alone in its concern. The city's religious institutions responded to the economic collapse with herculean efforts. Protestants and Catholics coupled an unprecedented expansion in charity with a new emphasis on industrial justice. In the depths of a depression that caused untold misery and hardship among those recognized as the industrious poor, Christianity and the labor movement forged a new relationship.

The emergence of a Social Gospel emphasizing industrial justice affected various churches quite differently. The first denomination to actively respond to the crisis in Philadelphia was the Protestant Episcopal Church. The Protestant Episcopal City Mission organized neighborhood kitchens that gave out 78,000 meals and provided relief to over 2,600 people in the Center City fifth ward alone. It gave employment to over 2,000 men in special works projects. Spurred in part by the advance of liberalism in the Anglican Church, Episcopalian clergymen and lay activists supplied many of the soldiers for a much-needed burst of expansion in church social work. In addition, many of the workers involved in secular associations, like the social settlements, were Episcopalians. Anna and Helen Devereux, Robert R. P. Bradford, and T. J. Taylor, among others, distinguished themselves through their work with the College Settlement Association, the Lighthouse, and the Women's Union in the Interest of Labor. Helen Devereux, especially, became a vigorous friend of unions and a frequent participant at meetings of the ULL. Although she started as a well-to-do charity worker, she spent many years in social reform, gravitating toward settlement work and women's labor organizations. In 1910, she was arrested while on the picket line with the striking female garment workers.[20]

Baptists also developed a strong Social-Gospel component in Philadelphia, but one quite different than the Episcopalians. Second in size only to the Methodists among Protestant churches in the city, Baptists, as part of the more reformed Calvinist wing of Protestantism, were more prominent among proponents of the New Theology. In Philadelphia, the church included several well-known liberals, including George Dana Boardman of the First Baptist Church, who helped start four missions in working-class districts. An early member of the Universal Peace Union that tried to arbitrate labor disputes, Boardman led a "self-sacrificing life among the poor" without the publicity accorded to men like Russell Conwell. Similarly, H. L. Wayland, who edited the local Baptist weekly, was a voice for liberalism. He, like Frank Goodchild, had devoted a great deal of time to Vrooman's Conference of Moral Workers. Finally, the extensive Baptist work among working-class immigrants owed a large debt to Samuel Zane Batten who preached in Philadelphia during the 1890s and again after 1910. Batten led a major campaign to start Italian- and Polish-language urban churches that would also provide much-needed financial and social assistance.[21]

Certainly, the commanding figure in Baptist social activism was Russell Conwell. His Baptist Temple in North Philadelphia set the standard for institutional churches and its work greatly expanded during the long depression of the 1890s. But Conwell also epitomized the torturous division that liberalism caused within the Baptist Church. While he, like Baptist ministers in general, raised large sums of money to assist the poor, he despised labor organizations for what he viewed as their assault on the liberty of the individual. Coercive labor leaders became an "ungodly aristocracy." Wayland, Batten, and the city Baptist Association agreed. Perhaps the large donations by such manufacturers as John P. Crozer and John Stetson accounted for a hesitancy to attack capitalism verbally, but probably more important was a long-term church commitment to personal liberty, dating from the colonial era. In any event, the Social Gospel within the city's Baptist Church, although sympathetic to the poor and unemployed and their lack of control over the conditions that plagued them, was not inclined toward any support for organized labor.[22]

In some churches the Social Gospel meant little more than an encouragement to increased charity. The Society of Friends, for one, had little involvement in new theological trends. While the Quakers had a long history of benevolence, the prosperity and remoteness of the Society's members made sympathy with the labor movement a distant possibility. The Catholic Church was, on the other hand, more entrenched in working-class neighborhoods. Its expansion of charitable work was critical to parishoners, but was accomplished without a commitment to a collective pursuit of industrial justice, despite the encyclical *Rerum Novarum*. Instead, the Philadelphia *Catholic Standard* actually was more suspicious of organized labor than it had been in the 1880s following what it viewed as its ill-fated support for the Knights of Labor.[23] Although the church was better situated to reach the urban working class, Catholicism paled next to Protestantism in controlling the dialogue of the Social Gospel.

Some Protestant denominations, however, shared Catholicism's caution concerning the Social Gospel. The New Theology exerted little influence on Philadelphia's Lutherans who exhibited a muted social conscience. *The Lutheran*, for instance, blamed the depression of 1893 on the waste of the working class. Ten years later the editor praised Lutherans for having remained aloof from the "enormous amount of confusion in the minds of Christians on great moral questions involved in the strife between labor and capital." Lutherans had not given into the reigning social passions, nor had they introduced the study of sociology or the "labor question" in their seminaries. Rather, the church had clung to its distinctive message and its moral and religious bearings.[24]

Lutherans, however, demonstrated that the Social Gospel could penetrate even conservative denominations. The church produced one of the most dynamic spokesmen for social Christianity in the city, the Reverend Edwin Heyl Delk. Delk moved increasingly toward a position at the far left of the political spectrum encompassing Social-Gospel Protestantism. By 1909, he not only supported trade unions but also argued that a "communistic spirit" was normal for the church. Socialism, he asserted, was a "movement for a truer realization of the kingdom of God here and now," and was "a work committed to the whole church." Delk was an exception, but Lutherans were hardly immune to urban liberalism, as the establishment of the Lutheran City Mission in 1902 demonstrates.[25]

The most dynamic people in behalf of Philadelphia Social-Gospel activities were the Presbyterians. While slow to adopt social Christianity, once Presbyterians did they quickly dominated the influential Social-Gospel associations. Spurred by the depression of the 1890s, such ministers as J. Gray Bolton, Charles Wood, Kemper Bocock, and Robert Ogden, all of whom toiled in working-class neighborhoods, led Presbyterians into social work with such vigor that the Philadelphia Presbytery grew by 38 percent between 1893 and 1901. Moreover, the church was perhaps the best equipped to meet the challenge of the depression. The Presbyterians had an active and prosperous group of laymen, including such leading merchant and manufacturing families as the Wanamakers, Disstons, Cramps, and Converses. In addition, they were decidedly evangelical in purpose, especially when compared with the other wealthy denomination, the Episcopalians. Calvinistic Presbyterians thus dominated the institutional church work in the city and built impressive records in such secular or nonsectarian organizations as the Interchurch Federation, the Church Society for the Advancement of the Interests of Labor (CAIL), and the YM and YWCAs.[26]

Presbyterians also distinguished themselves in cooperation with organized labor. Kemper Bocock became the first clergyman to sit as a delegate to the Central Labor Union (CLU). His successor, J. Gray Bolton, helped the CLU uncover a city filtration work scam that helped save union jobs.[27] It seems contradictory that a denomination supported by prosperous capitalists would join so actively in social reform, especially with organized labor. However, as Clyde Griffen has shown, many churches associated with early social Christianity obtained support from wealthy laymen.[28] To a certain degree, it was only well-endowed churches that could afford extensive social programs. In addition, many laymen found social criticism healthy even when they disagreed. Finally, there was a genuine Christianity among some businessmen who had supported older forms of benevolence. Just when these efforts crossed over the line that divided paternalistic from Social-Gospel sentiments was difficult to detect. It would have taken a great deal of vigilance and resolve for benevolent capitalists to desert congregations the moment the church expressed a social conscience.

Of course, another reason that compelled Protestant churches to develop social programs was to combat socialist tendencies among labor unions. Few liberal clergymen found collectivist strategies attractive, and Christian socialism had few adherents among Philadelphia's ministers. Although the depression had decimated the local labor movement, other signs pointed to an increasingly radical working class. The violence of the Homestead strike in 1892 was already on the minds of many religious leaders when the depression of 1893 brought the prospect of renewed agitation over unemployment and wage cuts. The militancy of and widespread support for the 1894 Pullman strike, as well as the specter of Jacob Coxey's unemployed army marching on Washington, shocked and upset many clergy and laymen. Samuel Wagenhals, for instance in the *Lutheran Church Review*, labeled the railroad workers "madmen" for trying "to array all the labor unions of the country against the law." Even such normally sympathetic publications as the *Outlook* and the *Christian Union* denounced the idea of labor solidarity as dangerous and foreign.[29]

The fact that socialism was suffering setbacks in the national labor movement suggests that the clergy's preoccupation with radicalism was perhaps out of proportion to the threat. Indeed, the socialists's call for a labor party within the Philadelphia ULL ultimately went down in defeat on a delegate vote of twenty-six to sixteen.[30] But for many Philadelphia ministers, labor militancy, political socialism, and even craft unionism were indistinguishable signs of radicalism.

Nevertheless, the city's unions exhibited some radical tendencies in the first years of the depression. Resisting wage cuts and layoffs, textile strikes occurred in 1893 and again in 1895, the latter involving thousands of workers in a lengthy battle against the employers' association. In 1894, cabinetmakers, garment workers, painters, brewery workers, and shoeworkers staged strikes and boycotts against employers. In December, more radical delegates to the ULL proposed resolutions supporting the Socialist Labor Party (SLP) in city elections.[31] The next year brought a bitter streetcar strike that resulted in rioting in working-class neighborhoods. Finally, the ULL admitted as members many of the unions connected with the United Hebrew and United German Trades, injecting the influence of the more politically minded Germans and Jews into debates.[32]

The lack of a socialist majority in the ULL continued, however, despite the absence of most of the conservative building trades unions from the League. Although craft unionists demonstrated a greater political activism during the 1890s, since much of their activity was contradictory it was by no means clear what it all signified. The joint sponsorship by the ULL and the Socialist Labor Party of a talk by British socialist John Burns collapsed amid SLP demands that it have the chairmanship. The ULL supported the SLP resolution denouncing a local judge who was abridging the free speech and encouraging the arrest of members of the Cigarmakers Union who were not yet citizens; yet the ULL also defeated by a vote of eleven to ten a resolution denouncing the arrests of anarchists.[33] Meanwhile, the Printers Union sent two socialist delegates—H. L. Minds and Fred Long—to the ULL, but also helped force the radical United Hebrew Trades out of the ULL. Finally, the Cigarmakers and the Hatters, two unions with large radical contingents in the 1890s, solicited support for their union labels among the Republican and Democratic parties. Philadelphia Hatters leader Edward Moore was soon to lead an attack on the large Jewish and socialist contingents in his union, while Cigarmakers leader John Kirchner became the most vocal opponent of socialism in the city's labor movement.[34]

After 1893, the activities of liberal Christian men and women ensured that labor organizations had a viable political alternative to socialism. In 1895, Unitarian minister W. I. Nichols introduced the Toynbee Society, a local organization headed by Social-Gospel clergy, to the ULL. The Society sought to help labor become sufficiently organized and obtain public support so that employers and workers could negotiate from equitable positions. Nichols felt that this would foster arbitration, reduce strikes, and steer unions "to practical measures, leaving to other organizations the consideration of social panaceas," presumably socialism. That same year, groups from the Baptist, Methodist, and Presbyterian Churches began work with the Bakers Union to abolish Sunday labor, and Holy Trinity Episcopal Church sponsored meetings soliciting the cooperation of the Civic Club, the Women's Christian Temperance Union and the Women's Union in the Interest of Labor on behalf of legislation limiting the hours of female and child labor.[35]

Christian-influenced voluntary organizations joined in this activism. Dr. M. V. Ball and Anna Davies, leaders of the College Settlement Association, provided financial support for working-class families during the strikes of garment and textile workers. By the turn of the century, the Consumers' League had galvanized middle-class women behind a demand for healthy conditions and fair wages for women workers. Anna Devereux, formerly of the Protestant Episcopal City Mission, and Florence Sanville carried the League's message to meetings of the ULL. Other groups like the New Century Guild, which prepared working-class women for more lucrative jobs, and the Octavia Hill Association, a reform group emulating the British woman who led the movement for better housing for the poor, brought Protestants into a close cooperation with unions on important issues for wage earners.[36]

By 1895, organized labor was building upon the support proffered principally by Protestant churches, even though there was a growing presence of Catholics and Jews in the ULL. The largely Jewish and German Bakers Union, for instance, stated that the Consumers' League, led by Protestant women, "will prove a powerful agency" in achieving labor's goals. Meanwhile, the union was presenting its case for the abolition of Sunday labor to various ministerial associations. In 1896, the Toynbee Society, with the ULL's support, initiated a bill in the state legislature that resulted in a law guaranteeing the rights of workers to organize without employer intimidation.[37] The emerging alliance of labor and Social-Gospel activists also turned to prominent

Republican Party reformers with its legislative program and obtained results. The Bakers Union thanked liberal reformer Clinton Woodruff for his work on a law mandating health and safety inspections in bakeshops. ULL president and legislative committee chair, the conservative George Chance, praised both the Clerical Brotherhood of the Protestant Episcopal Church and Senator Boies Penrose for their efforts on behalf of labor legislation in the state. Even the socialist Cigarmakers Union delegate, J. Mahlon Barnes, had kind words for Christian activists when he applauded John Wanamaker's work in mediating the streetcar workers' dispute and scored the labor paper, *Unity and Progress*, for "besmirching" Wanamaker's senatorial campaign.[38]

In the depths of the depression, with the labor movement largely in retreat, Christian reformers helped trade unions obtain legislation governing tenement-house manufacturing, female and child labor, safety and health conditions, and prison labor. In addition, other laws ostensibly freed organized labor from coercion, provided for an eight-hour workday on public works, gave unions the power to license building trades workers, and protected the union label from counterfeiters. By 1897, AFL president Samuel Gompers was able to point to George Chance's record of securing favorable legislation as a model, and hoped Chance's efforts would pay other dividends—"I trust too that you may be quite successful in bringing about healthier sentiments among the wage workers of Philadelphia so that they may more readily realize the necessity of organization on trade union lines."[39]

By 1898, then, Social-Gospel reformers had earned considerable good will among the city's labor movement. Members of the Toynbee Society regularly addressed ULL meetings on political matters; Anna Devereux of the Consumers' League and the Episcopal Church was ULL secretary; and Clinton Woodruff was the League's legal counsel. The ULL, a year later, began admitting Reverend Kemper Bocock to meetings as a fraternal delegate from the city's Christian Social Union. More importantly, the achievements of liberal Christianity bolstered moderate elements in the ULL, particularly after the more conservative building trades unions rejoined in 1898.

Still, the League's meetings were punctuated by name-calling between the socialists and George Chance, or with debates between socialists and moderates over the need for a labor party or the endorsement of Socialist Labor Party candidates. By 1900, the appeal of reform legislation waned for many trade unionists as manufacturers began blatantly violating the laws without penalty or, worse, successfully challenging the laws in court. Meanwhile, the city's unions began a rather remarkable resurgence. They resolved to implement the laws by force "above the sordid interest of those who care more for the Dollar than they do for the prosperity of those who obey the Divine injunction to 'earn their bread in the sweat of their face.'"[40] The failure of the initial efforts of Social-Gospel reformers to ensure industrial equality or class harmony perplexed Christian men and women. The dramatic growth of organized labor in the city presented them with an added incentive to redouble their efforts to achieve industrial justice.

A Plea for Honest and Righteous Dealing

The resurgence of the labor movement at the turn of the century continued, in large measure, the interactive dialogue with social Christianity. Philadelphia unionists emphasized the legitimacy and respectability of their cause by linking it to religion. Shortly after hosting the socialist skeptic, Ben Tillett, the city's labor movement applauded the stirring message of faith delivered by United Mine Workers leader John Mitchell: "As a boy I was brought up to believe that God conferred no more power or privilege upon one man than upon another, and, notwithstanding the declaration of the controllers of the trusts, I am not prepared to abandon the teachings of my mother."[41]

Other Philadelphia unionists echoed Mitchell's confidence that God was on the side of organized labor. Iron molder George Kemp emphasized the moral component of unionism: "Labor is worship"; workers should thus dedicate themselves through collective effort to "live up to [those] foundation principles of unionism." John White, a textile unionist, closed one speech with "a plea for honest and righteous dealing [between labor and capital] as laid down in the Scriptures."[42] The religious sanction of industrial justice, then, received much attention. The Union Label League handed out leaflets quoting prominent religious figures as well as Scripture to encourage consumers to buy only products bearing the union label. The Philadelphia labor weekly, the *New Era*, stated simply, "He has no religion who has no morality."[43]

The emergence of a large, moderate, Christian faction in the city's labor movement encouraged continued activism by Social-Gospel clergymen. Meetings of the Church Society for the Advancement of the Interests of Labor (CAIL), for instance, attracted union officers and business agents from the Stone Masons, Bricklayers, Upholsterers, Weavers, and Lacemakers. Meetings of local leaders of capital and labor, under religious auspices, obtained support from the building, printing, and several metal trades unions. Even the chairman of the Philadelphia Sabbath Association was invited to address the ULL several times in 1898 and 1899 on the value of organization and combination in pursuing the mutual interests of churches and labor.[44]

The regrouping and growth of the city's labor movement at the turn of the century had a moderate character. As the economy revived, the Printers replaced their socialist delegates to the ULL with more conservative men like George Chance, who was then elected ULL president. The Painters substituted the moderate James McGraith for its former delegate, socialist James Allen, and Joshua Morgan of the Machinists brought a more conservative viewpoint to ULL meetings than had his predecessor, William Delahay.[45] Equally important for the conservative character of the ULL was the re-entry of the building trades unions, which had refused to affiliate previously because of the belief that the League was controlled by socialist unions like the Cigarmakers. Building trades unions enjoyed an astounding growth spurt after 1897 as construction projects in the city boomed. The Carpenters signed up more than 1,000 new members in 1899 and the Paperhangers enrolled 600. Others, like the Plasterers, the Bricklayers, and the Elevator Constructors, won closed-shop agreements and the eight-hour workday, giving them considerable clout in the local labor movement. In 1902, the building trades unions erased all traces of the socialist connotations of the old ULL when they demanded that the League change its name to the Central Labor Union.[46]

Social-Gospel activists contributed to the resurgence of organized labor, encouraged by the moral tone of union leaders. Glassmakers president Denis Hayes claimed that his union's growth would enable it to surround members "with all the social and moral protection it possibly can." Liberal CAIL ministers A. J. Arkin and J. Poyntz Tyler contrasted those sentiments with the conditions they discovered when they took a United Garment Workers-guided tour of the nonunion, sweatshop clothing district. Arkin and Tyler denounced the garment manufacturers and helped the wives of Kensington union members to organize the Women's Union Label League as a vigilance committee to pressure local merchants to sell only union-made goods.[47]

One key component of the clergy's support for trade unions was the appearance of collective bargaining. Proposed by liberals in the National Civic Federation (where many nationally prominent Social-Gospel advocates were active), the trade agreement promised both fairness and industrial peace. As the American Federation of Labor grew from about 300,000 in 1897 to just under two million in 1904, the trade agreement became something of a panacea for liberal Christians fearing widespread labor conflict. Indeed, although Philadelphia Social-Gospel activists continued to promote reformist labor legislation, they increasingly looked to collective bargaining as local unions gained power. Between 1899 and 1903, sympathetic clergymen witnessed the signing of trade agreements by the Molders Union and the Foundrymen's Association, by the United Garment Workers and the Philadelphia Clothing Trades Association, and by the Allied Printing Trades Council and the Philadelphia Typothetae. Moreover, when bargaining broke down between the building trades unions and the Master Builders' Exchange, union leader Frank Feeney asked for the intervention of clergymen to avert a strike, asserting that union solidarity epitomized "the noble brotherhood of man brought into humble lives with the birth of the carpenter's son of Nazareth."[48]

Trade agreements, the expanding base of union moderates, the explicit evocation of Christian sentiments by union leaders, and the presence of Social-Gospel clergymen in labor organizations demonstrated the mutual benefits of a labor–religion alliance. Unions gained respectability and acceptance while achieving tangible gains in membership, wages, and working conditions. At the same time, liberal clergymen were contributing to industrial justice, the expansion of Christianity among the working class, and the prospects for labor peace and moderation.

The growth of mutual respect between organized labor and the Social Gospel was further enhanced by the appearance of clergymen who spoke the language of unionism. Nationally, the most prominent of these ministers was Charles Stelzle. At the turn of the century, Stelzle, a union machinist turned minister, formalized contact between organized labor and his church. In New York, he established a church-sponsored Labor Temple that provided local unions with a meeting place outside the saloon. He encouraged the exchange of fraternal delegates between ministerial associations and central labor unions, which led to Kemper Bocock's admission to the Philadelphia CLU. Finally, in 1903, he created a Department of Church and Labor within the Presbyterian Church, a mechanism that was soon to be adopted by the Methodists, Baptists, Congregationalists, and others.[49]

Stelzle presented his message in terms that workers understood. Shelby Smith, editor of Philadelphia's *Eastern Laborer*, commended Stelzle's style and delivery after one of his frequent visits to the city. He was not "theatric," nor was he given to "flights of oratory" or "bursts of eloquence." Instead, Stelzle's speeches resembled a conversation in the shop where he would "sit on his old tool chest and visit with his old associates." It was this style that caused literally hundreds of local labor newspapers and trade-union journals to carry Stelzle's weekly columns. By 1905, his messages appeared regularly in Philadelphia's *Trades' Union News*.[50] Moreover, labor people trusted him. They even called on him for assistance in matters concerning relations with local churches. When local Presbyterian churches began to use nonunion labor to erect new windows, for example, the CLU wrote Stelzle asking him to use his influence in the matter.[51]

The city produced its own counterparts to Stelzle. J. Gray Bolton, Kemper Bocock, Edwin Heyl Delk, and J. G. Bickerton, among others, earned the loyalty of labor and spearheaded local Progressive organizations. Delk was one of the few Lutherans to embrace organized labor, while Bolton, Bocock, and Bickerton had long careers of social activism in working-class wards. But only A. J. Arkin, of St. George's Episcopal Church in the working-class Port Richmond section near Kensington, spoke to labor from personal experience. A native of Germany, Arkin came to the United States in 1880 to join a socialist colony in South Dakota. When the colony collapsed he worked various jobs until he became involved in the labor movement as a member, and later an officer, of the Order of Railroad Telegraphers; later he joined the staff of a weekly labor newspaper in Chicago. These activities brought him into contact with the leading labor men in the country including Eugene Debs, whom he admired. After the failure of the labor paper, he relocated in Butte, Montana. There, under the influence of the local Episcopalian minister, he tried to escape the "feverish life" of the saloons and gambling houses in that "wide open mining town." After spending countless hours in the church library, he entered divinity school in the 1890s and took his first position at St. George's in 1901.[52]

Arkin, like Stelzle, won the trust of Philadelphia trade unionists. He chastized capitalists for utilizing sweatshop and child labor; as head of the local CAIL, he arranged debates between unionists and employers on such important issues as apprenticeship, the closed shop, and the usefulness of strikes. Meanwhile, Arkin served in nearly every Progressive association. He convinced the reformist Housing Association to build low-cost workingmen's homes near the playground he established, served as head of the local Coal and Stamp Savings Funds, raised money to send children on vacations, and advocated state-wide child labor laws. He also found time to successfully mediate labor disputes and direct a "Father's Club" at St. George's that frequently attracted union officials.[53]

While few ministers had the ability of Stelzle and Arkin to

communicate on equal terms with organized labor, unionists increasingly called upon clergymen to act as fraternal delegates, mediators, or spokesmen, as organized labor continued to seek legitimacy. Perhaps no other public event demonstrated the desire for respectability more than the reception accorded Presbyterian minister James B. Ely's tent meetings for workers. Beginning in 1902, Ely arranged for special Sunday services to be held at Lemon Hill in Fairmount Park each summer. He specifically invited union workers and provided prominent clergymen to give sermons on some social theme. More importantly, Ely's efforts appealed to the working class. The *Trades' Union News* applauded Ely and the few others who "had faith to believe that the working people of Philadelphia are not heathen by any means, and that if a service were keyed to their desires and tastes, with excellent music, they would respond."[54]

Philadelphia unions, in fact, did respond to the services. The CLU appointed delegates and frequently sent men to serve as ushers. The weekly meetings attracted between two and four thousand, while special services, such as those on Labor Day, drew over 15,000. Printer Shelby Smith claimed that the 1904 Labor Day "congregation was comparatively all [union] card men" and their families.[55] When cold weather halted the outdoor meetings, Harry Kurten of the Building Trades Council convinced Ely to continue the meetings at the People's Opera House in North Philadelphia. Many unions, especially in the building and printing trades, sent individuals or committees to speak, alternating with the popular clergymen who conferred legitimacy on such "constructive" union goals as collective bargaining and support for the union label. When the 1908 season began, the CLU advised unionists to "speak to him [Ely], tell him where you belong, assist him in his services, encourage him in whatever way you can. We should do something to show him we appreciate his assistance."[56]

Despite such optimistic examples, Social-Gospel Christians held many reservations about organized labor. As Kemper Bocock, the fraternal delegate to the CLU from the Christian Social Union, wrote in 1902:

> The socialist percentage of the membership of trades unions is growing, and trades-unionism as a whole is growing. . . . The result of this is not only a growing socialism among the wage workers, but, to a noticeable extent, a materialistic socialism, which claims to know Karl Marx for its father.

Bocock argued that if Christian men and women did not intervene with efforts to achieve greater social justice, then they would eventually be faced with a decision to vote for or against the socialist program.[57] Religious leaders nationwide agreed, predicting a crisis when socialistic labor would confront greedy capital.[58]

As the local labor movement became a more powerful force in the city, many clergymen made continued moderation and fair play a condition of their ongoing support. Social-Gospel leader Harry F. Ward, for example, challenged unions to abandon the strike and eliminate the "corruption, despotism, and violence that alienate public sympathy, but seem to be the inevitable accompaniment of the sudden acquisition of power." Similarly, Stelzle counseled unionists to "be patient. There is no short cut to the millennium. You will not correct all of the evils of your generation but your reasonable, definite, consistent campaign will surely bring some things to pass."[59]

Clergymen, in particular, railed against strikes because they frequently led to violence. A. J. Arkin proclaimed them "useless strife. . . . Warfare will not solve the labor problem." Stelzle asked for moderate labor leaders to come forward, and even sought the assistance of employers to bring this about. Manufacturers, argued Stelzle, should encourage the "best men" to participate in the leadership of unions so that "battles would be fought out in their meeting rooms, with reason and argument for weapons, instead of in the streets with bludgeons and cobblestones." Unions, meanwhile, should not strike but give employers a fair day's work, demonstrating that "a good class of citizen" made up the labor movement.[60]

Even more persistently, Social-Gospel advocates attempted to substitute social reform for socialism within the working class. Reverend J. Gray Bolton, who replaced Bocock as the Christian Social Union delegate to the CLU, stressed all that had been accomplished in the state legislature through a broad, cross-class alliance of good citizens, but suggested that the alliance would be compromised by even a hint of socialism. Others were more blunt. Stelzle, who called Karl Marx "a hater of Christianity," charged that "the Socialists are the Pharisees of the labor movement. Their profound contempt for everybody else who does not agree with their economic system is making them more enemies than they need to face."[61]

The alarm on the part of liberal clergymen appears, at first, to contradict all the progress made toward cooperation between organized labor and social Christianity. However, the moderate, nonsocialist control of the Central Labor Union, the development of trade agreements, and the presence of Social-Gospel activists on union councils did not eliminate labor militancy. When presented with the opportunity to redress long-term grievances against employers, the newly empowered trade-union movement, although avowedly not radical, proved more than willing to fight for incremental gains. Indeed, strike levels between 1902 and 1905 surpassed previous ones and were not equalled until the first world war. In 1903, Philadelphia's most strike-prone year, over 100,000 textile workers waged a citywide strike against long hours, low pay, and child labor, which culminated in a "children's march" to President Theodore Roosevelt's home in Oyster Bay, New York, led by the radical activist Mother Jones. That same year, even the supposedly conservative building trades unions engaged in actions perceived by some as dangerously radical. More than 75,000 construction workers tied up city projects when employers tried to eliminate sympathy strikes from the industry.[62]

Meanwhile, the socialist faction in the CLU kept liberal clergymen on the defensive. Philadelphia labor correspondent Charles Hawkins criticized the Protestant women who joined settlements and other voluntary organizations. "We find the wives and daughters of wealthy manufacturers spending time and money striving to better the conditions in one section of the city, while the husband and father, in another section, is creating a thousand fold more misery than the others can relieve."[63] Others, responding to church criticism of labor violence, pointed to employers who hired Pinkerton agents. Where was the fairness, asked CLU delegate William Huplits; "If the blacklist, why not the boycott?" In response, religious fraternal delegate J. Gray Bolton could only suggest moderation and patience.[64]

The socialist critique of such liberal Christian moderation became more trenchant in the decade after 1904 when court decisions, legal injunctions, and the employers' open-shop campaign struck at the very core of the labor movement. But the first decade of cooperation between organized labor and social Christianity promised to exert a moderating influence over class conflict. The previous tendency of Christian organizations to suspend operations rather than take sides during labor disputes dissipated. Instead, in the tense atmosphere of the 1903 textile strike, the Episcopalian-run Kensington Lighthouse settlement provided meeting space for the unions. At the strike's conclusion, Lighthouse director Robert Bradford explained his more enlightened policy.

> Such an uprising is the demagogue's opportunity, and he succeeds best in inflaming his hearers when the surroundings conduce to excitement. In the quiet, sober air of The Lighthouse, which is known for its honest sympathy with all who are in difficulty, there was much to restrain the temper of those who were labouring under the severe strain of a long strike. And it is safe to say that The Lighthouse played an important part in securing the calm, deliberate and sane discussion of the proper course to be pursued toward the textile employers and their property and toward the maintenance of law and order.[65]

In his self-congratulatory statements, Bradford neglected to mention that the strike had been defeated.

The Proper Course to be Pursued

After a decade of concerted action in support of responsible trade unionism, Social-Gospel advocates could take pride in their accomplishments. Social Christianity had been critical in moving American culture into greater sympathy with the concept of industrial justice. Journals like *The Survey* trumpeted the idea of injecting religion into social action. Prominent clergymen and lay leaders carried a religious spirit into social reform, which crested in a wave of social legislation. Not only did long hours of labor, slum housing, poverty, and many other social ills come under attack, but the reformers also posited dramatically new legislative remedies.[66]

No issue caused more concern to Christians than the labor problem. Genuine social concerns and the specter of radicalism forced Social-Gospel activists to increase their efforts to mediate and restore peace during labor conflicts. They felt that industrial peace depended upon the success of substantive collective bargaining and the emergence of moderate, Christian labor leaders. By 1904, clergical interaction with trade unions was firmly entrenched, as Social-Gospel Christians accepted collective action through trade unions, but only so long as unions were willing to eschew such devices as strikes and socialist politics. Clergymen, then, institutionalized their contacts with organized labor so that they could encourage the more moderate and nonsocialist labor leaders to assert themselves.

Cooperation with Social-Gospel Protestantism also had a strong appeal for many trade unionists. It gave unions credence as legitimate, respectable American institutions. For many workers in established crafts that were maintaining control of the workplace, this was an important quality. In particular, building, metal, and printing trades workers—the "labor aristocracy" of predominately well-paid, American-born, white males—welcomed Protestant support.[67] Furthermore, the endorsement of labor by liberal Christians allowed unions to press for significant political gains. Laws limiting the hours of female and child labor, providing for factory inspections, and insuring working-class families against industrial accidents promised substantial benefits.

At the same time, the middle road taken by Social-Gospel Christianity did not proceed unchallenged. For large segments of the working class—new immigrants, unskilled workers, and even craftsmen facing dynamic technological change—the moderate legislative achievements of Progressivism and craft unionism had little appeal. Unskilled workers in refineries, in the metal trades, and on the docks turned to militant industrial unionism or political socialism as their only hope of offsetting the power of industrial capitalism. Conversely, many Christians did not feel comfortable with even conservative unions. Evangelicals confronted Christianity with a choice of whether to continue the efforts to bring social science into church work or to withdraw into a strict reliance on fundamentalism. Beset by doubts on both sides, social Christianity could only hope for greater moderation and a calming of industrial turbulence; instead, employers launched a vigorous counter-attack against unionism and, by association, social Christianity.

5

Our Kind of Religion

ON January 30, 1918, over 150 young, female industrial workers from Kensington occupied the Philadelphia YWCA building during a board of managers meeting. Demanding a vote in the proceedings in accordance with their membership, the Kensington branch members hurled charges of "Prussianism," "autocratic domineering," and "fossilism" at the "gentle, elderly women" of the metropolitan board. The industrial workers complained of the board's recent firing of the extension department head and the eviction of eight women from their residence at the Kensington building. Anna C. Hudson, president of the metropolitan board, responded by calling on police to forcibly remove the young protesters from the board meeting, asserting that "the Y.W.C.A. could not permit any girls to come into it as industrial workers or as suffragists, or what not, but all must come in merely as Y.W.C.A. girls."[1]

Ironically, this event culminated three decades of effort by the city's Young Men's and Young Women's Christian Associations to appeal to industrial workers. What began in the 1880s as a cautious attempt to introduce evangelical Protestantism to young men and women in the manufacturing sections of the city had expanded into a concerted effort to improve conditions for industrial workers. This shift, caused by the emergence of social Christianity, transformed the YM and YWCA program from one promoting individualistic, evangelical self-help into one supporting collective social activism. In the process, however, their boardrooms became the scenes of intense conflicts. Pious, moralistic board members, many with close ties to the city's leading manufacturers, opposed the attempts of Social-Gospel staff persons to arouse a social conscience.

Conservative political and religious sentiments, as the conflict within the YWCA suggests, remained a potent force in the city's churches despite the emergence of social Christianity. Liberal support for social legislation and trade unionism, even with the goals of encouraging responsible and peaceful conflict resolution, aroused anger among many pious, middle-class Protestants and Catholics. Particularly in voluntary associations, which relied on the financial support of prominent lay people, working-class issues faced stern resistance. Nevertheless, the Social Gospel penetrated Christian associations of all types, making religion a contested terrain. The efforts of pious conservatives to stifle social activism brought class tensions out of the factory and into Christian halls, gymnasiums, and churches.

Ideas of Industry

Many older Christian voluntary associations in Philadelphia resisted changes associated with the Social Gospel. The provincial character of the local elite and their personal attachment to specific associations made many local organizations immune to national developments. In addition, many prominent Christians opposed social and labor reform because of self-interest. Such groups as the Home Missionary Society, the Western Soup Society, and the Union Benevolent Association, headed by Protestant merchants and manufacturers, feared the organization of the "dangerous classes" and rejected collectivist responses to the ills of capitalist society. Catholics, too, in the city's Federation of Catholic Societies, encouraged workers to "bear patiently your burden," and avoid being led astray by false friends of labor who engendered hatred. Voluntary associations, they felt, were particularly suited to a social control function that would check working-class independence through personal ties to local businessmen.[2]

Meanwhile, the voluntary societies that emerged alongside the

Social Gospel often saw no contradiction between the desire for social control and an ideal of social justice, especially since evangelical impulses existed within social Christianity. Settlements, for example, hoped to change the cultural patterns of immigrants and wage earners quite as much as they sought to lend assistance to the needy. The College Settlement Association asserted that in certain circumstances "ideas of begging, theft, almstaking, despondency, suicide can be substituted for ideas of industry, self-sufficiency, self-respect, cheerfulness, and the hope of a long life."[3]

The goal of middle-class, Christian settlement workers in such cases, then, was to shape a different response to urban, industrial society, a response that actually fit better with the needs of capitalist production. A part of their efforts consisted in reducing the layers of ethnic antagonisms and status hierarchies that existed within working-class neighborhoods, although they attacked ethnic cultures through a "filter of assumptions grounded in the dominant cultural perspective." They reinforced notions that all neighborhood ethnic groups were at the bottom of the social scale and that only by adopting the proper Protestant work ethic could they achieve the American standard of living. Although Protestant groups played the key role here, Catholics contributed as well; the growing Irish middle class, for instance, held approximately the same attitudes about Italian and Polish work habits as the Protestants did.[4]

Progressive groups like the Pennsylvania Child Labor Association often pursued their own cultural objectives at the expense of working-class needs. Led in Philadelphia by such prominent Christian social activists as Laura Platt, George Woodward, and Charity Organization Society head Mary Richmond, the association worked to ban female and child labor in factories, but did so without a similar commitment to insuring a decent "living wage" for working-class families. These and other middle-class advocates of protective legislation rarely understood that by legislating their domestic ideals they hindered immigrant families in their attempt to attain minimal security and blocked working-class women from acquiring better-paying factory jobs. Moreover, the association, except during the preparation of its 1906 exhibit showing factory conditions for children, refrained from all contact with organized labor. Mary Richmond, for one, criticized groups that were "bowled over by the first labor leader, or anarchist, or socialist" they met, and she steered the association away from such encounters.[5]

Catholic benevolent associations were more ambivalent about legislation but no more solicitous of trade unions. Their hesitancy about legislation stemmed from their fear of intervention by a Protestant government, particularly in family matters concerning child welfare. The *Catholic Standard and Times* denounced Protestant city officials for turning over a six-year-old Catholic orphan to the Presbyterian orphanage. Indeed, the church's major reason for demanding that its parishoners contribute to Catholic voluntary organizations was to avoid statist solutions.[6] Catholic resistance to social reform legislation began to soften, however, when priests and prominent lay activists discovered the even greater service that such legislation could play—that of undermining socialist sympathies within the working class. The church praised reform legislation in England and Belgium on just that basis. Meanwhile, the principal contact that Philadelphia Catholic voluntary associations had with labor was when they hosted talks by Father Peter Dietz, David Goldstein, and Peter Collins, three of the most vocal Catholic opponents of socialism in the labor movement.[7]

Inspired by the Social Gospel, Christian efforts to extend cultural evangelicalism even reached into the leisure sphere, as parks and playgrounds were established. In 1909, reformers in the Playgrounds Association of Philadelphia pressed for a thorough reorganization of the city's recreational facilities to make them better serve the work of Protestant uplift. They pointed to a basketball team that included a German, a Jew, a Pole, and an Irishman playing together under "rigid rules" that inculcated fair play, "self-control," and working "side by side for the honor of the team." As the association reported, "Here play has become a deep, wholesome Americanizing force."[8] The work of the Association resulted in a Philadelphia Public Playgrounds Commission that surveyed recreational facilities in other cities and obtained a substantial financial commitment from the city government to expand services. The rationale, as stated by the Commission, was the choice between "good citizenship" and "social unrest." The playground was the remedy for "mob violence, disregard of the rights of property, [and] contempt for lawful authority."[9]

As Social-Gospel advocates worked beside older voluntary associations, tensions began to emerge between social-justice ideals and social-control sentiments. The Charity Organization Society, with its "friendly visitors" to poor households and its harsh restrictions on receiving aid, opted for an earlier evangelical message but under a guise of new "scientific" charity. Similarly, most of the older Protestant social agencies in the city cooperated in the formation of a registration bureau so that a "standard of business efficiency" could be applied to benevolence.[10] Furthermore, such voluntary associations as the Law and Order Society and the Social Purity Alliance maintained their earlier individualistic evangelicalism despite having attracted activists from organizations more typically associated with Social-Gospel ideas. Many University Settlement workers, for instance, combined their striving for social justice with support for the Law and Order Society.[11]

The increasingly uneasy mix of social-justice sentiments and coercive evangelicalism that competed for control of Progressive-Era voluntary associations turned religion into an arena of conflict on the labor question. Many Protestant leaders doubted that social programs and a change in urban environment would lead more wage earners to Christianity. Revivalists, in particular, attacked the notion that poverty, tenements, or sweatshops were at the root of the problems facing an urban, industrial society. The generously funded campaigns of Reuben A. Torrey in 1905 and Billy Sunday in 1915 called for an activism associated with Bible study, prayer meetings, and prohibition movements as the answer to social unrest. Their solution involved coercive strategies to suppress vice, not support for trade unions, housing reformers, and Progressive legislation.[12]

Conflict, arising from the different methods of dealing with urban social unrest, materialized in specific churches. At the Christ Protestant Episcopal Church in downtown Philadelphia, the prominent parishoners had abandoned the working-class district surrounding the church for the suburbs or more fashionable city neighborhoods. The pastor, Reverend C. Ellis Stevens, however, made the church a "favorite place" for popular gatherings, including those connected to social and labor reform causes. But the vestry was still controlled by middle-class Christians who worried about declining attendance and the bad financial condition of the church, factors which they attributed to Stevens's outspoken support for social activism. Stevens denied the vestry's power to remove him, forcing the Episcopal Diocese to intervene on the congregation's behalf and find Stevens another church.[13]

Meanwhile, elements of the working class resisted Social-Gospel efforts to shape their culture. One small girl suspiciously questioned College Settlement workers about their motives: "Well this is all right for *us,* but what do *youse* get out of it? My father says youse ain't in this business for your health."[14] In fact, regardless of how effective settlements were in teaching middle-class domesticity and respectability to women and children, working-class males undermined that message. It was mainly the poorer, immigrant participants in rougher variations of working-class culture who combined natural caution with their desire to maintain a male-dominated family when dealing with middle-class groups opposed to working-class self-organization. Wage earners and immigrants also rejected the ideology behind parks, playgrounds, and the elaborate public pageants through which elite reformers hoped to temper working-class celebrations and recreation. Working-class neighborhoods remained isolated from holiday pageants, and immigrants carved out their own space in parks for drinking and rowdy parties, activities which the reformers undoubtedly condemned.[15]

Consequently, proponents of social Christianity felt that voluntary organizations needed to go even further to demonstrate their support for working-class objectives. Some individuals, like Anna Davies of the College Settlement, did go far to prove their sincerity. During a garment workers' strike in 1909–10, she ran "tag days" to raise strike funds, organized assistance for strikers' families, and even went to jail for helping on the picket line. Another young Protestant, Florence Sanville, began a reform career as a religious opponent of female and child labor. She quickly recognized, however, that middle-class domestic ideals could not address the needs of working-class families. She then extended her activities, organizing support for working-class women in the Consumers' League, carrying the messages of the Women's Union Label League to the Central Labor Union, and writing scathing indictments of sweatshop and factory labor for such publications as *The Survey*. Still, she felt her work did not reach the heart of the matter. In 1914, she left the Consumers' League to join and eventually head the local office of the Women's Trade Union League.[16]

Nevertheless, many voluntary associations stifled the efforts of Christians to lend support to working-class activism. After the turn of the century, a widening breach appeared in the ranks of the vast array of religious organizations. Liberal and conservative Christians, particularly in Protestant denominations, competed for dominance in proposing different solutions to urban problems, often within the same voluntary associations. Both groups sought to win wage earners over to a Christian America; the differences arose over the best means to attain that goal. Nowhere was this division more evident than in the area of industrial strife. Many of the wealthy backers of voluntary associations refused to place any confidence in moderate trade unions as a possible remedy for labor conflict. Self-interest and an evangelical ethos stressing individualism combined to thwart liberal pro-union sentiments. Although Social-Gospel ministers had a resounding voice within Protestant clergical bodies, they had less influence in many voluntary associations.[17]

For the pious, conservative Christians who rejected even moderate trade unionism, perhaps no voluntary association received more assistance or promised more hope of evangelizing the working class than the YM and YWCAs. Their boards of directors included the most prominent Protestant men and women in the city; their fund-raising campaigns could earn over a million dollars; they had their own press, their own buildings, and even their own professionally trained staff. For many, they epitomized the promise of a Christian America. But in practice, they embodied the tensions that splintered voluntary organizations and divided Christianity. In short, because the Ys revealed in dramatic fashion how religion became entangled simultaneously with ideas of social justice *and* social control, they present a case study of the ways in which class struggle made Christian voluntary organizations an arena of conflict.

Well-Equipped Buildings

Neither the Young Men's nor the Young Women's Christian Association began with a particular interest in working-class men and women. Founded in 1855, the early YMCAs focused on providing a Christian environment for young clerks, especially those moving into an urban setting for the first time. The YWCA dated its founding from 1870, although it functioned under the name Women's Christian Association until the turn of the century. Like its male counterpart, the YWCA acted primarily as a buffer organization, helping newly arrived working women reconcile a rural American past with the realities of their new industrial situation. Both organizations began by providing shelter and an atmosphere of Christian nurture, broadly assisting churches in promoting personal piety through an associated effort. In the difficult economic times of Gilded-Age Philadelphia, however, the Ys gradually branched out, opening services to new groups, including blacks and immigrants, and sponsoring inexpensive lunches, recreational programs, vocational training, and employment bureaus. By the 1890s, they functioned almost like institutional churches.[18]

For the middle- and upper-class men and women who served on the YM and YWCA boards, these efforts represented an old-fashioned idea of Christian charity. By-laws required that board members be attached to evangelical Protestant churches. Furthermore, the boards were comprised of members of the leading manufacturing and commercial families in the city. The YMCA boasted of the 268 "business men" constituting the various managing boards of the city association, while the YWCA boards included important manufacturing names like Disston, Dornan, and Collins (producers of saws, textiles, and paper boxes, respectively). Some identified the Ys as the "business side of religion," led by businessmen in a business-like spirit.[19]

Well into the 1890s, the Ys continued to concentrate on white-collar workers residing primarily in center city, or the more prosperous workers and middle-class residents in places like Germantown. The YMCA did not start a branch in working-class Kensington until 1885, and the Women's Christian Association waited until 1891. Even then, such working-class branches were underfunded and limited in scope to vocational self-help programs. Wealthy backers of Y programs, in large part, took care of their own workers through extensive factory-oriented welfare programs that reinforced the paternalistic atmosphere of the factory. Only when workers refused to participate in company welfare schemes did manufacturers intensify their support for the Ys in the industrial sections of the city.[20]

The new branches in working-class wards, however, did maintain the earlier evangelical emphases of YM and YWCA board members. The YMCA board viewed its goal as merely extending the benefits and moral tone of Christian philanthropy. The men's Kensington branch, for instance, helped authorities keep a closer watch on saloons in that section of the city, and one of its proudest acquisitions was an ice water fountain donated by the Women's Christian Temperance Union.[21] The Women's Kensington branch was concerned largely with dressmaking, cutting, and millinery classes that aimed to provide Christian-inspired self-help for women in low-income jobs. It did not offer low-cost meals or boarding until 1895.[22] Although both of the Ys expanded and varied their services in working-class districts in the 1890s, the emphasis remained more evangelical than social. Eventually, the YMCA board congratulated itself on the better material standard of living and higher moral condition of Philadelphia's working class.

In large measure, the conservative approach of the Ys reflected the interests of their major benefactors. When the National YMCA initiated "industrial work" in the 1880s in its special "railroad branches," it "completely allied itself with the employing class in a paternalistic service to workers." Facilities, often paid for by the railroads, routinely discontinued operation during strikes. Similarly, although these "railroad YMCAs" offered benefit programs for employees, many workers refused to participate. One Philadelphia railroad worker told the state labor bureau that company-run benefit systems "meant either lower wages for [the employees] or that they were to suffer in some way if the organization should flourish."[23]

Metropolitan YM and YWCAs, unlike the railroad branches, were not under the control of a single company, but the local economic elite did dominate the boards. In Philadelphia, a $100,000 contribution from traction magnate Peter Widener and $10,000 from hat manufacturer John B. Stetson made up a significant portion of the YMCA building fund. Baldwin Locomotives president Alba Johnson, textile manufacturer Henry Bromley, and merchant John Wanamaker led fundraising drives for both the YM and YWCA.[24] Thus, control by the commercial and manufacturing interests of the city generally shaped the programs of the Ys.

Through the 1890s, the professional staffs of the Ys heeded the wishes of the board members. When Kensington YMCA secretary Harry Heebner wanted to further the interests of his branch in 1899, he quickly assembled a group of businessmen and clergymen. The association's annual report for 1903 stated simply that in "America we are engaged not in pulling each other down to a common level but in lifting up to a higher plane." The YMCA proudly proclaimed that it "found no yawning chasm between Christianity as represented by the Association and the industrial forces of our city."[25] YWCA industrial department head Florence Simms captured the tone of the early industrial work when she recalled her own experiences: "We had factory meetings at noon at which we presented our kind of religion. . . . I am ashamed to tell you . . . that I did not even know what wages [the workers] earned. I am ashamed to tell you . . . that I was not concerned about the hours they worked."[26]

The social conscience of the Ys remained unchanged into the twentieth century despite advancing Social-Gospel theology. In 1903, the Philadelphia YMCA characterized its role as a mediating force for paternalistic employers. "Experience has shown," its annual report declared, "that employers, however generous their intentions," cannot overcome the suspicions of their workers toward welfare services. Thus, "well equipped buildings, provided by employers, after a full experiment, have been turned over to organized branches" of the YMCA. The report concluded candidly that "men distrust or else disregard such efforts" when controlled exclusively by management.[27]

The YWCA likewise interceded for manufacturers. Besides the Kensington and Falls branches, which were centrally located in textile districts to provide services for many different factories, the North American Lace Company and the A. M. Collins Manufacturing Company built and financed branches for female workers.[28] In these Ys, Protestant men and women provided vocational and homemaking classes, gymnasiums, swimming pools, cheap lodgings, inexpensive meals, and a variety of social clubs, all with a less obvious taint of employer domination. But the Ys were not neutral regarding organized labor. Buildings were closed to union meetings, industrial training courses often cooperated with manufacturers seeking to undercut union apprenticeships, and the Ys routinely emphasized a middle-class work ethic.[29]

A large part of YM and YWCA outreach to industrial workers came through factory evangelizing. The staffs conducted numerous noon-hour shop meetings, including music, talks on hygiene, sermons by popular ministers, and, at times, even calisthenics. In 1911, the YWCA reached approximately 1300 young women per month with its twenty factory religious services. During one Lenten season the extension program increased its work at the National Biscuit Company, where it held a series of Friday night religious meetings.[30] The YMCA, a decade earlier, had a similar concentrated effort at Niles Bement's and William Sellers's machine tools factories, holding seventeen lunch-time meetings for an average of over 200 workers. In Kensington, the YMCA helped form two brotherhood of Christian workingmen groups, while Cramp's Shipyard consistently provided huge audiences and a congenial atmosphere for YMCA evangelism. These employers also happened to be some of the most notorious anti-union manufacturers in the city.[31]

Employers must have felt their contributions to the Ys were well worth the cost. As one manufacturer reported, "The morals of the shops are greatly improved. Men are cleaner, happier, freer from vulgarity and profanity; more sober and industrious." In another shop, a foreman who was a "very staunch Catholic" said he would be glad to have the Ys "hold a meeting *every noon*, for the afternoon following the meeting men accomplished more with less friction than at any other time." S. G. Watkins, a foreman at the Otis Elevator Works factory in Philadelphia, wrote to the YMCA about the religious conversions and the "change of atmosphere" in his shop, while at other factories employers offered bonuses to temperate workers.[32]

The YWCA performed a similar service for employers. At meetings, female industrial workers received bits of advice like "I will never let play serve as the ends of existence, but always it shall be used to make me a better worker and a richer soul." Mary Channing Wister, wife of western novelist Owen Wister, complained to another gathering that "responsibility of citizenship is seldom brought to bear upon a child's mind, hence the attitude is taken, What does the country owe me? not What do I owe my country?"[33] The Ys' service to employers in promoting sobriety, stability, industriousness, and efficiency was perhaps only overshadowed by its offer to bring "the power of Christianity" into labor relations. "The opportunity is presented to manufacturers and heads of other corporations" to utilize the YMCA to solve industrial problems, volunteered the 1906 annual report. It made no such promise to trade unions.[34]

Well into the Progressive Era, then, segments of the Philadelphia YM and YWCAs resisted the Social Gospel. Buffered by the finances and ideology of the local manufacturing elite, many Y staff persons ignored broader social questions. The associations prospered and, what is more, they allowed the professional staffs to feel that they were doing something for unfortunate working-class men and women. At the same time, the wealthy benefactors could point to the thousands of members who took advantage of an uplifting Christian philanthropy for their recreational, educational, and moral self-help. The rumblings of trade unionists and working-class activists against Y-sponsored trade schools or the awarding of Y construction contracts to non-union firms seemed petty by comparison. The Ys appeared to offer widespread opportunities for participation in important voluntary organizations that worked alongside the churches. Perhaps even more than the institutional missions, the YM and YWCAs held out hope to conservative elements of Christian Philadelphia for directing working-class activities into acceptable channels.

Dislodging the Christian, Praying Women

After the turn of the century, it became increasingly difficult for voluntary organizations to ignore social issues. Desiring participation from the working class, middle and upper-class leaders had to concede some autonomy and initiative to the people they were trying to attract to Christian associations. This meant lending support to the goals and objectives of wage earners, especially since organizations like the Ys were asking for a commitment of time and money, things dear to working-class people. To fulfill their mission among workers, then, the Ys had to relegate some of their space and resources to activities that strayed from their more narrow evangelical emphasis.

This concession of autonomy became more problematic following the widening breach within Protestantism caused by the Social Gospel. As liberal advocates of social Christianity increasingly challenged the conservative, benevolent approach to the problems of urban society, the professional staffs of the Ys likewise diverged from the goals of the local manufacturing elite. Social-Gospel activists had their own expectations for voluntary associations such as the Ys. They sought to help working-class participants solve problems through collective action rather than individual self-help and piety. The national YM and YWCAs gravitated toward this Progressive Social-Gospel approach to the "labor problem" after the turn of the century. Such leaders as Grace Dodge, Florence Simms, Peter Roberts, and Charles R. Towson sought a more activist role for the YW and YMCAs in ameliorating the social problems faced by American workers. Influenced by a Protestant-spurred "civic awakening" and a notion that corporations were corrupting the political and moral fiber of urban society, they fostered a new attitude in the Ys.[35]

National associations also benefited from being further removed from their financial benefactors, as it allowed them to develop, at a safe distance, a stronger institutional logic concerning their programs and their social commitments. The national Ys consequently adopted Progressivism's environmentalist approach, asserting that better material, moral, and social conditions would produce better people. This conviction had to be implemented in the blighted, crowded working-class sections of the cities. At the same time, the national Y leadership turned increasingly to collectivist strategies, fighting to place workers on an equal footing with their employers by supporting trade unions, collective bargaining, and arbitration. Progressive staff members argued that these strategies would strengthen the appeal of the associations among the working class and, in the long run, increase membership and make them more financially independent.[36]

The Progressivism of the national associations penetrated the local Ys more slowly. Despite the best intentions of activists at the national level to train and employ staff persons motivated by social Christianity, the control of city boards by the local corporate elite in such places as Philadelphia impeded their efforts. Largely autonomous city boards resisted national policies that did not match their own interests—a factor in many voluntary organizations that were active principally in a local context and were financially dependent upon local supporters. In Philadelphia, the large number of manufacturers either living near their place of business or with parochial interests added to the vibrancy and localism of the city's Ys,[37] but also tended to cut them off from the Progressivism of the national associations. In fact, the close ties of the Ys to the business classes provided less of an opportunity for the expression of social concerns than did church work.

The Philadelphia YMCA nevertheless made a significant contribution to the development of Y industrial work. Professional field worker Charles R. Towson, conducting association work for the Pennsylvania Railroad Company in Philadelphia, took over a moribund industrial department in 1907. In his first action, he selected Kensington for an experimental effort to reach factory workers. During the next two years, the industrial department and the metropolitan YMCA financed a plan calling for the hiring of three full-time field workers, or secretaries, by the Kensington branch to carry on an intensive program of shop meetings and special events to build up membership in the city's largest industrial district. Towson received a pledge from the metropolitan board for half of the $10,000 needed for the work.[38]

Towson was a vocal advocate of the Social Gospel. In the Kensington program, he sought cooperation with the existing trade unions in the textile and metal industries, hoping to secure collective bargaining and fair wages for the workers in that troubled section. He organized large meetings for union workers, many of whom had participated in violent labor conflicts between 1903 and 1907. The Y rented theaters and popular halls for meetings addressed by Social-Gospel clergymen or lay spokespersons on some important topic for organized labor. In October 1907, shortly after inaugurating the Kensington experiment, Towson arranged for Charles Stelzle to come to Philadelphia. In several separate meetings, Stelzle counseled workers to join the respectable unions of their trade, and lent support to an iron molders' strike then in progress. Craft unionists turned out by the thousands to hear Stelzle chastize such employer organizations as the Metal Manufacturers' Association for their opposition to union workers and collective bargaining.[39]

The pro-union sentiments of Towson and the Kensington field workers quickly met resistance from wealthy YMCA backers. Within six months, field worker C. C. Robinson was complaining that the board was not supporting the plan. Funds promised by the metropolitan board, upon which the Kensington branch depended, were not forthcoming, so that the branch was soon $5,000 in debt. The Kensington managers considered calling a halt to the experiment as early as March 1908, only six months into the two-year plan. Without assistance from the wealthy local backers of the YMCA, the industrial experiment limped into its second year. The chastized Kensington YMCA did little to invigorate the program the second year, so that by January 1909 Towson had removed all of his industrial specialists from the city for reassignment in the coal fields.[40]

The failure of Towson's experiment, however, did not stem the growing social consciousness of YMCA staff. Social Christianity in Philadelphia gained wider visibility in December 1908 at the founding convention of the Federal Council of Churches of Christ in America, which touched off a flurry of activity that reinforced Social-Gospel views of YMCA professionals. In particular, the council's report on "The Church and Modern Industry," which condemned corporate selfishness and asserted that workers should organize for collective social, moral, and material advancement, won support from unionists and Progressives. Glass Bottle Blowers president Denis Hayes claimed that it was "almost like the dawning of the millennium" to read the council's pronouncements. Further, the report also impacted tremendously on the staffs of voluntary associations, influencing the thinking of Protestants about trade unions.[41]

This surge in social Christianity invigorated the Ys. By 1911, the inspired professionals on the YMCA staff involved the association in one of the major Federal Council undertakings, a revival campaign called the Men and Religion Forward Movement. The revivals, led by YMCA activist Fred B. Smith, presented a Social-Gospel message favorable to organized labor and enlisted such prominent people as Jane Addams, Raymond Robins, Graham Taylor, and United Mine Workers president John Mitchell. In Philadelphia, YMCA education secretary William Easton coordinated the campaign, committing the association to full cooperation.[42]

Although the revivals concentrated on men and boys, they meshed with a growing social awareness in the YWCA, under the leadership of Emilie Green. YWCA professional staff members were developing a close relationship to the ideals of the Federal Council through the national association's training program. Locally, they expanded the work of their Federated Industrial Clubs and held large gatherings for women workers on labor law, industrial conditions, and other social issues. At YWCA-sponsored meetings and socials for union members, Margaret Dreier Robins of the Women's Trade Union League and Florence Kelley of the Consumers' League counseled women on their legal rights under current labor laws and promoted union organizing.[43]

The social Christianity of the Ys spread beyond the boundaries of Protestant young men and women. Catholics and Jews began making use of Y facilities and joining the industrial clubs. The YWCA, for instance, sponsored talks by Jewish labor activists Pauline Newman and Rose Schneiderman for Jewish garment workers. The success of the YMCA among Catholic youths was noted by the *Catholic Standard and Times*, which railed against its supposed "non-sectarianism." The paper denounced the religious message of the Ys, asserting that its appeal was "dangerous" to Catholics. In response, the church began its own rivals to the Ys and kept up a steady attack on the associations. Nevertheless, Catholic and Jewish immigrants continued to join Ys in working-class neighborhoods, encouraged by the Social-Gospel inspiration of the professional staff.[44]

Moreso than immigrants, organized labor took advantage of this atmosphere to inaugurate a major recruiting drive. Sensing a change in attitude expressed by the dominant religious and voluntary organizations in the city, unions pressed for gains through their own series of "revivals" called the Labor Forward Movement. This campaign, which lasted for two years in Philadelphia with generous support from the American Federation of Labor, revitalized a weak trade-union movement in the city. And despite a generally anti-labor city government—neither the Republican machine nor the Progressive challengers particularly courted unions—organized labor made substantial gains in many industries in the city.[45]

Organized labor's efforts in Philadelphia led wealthy supporters of the Ys to exert stricter control over the activities of the associations. The YMCA board responded to the strikes that followed trade-union growth by closing its facilities to any organization "not under the control of the Board of Managers." At that very same meeting, however, the board decided to visit "certain business men" to convince more members of the local merchant and manufacturing elite to serve on the management committee. It also offered the use of YMCA buildings for the meetings of businessmen's organizations. Furthermore, the manufacturer-controlled board joined with the rabidly anti-union Metal Manufacturers' Association in establishing a trade school where young men would learn metal trades work outside the union apprenticeship system.[46]

The election of Anna C. Hudson to the presidency of the metropolitan YWCA in 1914 brought out similar anti-working-class policies in the women's association. In cooperation with the wives of several prominent manufacturers, she tightened her grip over the branches and departments under the board's jurisdiction, particularly the North American Lace Company, the Kensington branch, and the extension department, all of which had harbored activists with Social-Gospel and pro-union sentiments. Hudson's election represented the triumph of the conservative, pietistic wing of the board. In fact, one week after her assumption of the presidency, the board banned dancing from the YWCA. This specifically targeted the Kensington branch, which had allowed immigrant and working-class women to hold dances. One Kensington member asserted that "all over the world" there was mixed dancing except at the Philadelphia YWCA.[47]

In January 1915, Billy Sunday's Philadelphia revival campaign bolstered the conservative tendencies of the YWCA board. The metropolitan leaders appointed a group to work with the evangelist, then hired three secretaries to take up the work of the Sunday campaign—especially in the areas of temperance and Sabbath observance—when it ended. Sunday's message also included an attack on the Social-Gospel orientation of liberal Protestantism, specifically its pro-trade-union sympathies. Not surprisingly, Sunday's well-financed revival followed on the heels of the Labor

Forward Movement and the upsurge of strikes in 1914. The *Public Ledger* even claimed that the revival was "financed by millionaires. 'Billy' Sunday is the best strike breaker the country has produced, and they are willing to pay him for strike breaking."[48] The Philadelphia YWCA board heartily concurred with Billy Sunday's social message.

The efforts of the YM and YWCA boards to stifle any pro-trade-union sympathies challenged the ideal of broad participation that was at the core of Protestant voluntary associations. Male working-class attendance dropped off so dramatically in Kensington that in 1917 the branch suspended its service department. War work revived branch secretary Harry Heebner's position, but most YMCA staff members contented themselves with a very limited role in providing assistance to working-class groups.[49] The YMCAs, in many cities like Philadelphia, became little more than the gymnasiums and recreational centers that most people know today, without the evangelical role that they had at the turn of the century.

In contrast to the experience of the YMCAs, the conservative board of the YWCA faced a more dramatic and determined response when progressive staff members openly challenged the board. In July 1915, extension department head Estelle Stauffer scheduled Association Hall for an address by Rose Schneiderman of the Women's Trade Union League, while Eunice Lightowler of the Kensington branch continued to coordinate activities with the textile unions in her district. Hudson and her conservative supporters, however, moved to force out these pro-labor activists. They demanded the resignation of Stauffer and placed Lightowler on an extended leave of absence, citing the financial problems that were plaguing the Kensington branch as manufacturers withdrew their once plentiful donations.[50]

New staff members nevertheless continued opposition to the board's anti-labor policies. Significantly, they had been trained and educated by the national board and had loyalties to the liberal national rather than the more parochial local association. In particular, two extension secretaries, Ethel Durnall and Helen Button, encouraged industrial clubs to join the Consumers' League.

There, the working-class women were "interesting themselves in the work of the League" and cooperating with women from settlement houses, trade unions, and other reform causes. Proud of their successes, the extension secretaries asked for a greater commitment from the metropolitan board. When refused, Durnall criticized the board for its inaction, but Hudson named herself and the wife of carpet manufacturer Joseph Dornan to investigate the complaint. Two months later, Durnall overstepped the limits of the board's patience. After Jennie Disston, widow of saw manufacturer Samuel Disston, tabled a letter from the Consumers' League asking for YWCA assistance in enforcing the state eight-hour law for women, Durnall reported that her industrial clubs had been investigating on their own and had turned in the names of seven violators of the law to the state labor commissioner. Less than a month later, Disston led the movement to do away with all extension secretaries "on account of financial difficulties."[51]

Anti-labor sentiment spilled over into the YWCA board's attitudes toward ethnic groups. Until 1917, being a member of an evangelical Protestant church was a condition for membership in the YWCA, although Y secretaries in working-class neighborhoods had overlooked that requirement in their outreach efforts. Indeed, in 1916 and 1917, the extension department organized a club of Italian women, and the Kensington branch admitted many Jewish workers who wanted to use the facilities. When the national YWCA abolished the old evangelical basis in 1917, the Kensington branch stated publicly that no discrimination as to religion or nationality would be made regarding membership. The Philadelphia metropolitan board, however, fearing immigrant working-class activism, voted to stand by the old requirements. It ordered the Kensington secretary to bar the "undesirable" women being admitted at her branch. In a largely immigrant and working-class section of the city, this policy decreased both membership and participation.[52]

The battle between the progressive and conservative forces in the Philadelphia YWCA finally peaked in November 1917, when the city board decided to abolish the Federated Industrial

Clubs, which were often accused of being incipient trade unions. When Ruth McCombs—the fifth extension department head in three years—refused to give up the clubs, the board forced her to resign. Over 150 Kensington branch members drew up a petition protesting the action and stating their pride in their industrial clubs. "Our club life," the petition asserted, "has done much to develop team work among us, as well as given us a knowledge of parliamentary proceedings." This capacity for working-class self-organization obviously made many YWCA board members uncomfortable; the board responded by evicting eight petition signers from their residence in the Kensington branch building.[53]

At this point, the national YWCA interceded in the struggle, much to the consternation of the city board. Mary James Vaux, a field representative for the national association, listened to the Kensington women's protest at the January 30, 1918 meeting, during which police forced the industrial women from the building. She then brought suit against the board to halt the evictions and to force the board to allow all members who attended the annual meetings a vote in the proceedings. This was in keeping with the directives of the national YWCA, but had never been put into practice in Philadelphia. Vaux, a wealthy Social-Gospel advocate involved in numerous Progressive causes, enlisted a number of other Progressives to fight the metropolitan board "old guard." The "insurgents," as they were dubbed by the press, were all influenced by the Social Gospel and were sympathetic to the pro-labor activists on the YWCA staff. They carried on the court battle for over a year, obtaining widespread publicity for their cause. In December 1919, a judge finally awarded the insurgents control over the city association.[54] It had taken more than a decade of conflict to firmly implant the Social Gospel in the Philadelphia YWCA.

The transformation of YWCA industrial work was, however, more than simply a show of sympathy with the labor movement. Protestant concern for the working class blended with other factors to make the struggle for control assume a larger significance. One of the old guard summed up the conflict as an attempt by "society women" to "secularize the Association, destroy the home influence," and dislodge "the Christian, praying women" of the YWCA. Yet, it was more than opposition to piety that galvanized the insurgents. They opposed the patriarchal nature of middle-class domesticity that prevented women from obtaining political power. The growing women's suffrage movement encouraged many Progressive women to seek a gender solidarity that crossed class lines and paid less attention to cultural differences.[55] With this in mind, it becomes still easier to explain why the YMCA, directed by the husbands of YWCA board members, did not follow a Progressive course with more determination. The leaders of the YMCA lacked a similarly compelling reason to attack class privilege and ethnic antagonisms.

Therefore, the liberal–conservative division within Christianity proved extremely problematic for the YM and YWCAs. Attempts to reach large numbers of immigrants, blacks, and wage earners, spurred in part by the energy of social Christianity, altered the programs and activities of the Ys. In a time of growing social conflict, voluntary groups either embraced new ideas or retreated from their broader goal of encouraging a widespread expansion of Christianity. In Philadelphia, the YMCA followed the second route. The YWCA, on the other hand, took a path that thrust the association into the middle of the Progressive movement, albeit after a long struggle. The YWCA developed vigorous support for working-class organization that would lead to cooperation with the Bryn Mawr school for women workers in the 1920s and would make the Kensington YWCA building an important center for industrial union activity in the 1930s.[56]

Breathing the Spirit of True Religion

In the early twentieth century, the Social Gospel forced a reconsideration of Christian duty in resolving social conflict. However, religious liberalism never entirely overwhelmed the more traditional emphasis on individual piety that was at the root of Protestant evangelicalism. The industrial unrest characterizing the period prior to World War I enhanced the resolve of conservative

Christians and added to their numbers, not only in the Protestant churches but also in the Catholic Church. In Philadelphia, the *Catholic Standard and Times* applauded the efforts of the Militia of Christ, an organization of Catholic priests, businessmen, and union leaders intent upon rooting out socialist sympathies in the labor movement.[57] Meanwhile, Reverend M. C. Stone of the Protestant Episcopal Church—the congregation at the forefront of the Social Gospel in the city—organized a paramilitary club. The Stone Men's League, which expressed zealous anti-immigrant and anti-labor sentiments, and recruited many prominent businessmen as well as nativistic, working-class Protestants.[58]

In general, the first decades of the twentieth century thrust religion into the center of conflict over the future shape of industrial society. Particularly in Christian voluntary associations, the rise of the Social Gospel clashed with more conservative doctrine. The attorney for the "old guard" in the YWCA claimed that the insurgents were not Christians, for they were "not breathing the spirit of true religion."[59] The lines of division were no longer simply Catholic versus Protestant, although that conflict certainly persisted and expressed some of the discomfort that middle-class Protestants felt about the changes in urban, industrial America. Instead, the conflict was also among Protestants and among Catholics, divided by liberal and conservative perspectives, and between Christians of all varieties and the irreligious, some of whom posited drastic social upheaval as the proper solution for an exploitative, capitalistic society.[60]

6

A Trade-Union Gospel

ON November 13, 1914, Philadelphia trade unionists sponsored the largest labor parade in the city's history. Coinciding with the convention of the American Federation of Labor, the parade proudly exhibited the recent growth of local unionism. In a city renowned for the recent weakness of its labor movement, the floats, bands, and over 100,000 costumed marchers surprised AFL delegates. Even more astounding to visiting trade unionists, the renewed vigor of Philadelphia trade unionism drew conspicuously on an earlier campaign of religious revivalism. Impressed with this show of spirit, the AFL resolved to bankroll the continuation of the organizing drive known as the Labor Forward Movement. To encourage this support, one Labor Forward evangelist reiterated the links to Christianity: "There is no work being done that is greater, more holy nor more ennobling than the organizing of workingmen and wage earners."[1]

Given the limitations that most Christians placed on their interaction with organized labor, it seems strange that trade unions would emphasize a connection with religion in organizing workers. Yet, the Labor Forward campaign was filled with contradictions. It was the most energetic organizing drive in Philadelphia between the era of the Knights of Labor and the CIO, but its base was overwhelmingly in the craft unions. While speaking principally to native-born white males, it provided women, immigrants, and unskilled industrial workers with an entering wedge into a restrictive labor-movement culture (a wedge that would widen during the more favorable circumstances of World War I). Trade-union evangelists were attempting to restore a more spirited character and a more expansive vision to the labor movement.

Locating the Labor Forward Movement squarely between the millennial outlook of the Knights and the industrial union upsurge dominated by non-Protestant ethnic groups in the 1930s, then, highlights the contradictory forces pulling at the labor movement as the Progressive Era ended. On the one hand, the Social Gospel and Wilsonian liberalism offered organized labor opportunities for achieving its goals within the norms of the larger society. Moreover, the evangelical dimensions of Labor Forward were rooted in the particular culture and ideology of craft unionism. On the other hand, industrial capitalism was destroying the basis of craft unionism at the same time that industrial workers, immigrants, and women were challenging the restrictions on membership and the limited social and political horizons of the trade-union movement. This made the identification with moderate, reformist Protestantism a highly charged political issue.

"Errors Made by Organized Labor"

The Reverend James B. Ely opened the 1904 season of his evangelistic "tent work" with a strange twist. The announced topic of his sermon, "Justice and Mercy, or a Suggested Motto for Labor Unions," earned early praise from the Philadelphia labor movement. The *Trades' Union News* encouraged union members and their families to attend, as Ely was a proven friend of organized labor. Thousands of working-class families journeyed to Lemon Hill in Fairmount Park on Labor Sunday (the Sunday before Labor Day) to hear his message. But Ely stunned the largely working-class crowd, stating that labor frequently did not give a fair day's work although they expected a fair day's wage. He then proceeded to talk about dissention within unions and the impracticality of much of organized labor's political program. Numerous union workers in the audience "were rather surprised at the turn that Mr. Ely's sermon took, for he talked at length . . . against the errors made by organized labor," according to labor editor Shelby Smith, a proponent of Ely's tent work.[2]

It is impossible to say how many union families never returned for subsequent tent meetings, particularly because speakers at later meetings included such critics of unionism as Baptist minister Russell Conwell, in addition to prolabor clergymen. Yet, less than two months after Ely's Labor Sunday sermon, he gained the cooperation of Harry Kurten of the Building Trades Council to continue the Sunday meetings through the winter in the People's Opera House. The Central Labor Union also appointed a committee to confer with Ely on "undemoninational Sunday afternoon meetings" aimed at establishing labor–capital harmony. In fact, Ely's evangelistic work continued to draw thousands of working-class people until he left the city during World War I.[3]

Such seemingly illogical events demonstrate, in part, just how deeply rooted religion was in working-class life. Wage earners turned to Christianity both for cultural reasons and for individual strength, regardless of the social message of particular clergy. Historian Herbert Gutman, for instance, has identified several strains of working-class religious sentiment. Many wage earners found comfort in a despairing, premillennial pessimism that promised a better life upon Christ's second coming. Others found inspiration for the daily struggle of trade unionism in a postmillennial optimism, hoping to create God's kingdom on earth. In either guise, the religious sentiments of workers were not always an accurate gauge of their commitment to trade unionism. When questioned about the large crowds of Philadelphia workers who attended the revival meetings of conservative evangelist Billy Sunday, for instance, printer Ernest Kraft explained, "I think Billy Sunday is doing a fine work. I believe in God myself, you see."[4]

If anything, the city's religious bodies were gaining ground in the early twentieth century. Between 1890 and 1910, the ratio of Philadelphians formally attached to Protestant or Catholic churches increased from less than one of every three to almost one of every two. Given that formal membership seriously understates an acknowledgement of religious preference or loose attachment to a particular denomination, and judging from the continued popularity of evangelist preachers and revivals, it seems safe to say that a significant and steadily rising segment of the population accepted, if not embraced, Christianity to a certain degree.[5]

There are other signs that a popular Christianity exerted influence far beyond its formal members. Carpet weaver William Hartley, for one, was raised in a nondenominational "Protestant" household, and was a member and also regularly went to the YMCA to play the piano. It is impossible to say how much of the YMCA's evangelicalism men like Hartley absorbed, but it is clear that religion was stronger than church attendance would indicate: Parents who were not attached to churches themselves often sent children to the Ys or Sunday schools for some religious training; others held religious beliefs but were too poor to make what they felt was the proper showing in dress and religious donations. In addition, many churches themselves abandoned potential members because of the inability to sustain church activities in poorer neighborhoods. Although such actions by the churches may have generated cynicism among workers, it is unlikely that they destroyed all vestiges of religious belief or preference. Numerous working-class spokespersons claimed that it was only time and money, not secularism, that kept wage-earners out of a church on Sunday.[6]

Local Protestant leadership also helped shape popular attitudes about respectable behavior, particularly for those hoping to distance themselves from rougher aspects of working-class culture. The vast number of Catholic temperance societies reflected more of "an English and American Protestant influence" than the traditions of rural European Catholicism. According to Irish historian Dennis Clark, Catholics similarly adopted Victorian Protestant ideas about family, deportment, and sex. Even the church hierarchy adapted to American cultural influences, drawing heavily upon the forms of Protestant revivalism and the Victorian attraction to ritual in maintaining congregations in working-class neighborhoods.[7]

Radicals too acknowledged the powers of popular religion and its hold over the working class, although in most cases it took the form of ridicule and parody. The Industrial Workers of the World (IWW) frequently borrowed familiar gospel hymns, which they rewrote into humorous songs like the sarcastic "you'll get pie in the sky when you die," a parody on "The Sweet Bye and Bye." Yet while IWW songwriters parodied many hymns, they also exploited the power of gospel music in creating their most memorable inspirational songs, in particular the use of "The Battle Hymn of the Republic" for their stirring "Solidarity Forever." Other groups on the Left took popular forms of religious expression much more seriously. Socialists began their own versions of the Sunday school, and they often held camp meetings that drew upon Protestant revivalism. The greatest radical speaker of the time, Eugene V. Debs, owed much of his oratorical success to the millennialist fervor and the popular religious imagery of his midwestern Protestant background, which he utilized to denounce capitalism in terms the common man understood.[8]

In this context, the attraction to Ely's tent work becomes less puzzling. The evangelistic meetings offered a pleasant atmosphere, plenty of gospel music, and a less forbidding setting than many churches. Wage earners and their families could attend without the formal dress and financial commitment expected by a church. Understandably, workers inevitably withdrew from those churches where they had to mix with the elite. Their reasons included the "sober" but "costly" dress, "cultured" manners, "formal music, and a pervading intellectualism" that characterized the wealthy. One astute observer of the working class, journalist Al Priddy, suggested that wage earners felt more comfortable in their "own churches." An English immigrant told Priddy that despite his general approval of the local middle-class church and its congregation, there was "no use talking, we don't move in the same class. We have our own ways and it's better so. We surely feel better by ourselves."[9]

The class segregation desired by many wage-earning churchgoers did not demand that ministers offer a uniformly pro-labor message. In fact, Priddy found that few working-class churches devoted much attention to the "labor problem." Feeling that workers discussed labor issues on other days, ministers in working-class churches usually delivered a religious message.[10] The success of Ely's tent work thus attests to the importance of religion's spiritual rather than political role. A dynamic speaker like Russell Conwell was perhaps just as likely to appeal to a devoted Baptist trade unionist as was an uninspiring Social-Gospel minister; chiliastic Christian pessimism was just as likely to attract workers as was postmillennial optimism. In most cases, religious commitment preceded political ideology.

All this suggests the complexity of the appeal of the Social Gospel for ordinary working people. While anti-labor sermons frequently drew the wrath of trade unionists, the respectability conferred by church membership had its greatest attraction to the same ranks of the working class from which the labor movement drew its adherents. Given the trade-union devotion to the principles of education, self-improvement, and "manly" independence, loyalty to both unionism and religion is understandable. In fact, Sunday religious observance mirrored ideas about home life—including the family wage, temperance, and the advocacy of "one day's rest in seven"—that were important mobilizing issues for organized labor. Philadelphia Glass Bottle Blowers president Denis Hayes, for example, stated that his union advocated these issues so "that men are in better condition to exercise the religious and social obligations belonging to Sunday."[11] Labor preacher Charles Stelzle felt it was no coincidence that married men were not only more likely to attend church but also more likely to be in a union. Moreover, this dual loyalty to both religious inspiration and union principles was most marked among the best-paid, most highly skilled workers.[12]

The expansion of particular Christian denominations also testifies to the complicated link between working-class church attendance and specific pro-union Social-Gospel sentiments. The most rapidly growing church in Philadelphia was the Catholic Church, hardly known for pro-labor sympathies in the Progressive Era.[13] Close behind were the Baptists and Lutherans, two of the least pro-union Protestant denominations. The Presbyterians and Episcopalians, which had the best reputations for being sympathetic to labor, grew at a slower rate than the city's religious bodies as a whole. But these rates of growth also reveal ambiguity concerning an evangelical–liturgical split. More evangelically inclined denominations (Baptists, Methodists, Presbyterians) were divided between rapidly growing and more stagnant denominations, as was also the case for such ritualistic churches as the Lutherans, Episcopalians, and Catholics.[14]

Ely's startling observations at the opening of the tent meetings in 1904 thus caused barely a ripple in the local labor movement. In fact, one trade unionist, iron molder George Kemp, agreed that workers needed to give a fair day's work. "Labor worthily performed is only duty, and duty faithfully rendered glorifies God," he wrote.[15] In general, Philadelphia trade unionists commended the fact that Ely offered services geared to the tastes of the wage earner. His efforts, as well as those of many ministers in working-class neighborhoods, appeared to lend legitimacy to the labor movement. Never before had Protestants been so consciously solicitous of organized labor. Although some speakers raised the eyebrows of trade unionists, most workers probably did not attend just to hear laudatory remarks.

Even though Christian workers attended religious services regardless of the political message, the emergence of Social-Gospel theology made it easier for union members to mix labor activism with being a good Christian. Bookbinder Alf Bieber asserted that the church and labor were "unconsciously drawing closer together." Some, like shoemaker Henry Goodwin, could state, "I have always been a trade-union man, and I have endeavored to live up to its principles," but "I feel also that I am a Christian. I endeavor to live a Christian life, and my charity comes to my relief when I find" needy men, women, and children. Christians in the labor movement no doubt reinforced their commitment when local ministers like Keith Cherry and Edward Randolph praised the moral virtues of trade unionism or when the YMCA and the Salvation Army insisted on union-label products.[16]

By 1904, Philadelphia trade unionists had ample reason to feel that the time was never better for the cooperation of organized labor and mainstream Christianity. Social Gospellers encouraged the recognition of trade unions, clergymen sat as fraternal delegates to the Central Labor Union, and reformers pressed for labor legislation. This increased legitimacy and respectability complemented the substantial upswing of the trade union movement. Nationally, the AFL grew from around 300,000 members in 1897 to just under two million, ushering in the era of the national trade agreement. Union treasuries ballooned, allowing labor organizations to surround members "with all the social and moral protection which [they] possibly can."[17] Although unions still centered on the skilled, white, male elite of the working class, the potential for growth appeared unlimited.

Philadelphia workers witnessed this same expansion. Cigarmakers Local 100 grew by 500 members in 1900. In the building trades, Local 8 of the Carpenters and Local 9 of the Paperhangers experienced an unprecedented growth, allowing the Paperhangers to employ a full-time business agent for the first time in 1899.[18] In the metal trades, over 90 percent of the patternmakers were in union shops, and the Iron Molders enforced the closed shop in all but three factories in the city. Printers, garment workers, and textile workers all formed councils to coordinate organizing drives and union negotiations. Between 1899 and 1903, the number of affiliated locals in the city mushroomed from 140 to 213.[19]

Organized labor's new power contributed to gains in recognition and collective bargaining. In 1903, the Philadelphia Clothing Trades Association negotiated a contract for over 5,000 workers in the men's garment industry which called for the eight-hour workday and wage increases. That same year, the Philadelphia Typothetae, an association of printing employers, recognized the Allied Printing Trades Council through a three-year contract. The Iron Molders signed a nationwide agreement with the Foundrymen's Association and forced its acceptance on numerous small establishments in Philadelphia through a series of individual strikes.[20] In 1904, the building trades orchestrated one of the most startling victories when they forced all the major contractors in the city to accept their right to engage in sympathy strikes in addition to winning major wage increases.[21]

Backing from middle-class Protestants further enhanced labor's strength. Clergymen interceded on behalf of the building trades workers, encouraging the Master Builders' Exchange to accept union conditions. Middle-class women like Anna Davies and Florence Sanville participated in the Consumers' League, the Women's Trade Union League, and union-label agitation against unfair labor conditions in the cigar and clothing industries.[22] Just as critical was their assistance in the agitation for labor legislation. Between 1897 and 1907, a veritable flood of acts regulated child labor, factory inspections, sweatshops, bakeries, employer liability for injuries, and even the counterfeiting of union labels. In Philadelphia, union power and middle-class reformers ensured that all city printing was done in union shops and that union scales applied to all city construction projects.[23]

Social-Gospel ideas, by conferring legitimacy on the labor movement, however, helped change the character of the religious sentiments of trade unionists. The limited acceptance of respectable labor organizations into the mainstream of Christian culture abated the force of millennial, sect-like religiosity. The years of struggle to be accepted by the Church finally reaped rewards for labor. No longer on the margins of American society, labor activists could point to clergymen who asserted trade unionism's role in "the uplifting of human society." For one, the Reverend Edward Randolph of the city's Trinity Methodist Church commended labor's support for arbitration, its improvement of "civil government" by championing sanitation and child labor laws, and its importance in "Americanizing" the immigrant. Trade unions, Randolph continued, "have created a brotherhood of laborers, who bear one another's burdens and share each other's successes," not unlike true Christians.[24]

Protestant churches were particularly evident in this trend. The Central Labor Union (CLU) organ, the *New Era*, applauded Methodist minister Louis Bank's claim that next to Christianity, organized labor was the worker's best friend. The work of Presbyterians Kemper Bocock and J. Gray Bolton on behalf of the CLU won consistent praise, and for two weeks the *Trades' Union News* headlined the condemnation of sweatshops by two Episcopalian ministers. When the Union Label League printed leaflets encouraging patronage of union-made products, the literature contained quotes from prominent local Protestants as well as from the Scriptures.[25]

For a number of reasons, the Catholic Church was unable to provide organized labor with support equal to that offered by Protestant churches despite the growing influence of Catholicism in the working class. Of principal importance was the fact that Catholicism was still "a suspect church in a hostile host culture," according to Catholic historian Joseph McShane. As such, any active support for mass organizations criticizing American political or economic relationships would make the Church appear too radical, a position certain to arouse nativist animosities. Secondly, the Church feared and often censured secret societies and socialist thought, both of which remained present in the labor movement. Finally, Catholics were wary of cooperating with reform movements because they were too frequently associated with the evangelical objectives of American Protestantism. In such an atmosphere, the American Catholic Church was reluctant to confront social issues and did not develop a body of social thought able to rival either the Protestant Social Gospel or socialism in appeal to the working class.[26]

The labor movement nevertheless included many Catholic trade unionists. Organized labor's religious character, in fact, became uncoupled from sectarianism and creeds. As trade unionism gained acceptance from the dominant religious culture, the beliefs and attitudes of labor activists lost much of their edge. The popular Christianity of trade unionists grew to be less marked by the fierce commitment to the fellowship of believers, the millennialist visions, and the attachment to religious inspiration that had characterized the Knights of Labor. Rather, more formal religious connections—either to a church or through the exchange of fraternal delegates by the CLU and the local ministers—combined with greater expectations for positive and concrete results from religious activity and a more pragmatic approach to religious participation to increasingly typify the Christianity of trade unionists in the early twentieth century.

Under such conditions, Catholic labor activists routinely, if perhaps uneasily, attached themselves to a trade-union Christianity with a decidedly Protestant complexion. At the founding meeting of the liberal, Protestant Federal Council of Churches of Christ in America (FCC), Catholic unionists Denis Hayes and Frank Feeney shared the podium and praised the FCC's "social creed." Despite the growing Catholic presence in the city's unions, the CLU exchanged fraternal delegates only with Protestant churches; Catholic priests were conspicuously absent at CLU gatherings.

When Presbyterian minister Charles Stelzle, a noted friend of labor, spoke at the YMCA hall, it was largely the Catholics in the CLU who voted to end the regular meeting and reconvene where they could lend support to the labor preacher.[27] These episodes do not speak of a declining religiosity among trade unionists but rather to the altered character of their religious sentiments.

Consequently, from the vantage point of a resurgent labor movement, activists could ignore such criticism as the Reverend Ely levelled in his 1904 sermon. Organized labor seemed firmly ensconced within the norms of society. Trade unionists paraded this respectability, in large measure because it mirrored their hopes and dreams.[28] Protestantism, consequently, was more than a legitimizing notion. Indeed, religious sentiment went far deeper and blended with a commitment to the uplifting power of unionism. At times even socialists attached themselves as much as possible to Protestant values and culture. Amid a dramatic upsurge of labor in the early twentieth century, Christian respectability appeared more a unifying element than a divisive factor.

Christian Labor in the Enemy's Country

The blending of Protestant culture and labor power did have boundaries. Within the working class, the Christian message adopted by organized labor was less comforting and fulfilling for new immigrants, unskilled industrial workers, blacks, and women. For various reasons, these groups could not be easily assimilated into the "brotherhood of laborers" praised by the Methodist minister Edward Randolph. Furthermore, Christian support for labor rested principally upon the use of voluntaristic solutions to achieve industrial peace. However, effective moral suasion and voluntaristic solutions need a relatively equal distribution of power between labor and capital, a situation that beginning in 1904 employers took great pains to undermine. Thus, the alliance of Protestantism and organized labor not only excluded large elements of the working class but also proved unequal to the task of gaining acceptance from capital.

As organized labor demonstrated its considerable growth in a flurry of strikes and public demonstrations in 1903–04, employers began mobilizing for a counterattack. In the city's second largest industry, a group of executives from small and medium-sized companies organized the Metal Manufacturers' Association (MMA). Patterned after associations recently begun in Cleveland and Cincinnati, the MMA declared its intention to bring the open, nonunion shop to the Philadelphia metal trades. The association began a labor bureau to recruit nonunion machinists, molders, blacksmiths, patternmakers, and polishers and to screen out pro-union mechanics. Within two years, the MMA had over 50 members employing more than 5,000 metal workers. It stopped the competition among firms for skilled labor and organized a solid defense against union demands.[29]

Open shop ideas spread to other industries. In men's clothing, smaller firms outvoted the large companies in 1904 and began a struggle to oust unions. The Philadelphia Clothing Trades Association issued a public statement complaining that "for the past year the United Garment Workers have had complete control of all of our shops. . . . There was a lack of order and discipline, but worst of all a constant restriction" was placed on output.[30] Members of the Philadelphia Typothetae united to reject the Typographical Union's demand for an eight-hour workday, and to end collective bargaining in the printing industry. In textile mills, the 1903 strike so unified employers that they decided as a group which holidays to grant employees.[31]

Employers revived a number of methods to undermine union control of craft labor markets. Renewed attention to trade training allowed employers to substitute nonunion young men and women for union workers. For example, Roelof's hat factory broke off relations with the United Hatters after employing hastily trained apprentices. The Bricklayers' Company of Philadelphia revitalized its trade school to train journeymen outside the influence of unions.[32] In this area, Christianity actually bolstered anti-union activities. Clergymen like Russell Conwell, arguing that acquiring a trade should be available to all children, established church-sponsored trade schools, none of which allowed union input because of labor's restrictive practices. The YMCA meanwhile even provided trade training for the anti-union MMA.[33]

Technological change further assisted employers in their assault on labor. Large tobacco companies stepped up their use of molds, hand bunchers, and suction tables to enable unskilled women to make a decent cigar. In metal plants, molding machines allowed the replacement of skilled molders. In the glass industry, the introduction and improvement of jar-making machinery by 1904 severely reduced the need for highly skilled bottle blowers. Even the building trades were not immune. The development of plaster partition block eliminated much of the inside work of masons, and prefabricated doors and windows enabled carpenters to be replaced by semiskilled factory workers.[34]

When technological improvements were not available, employers experimented with reorganizing the labor process to take control away from craft workers. The most elaborate example was Frederick Taylor's use of detailed directions to abolish all decision-making by machinists. More common, however, was an intensified division of labor and the implementation of piece work. The Autocar Company, for one, took advantage of worker unrest by getting "rid of a lot of dead wood and disgruntled men, who would undoubtedly have given us considerable trouble in the future" and inaugurating "the piece-work system." The MMA, in particular, resorted to piece work and incentive systems to extract greater productivity from workers.[35]

Vital to the employers' ability to gain control over craft production was the sheer force of their power and wealth. In the metal trades, the manufacturers simply extended their recruitment efforts, which flooded the city with machinists, molders, and polishers and allowed the manufacturers to blacklist unionists. In the building trades, large intercity construction firms emerged, capable of sending large numbers of carpenters, sheet metal workers, masons, and electrical workers from one city to another. Similarly, employers in the garment, bottle, printing, and textile industries formed powerful alliances to crush the control of craft workers in their trades.[36] These employer associations demanded unity. The MMA expelled the Girard Iron Works for negotiating with unions. Machinists leader Edward Keenan told the Commission on Industrial Relations that some companies secretly negotiated with his union, but refused to allow public notification of a contract for fear that other companies would retaliate and undermine their businesses.[37]

The open shop movement unified the diverse strategies employed within individual trades. More importantly, it allowed Philadelphia manufacturers to resist unionism under a more favorable light, as they asserted that the open shop was a moral issue. Two members of the MMA, Arthur Falkenau and Stanley Flagg, told the Christian Social Union that unions restricted output and prevented workers from earning better wages. Unions also blocked the entry into trades of young men and women who could not obtain a union apprenticeship. In addition, they hindered progress by rejecting labor-saving inventions and innovations that could lower the cost of products. Over the following decade, manufacturers hammered their arguments at the public through business and "civic" publications. The high moral tone of their individualistic arguments convinced many Christians who were already unhappy with the collectivist drift of Social-Gospel sentiments. In addition, they received support from many erstwhile Progressives who viewed efficiency and productivity as the answer to poverty.[38]

The results of this employer offensive were startling. By 1907, only four small foundries continued agreements with the Iron Molders Union following a two-year lockout. The Boiler Makers had only 300 union members among 5,000 workers. Following the defeat of the printers' strike in 1905, the Typographical Union had only about one-third of the 3,000 printers in the city organized. Of the daily newspapers (usually a union stronghold) only three of eight were union shops.[39] The United Garment Workers rapidly became weak and ineffectual following the 1904 lockout. Similarly, in 1907 the weavers, usually the core of unionism in textiles, succumbed to intimidation by Pinkerton agents and the recruitment of strikebreakers. This is to say nothing of the truly immense establishments like Cramp's Shipyard, the Baldwin Locomotive Works, and Midvale Steel, where unionism had made no headway in the twentieth century.[40]

In just three short years, the open shop movement halted the growth of organized labor. Philadelphia became the self-proclaimed "scab recruiting station" of the country, according to the *Machinists' Monthly Journal*. But the metal trades were not the only ones weakened. Printer Shelby Smith stated that Philadelphia was the "enemy's country." In neither the men's nor the women's garment industries was unionism particularly strong. Even in many of the building trades, organized labor sank to a low level. The Sheet Metal Workers, for instance, were unable to obtain a contract anywhere in the city.[41]

Throughout this period, the structure of unionism became a major source of labor's vulnerability. Despite their growth before 1904, unions never made a significant commitment to organizing women, ethnics, blacks, or the unskilled. The employer attack and the onset of an economic recession in 1907 heightened these ethnic, gender, and racial antagonisms, creating a "splintered world" of labor.

For years, blacks had been systematically excluded from local unions. Local 77 of the Musicians even prevented the formation of a separate black local within their territory. In the building trades, union-controlled jobs relegated blacks to the poorest-paying laborer positions, despite the presence of a considerable number of black building trades workers in the city. In other industries, like metal manufacturing, white workers helped exclude blacks from all but the dirtiest and most menial jobs and made no effort to organize these unskilled occupations. Consequently, wherever blacks managed to obtain an occupational toehold, they were in effect a potential source of strikebreakers and anti-union labor. Famous black sociologist W. E. B. Du Bois summed up the situation for black workers in the city. "He cannot become a mechanic except for small transient jobs, and he cannot join a trades union."[42]

Unionists exhibited little more sensitivity toward immigrants. In the men's clothing industry the United Garment Workers (UGW) primarily protected the Irish, Germans, and Americans who dominated Cutters Local 110. Jews and Italians, concentrated in most of the other parts of the trade, correspondingly had no interest in the UGW except during periodic strikes. Some organizers—often ones imbued with a militant brand of Protestantism —exhibited a more blatant prejudice against immigrants. UGW leader Tunie Symonds, for one, blamed the poor state of Philadelphia's garment district on the Jewish and Italian immigrants who lived in crowded, unsanitary conditions. Symonds had no interest in working with such people. Similarly, the anti-Semitic United Hatters leader Edward Moore smeared organizing drives by the Hatters. Until Musicians Local 77 finally reached an agreement with Jewish players in 1907, ethnic hostilities caused bad feelings. Yet, over the next two years, Local 77 experienced similar difficulties with Italian and Hungarian musicians. Textile workers were also clannish, and their unions restricted membership to certain ethnic groups well into the twentieth century. This made for a high degree of unity within the craft, but it also generated a good deal of resentment among the groups excluded from skilled jobs.[43]

Women were even more afflicted by the narrowness of craft unionism. Females accounted for over one-quarter of the workforce, but either by design or neglect unions systematically limited their participation. In textiles, where they comprised over half the workforce, craft organizations segmented women in the least skilled jobs and excluded them from membership. When women did break into unions, the night-time, male-dominated meetings, held in saloons or lodges discouraged their attendance.[44] In the cigar industry, the male hand-rollers at first refused to organize less-skilled women, then organized but relegated them to a second-class status, despite the increased dominance of women in the trade. Women were forced to develop their own work culture that was separate from, and often hostile to, the male hand-rollers. Although the Printers allowed women, they rarely made any attempt to involve them in the social and cultural life that was integral to building craft union solidarity.[45]

Through an ironic twist, organized labor's Christian tenets actually worked against the incorporation of women, who otherwise might have been most receptive to its sentiments. Patriarchal notions of the family wage appealed to elements of the working class both by reducing labor market competition and protecting women and children, but they also reinforced male dominance and discouraged trade unions from organizing women who, males argued, should be at home.[46] Consequently, women in the workforce benefitted little from labor's Christian gospel.

By largely excluding blacks, ethnics, and women, the labor movement created a tremendous pool of workers who were potential competitors for jobs. Especially at a time when manufacturers were undermining various crafts, this meant that unions were losing control over local and even national labor markets. In a wide variety of trades, including the burgeoning electrical industry, the factory prefabrication of materials used in construction, the mechanization of press feeding and typesetting, and the devices used for cigarmaking, employers began replacing the male, ethnic craft workers with semiskilled women and new immigrants. Unions had little influence with these workers. Indeed, the exclusiveness of craft unions, particularly through the high dues and initiation fees that unions charged, proved a barrier to organizing. Furthermore, much of the cultural underpinnings of craft unions—Victorian respectability, male separatism, pietistic self-improvement—was either repugnant or alien to the female, black, or immigrant industrial workers.[47]

Organized labor eventually made some attempts to adapt. The Carpenters, for example, began organizing mill workers to protect their jurisdiction over "all that's made of wood." The Cigarmakers and Electrical Workers began including semiskilled machine rollers and linemen, adopting a quasi-industrial-union structure. The United Garment Workers created ethnic locals for pantsworkers, shirtmakers, and coatmakers. The Printers and the Bookbinders established women's locals or auxiliaries. In the upsurge between 1898 and 1904, union growth, by necessity, included many semiskilled, women, and immigrant workers. But in most cases, craft workers did not accord the new members an equal status within the union. Instead, unions set up special categories which forbade these semiskilled workers from entering the craft domain, even in the same trade. In some cases, union rules barred these members from the top offices, while the organization channeled most of its attention and funds to the skilled elite.

In effect, unions expanded to include the semiskilled merely to protect their hold on the labor markets and the dominance of the older craft workers who had no commitment to equality.[48]

Thus, despite the optimism of organized labor in 1904, trade unions stagnated. Faced with a concerted effort on the part of manufacturers to roll back union gains and uncomfortable with the idea of organizing large numbers of women, blacks, immigrants, and industrial workers, labor quickly retreated to a conservative, defensive position. To a certain degree, this reflected the increasing bureaucratization of the union movement. The rise of "business unionism," with its emphasis on benefits and large treasuries, encouraged the high dues and initiation fees that repelled the less prosperous immigrants and semiskilled workers. Administering these funds required paid, professional business agents and officers who looked more to the preservation of the union than to its growth. Union leaders thus became reluctant to sanction strikes that would drain treasuries, or to expend significant funds on organizing. Instead they turned inward, preserving the organization for the shrinking numbers of craft workers who maintained control over working conditions and labor markets.[49]

Nowhere was the growing conservatism of Philadelphia labor more evident than in the political arena. Frank Feeney, president of the Elevator Constructors and a leader of both the CLU and the Building Trades Council, channeled labor's political initiatives into the Republican machine in 1905. This was an abrupt change for Feeney, who as late as 1902 had challenged the machine as a Democratic candidate for city council. A political intriguer from the Retail Clerks, Martin Mulhall, later claimed that he had purchased Feeney's support with money from the National Association of Manufacturers, although Feeney was later cleared of that specific charge. Nevertheless, Feeney ruled the CLU from 1905 until the AFL expelled him in 1908 for being on the payroll of the city government and the contractors' association—positions in conflict with his leadership of the Building Trades Council.[50]

Feeney, however, points out the direction in which the labor leaders most closely associated with Christianity were heading.

Indeed, Feeney and others, who were intent upon emphasizing the moderate respectability of labor, were busy severing connections with a broader social and political program promoted by labor's more radical wing. Feeney, of old immigrant stock and based in an exclusive craft, rejected alliances with new immigrants, women, and the unskilled, knowing they could jeopardize his standing and political influence. Although an Irish Catholic, he felt more at home with middle-class Protestant reformers than with the Italian garment workers of South Philadelphia.

In similar fashion, support for the machine gained favor with a number of unions attempting to regroup from the open shop offensive. The Allied Printing Trades Council, for instance, following the defeat of the Printers in the 1905 strike, came increasingly to count upon the machine to have all city government printing and bookbinding done in union shops. With most local newspapers nonunion, city contracts kept union shops afloat and members employed. Meanwhile, the reformers, led by future Progressive mayor Rudolf Blankenburg, had their campaign printing done in nonunion shops.[51] Likewise, in the 1906 Senate campaign, the CLU endorsed GOP machine leader Boies Penrose over reform Democrat Lewis Emery because of the former's support for the employers' liability act. In classic AFL fashion, the *Trades' Union News* argued for the machine above reform candidates or third-party alternatives: "We will stand by our friends and administer a stinging rebuke to men or parties who have been either indifferent, negligent or hostile" to labor.[52]

In 1907, the CLU ignored the objections of both Democrats and socialists, and endorsed the incumbent mayor John Reyburn. Machinists leader John Gilbert argued that Reyburn was a fair employer who responded to issues raised by his employees. In his own plant, the mayor demonstrated "the sincerity of his friendship for workingmen." Moreover, the machine appointed many labor leaders to positions in the city or state government. John Price Jackson became head of the state labor department, while Tunie Symonds (of the United Garment Workers), and several other ex-labor activists were appointed as factory inspectors.

Feeney's own political plum was head of the city's bureau of elevator inspection. The patronage of the machine, through city contracts stipulating union conditions, meshed with the growing careerism of union activists.[53]

Support for the machine signalled both a break with the socialists in the CLU and a major crack in labor unity. The CLU began publishing its own newspaper in 1904 and eliminated socialist support. By 1907, the CLU had blocked socialist participation in its May Day parade. "The action of the Philadelphia labor unions in summarily ejecting the socialistic or lawless agitators from their ranks" was "reassuring" to printer Shelby Smith.[54] This represented a significant shift from the friendly cooperation that the CLU and socialists had enjoyed as late as 1903. That many socialists were also new immigrants widened the chasm.

The CLU's retreat to the machine, however, did more than just drive out the socialists. The machine protected only a small number of craft workers and, even there, quite frequently just the leaders. Garment workers, cigarmakers, and machinists, among others, began complaining that CLU politics benefitted a privileged few. Women, immigrants, and industrial workers, in addition to hard-pressed craft workers, began clamoring for a change. Even within the building trades, criticism emerged. James White of the Granite Cutters explained that his local left the CLU because "for years" it was "run for the benefit of a political machine."[55]

By 1908, then, organized labor's influence in the city was stagnating. The employer offensive, changes in the production process, and the political and social outlook of craft unionism combined to shatter the optimistic vision that characterized labor's alliance with Social-Gospel Christianity in 1904. The voluntary settlement of labor disputes advocated by local religious leaders did not restrain powerful employers intent upon destroying unions, and a respectable, Christian trade unionism had little appeal beyond a small craft elite. The house of labor appeared to be crumbling from the outside and from within.

Socialism or Humanity?

As employers attacked organized labor, Christian respectability became increasingly important to craft-union leaders. *The Trades' Union News* ran weekly columns from labor preacher Charles Stelzle. The CLU became involved with middle-class agitation against tuberculosis and worked closely with the Consumers' League in helping to expose the evils of sweatshop labor. The Union Label League joined with prominent Protestant reform groups in preparing an exhibit uncovering the horrors of child labor. Finally, the CLU continued to seat a fraternal delegate from the Christian Social Union.[56]

In many ways, the support of Social-Gospel Protestants provided the one stronghold of organized labor's legitimacy in Philadelphia. Denis Hayes of the Glass Bottle Blowers emphasized this link when he told the Labor Sunday audience at Lemon Hill that "our faith in organized labor is equal to our religious faith and above our political faith." Given the experience of Philadelphia unions with politics, he probably voiced a widespread sentiment. Nevertheless, labors' public image was necessarily improved when prominent union leaders shared a platform with founders of the liberal Federal Council of Churches of Christ in America in December 1908. They read the Council's principles, which included support for unions and collective bargaining, and closed by singing "Onward Christian Soldiers."[57]

The price of Social-Gospel support, however, was a commitment to moderation. Religious leaders counseled against independent politics, hasty or violent strikes, and radical sentiments. The tone and message of labor preachers like Stelzle increasingly stressed patience, compromise, mutual respect, and above all antisocialism. "The church can not and should not adopt and advocate socialism," Stelzle repeatedly asserted. "I would protest against having forced upon me by the church any social system with which I do not agree."[58]

Stelzle's message attracted vigorous support from Irish Catholic trade unionists who dominated the local building trades unions, particularly because it blended with the vocal antisocialism of the Catholic clergy.[59] Yet, by coming from mainstream Protestants, this message seemed to carry more weight. Irish Catholic support for Stelzle, however, was more than a gamble to acquire political influence; the reform initiatives, the Christian sentiments, and the desire for respectability all spoke to genuine, deeply held beliefs of the majority of craft unionists. Moreover, Protestant support provided a justification for continuing their craft-union program at a time when unions were under attack from above and below.

Local labor struggles increasingly forced conservative craft unionists to separate themselves from "irresponsible" elements of the working class. In 1908, radicals in the International Brotherhood of Electrical Workers (IBEW) challenged the corrupt, self-serving leadership of president Frank McNulty. The IBEW contained two factions—workers in the building trades who did inside wiring work, and outside (line) workers who strung cables. The inside workers dominated the union and made much higher wages due to their being in the building trades. These inside workers relegated outside workers to a second-class status in the union, forbidding them from taking an inside job without paying an additional fee and passing an examination. Equally important, the union devoted little money to assisting the outside workers. Complaining of corruption and advocating a form of industrial unionism, the line workers rebelled. Nearly three-fourths of the IBEW members joined the rebels, including most of the members of Philadelphia IBEW Local 98. Yet, the AFL continued to recognize the corrupt remnant, and the local Building Trades Council helped organize a new local that undermined Local 98 on construction jobs. Such actions threw the rebel IBEW members into league with the socialists from whom they received unqualified support.[60]

Only a year later, female garment workers, mostly outside the garment unions, organized against exploitative conditions in the shirtwaist trade. Following the example set by their sisters in New York, Philadelphia waistmakers demanded a nine-hour day, uniform wage scales, and recognition for their new union. Prominent women, including Florence Sanville and Fanny Cochran of the

Consumers' League and College Settlement Association leader Anna Davies, joined the waistmakers on the picket line and organized fund raisers. Young women from Bryn Mawr College patrolled the streets with placards demanding justice for the waistmakers. Although the CLU sympathized with the strike, women outside the union establishment generated most of the support which ultimately led to a partial victory.[61] Militant actions by women, not assistance from male-dominated unions, forced a settlement, demonstrating to many workers that there were alternatives to conservative craft-union tactics.

Within weeks of the garment workers' action, streetcar workers began their second strike in nine months against the Philadelphia Rapid Transit Company (PRT). The immediate cause of the February 1910 conflict was the PRT's firing of 173 union members. But since May 1909, Division 477 of the Amalgamated Association of Street Car and Electric Railway Men of America had been fighting for a nine-hour day, the abolition of swing shifts, and an hourly wage of 25 cents. In June 1909, the Amalgamated and the PRT reached a compromise. Within six months, however, the company cancelled the negotiated raises, inaugurated an elaborate welfare plan, and fired seven employees who were openly critical of the actions. On February 15, despite efforts by Republican machine leader James McNichol to obtain a compromise, the Amalgamated broke off negotiations and the PRT retaliated by firing 173 union members.[62]

Events rapidly turned the PRT strike into a mass uprising. Streetcar workers were uniquely positioned to obtain widespread support. The large PRT workforce gathered for work at centrally located roundhouses that provided convenient rallying points for strikers and sympathizers. More importantly, the streetcar ride proved an excellent means of informally spreading the strike message. Finally, most other workers saw the PRT as a source of exploitation and corruption, forcing employees to work long shifts in open, drafty cars for very low wages. The mayor's quick dispatching of police and private militia companies to suppress demonstrations symbolized the company's arrogance and power, and incensed crowds of workers and their supporters. Throngs challenged police in Germantown, Kensington, and at the Baldwin Locomotive Works in center city. Sympathizers smashed streetcar windows and destroyed PRT property. When the mayor arrested the presidents of the Amalgamated and the CLU and called in the National Guard, infuriated workers called for a general strike.[63]

Approximately 100,000 workers walked off their jobs in early March; in working-class districts like Kensington, industry came to a standstill. In the metal trades, textiles, and even such non-union bastions as Baldwin Locomotives, workers asserted that the "time has come when we must assert ourselves." Such an uprising even impelled cautious building trades unionists to join the strike, which seemed to capture organized labor's frustration at its embattled position. One worker stated that "this fight is not confined to that one union. It is an attack on organized labor, and threatens the life of every union in the country."[64]

The general strike lasted until March 27, but police violence and the arrival of the National Guard restored order earlier. The moderate Pennsylvania Federation of Labor also backed off from further confrontations. During the strike, however, over 20,000 workers joined unions. Many factories, like Baldwin's, were organized for the first time. As the CLU's general strike committee declared, "No longer can Philadelphia be pointed to by the rest of the country as a 'scab' town to be shunned."[65]

At the same time, the struggle revived the Left in the Philadelphia labor movement. Socialists played an important role in mobilizing support for the strike. Speeches by Eugene Debs and Elizabeth Gurley Flynn, although banned by the mayor, drew huge crowds. Local socialist leaders Charles Ervin, Luella Twining, and Joseph Cohen produced leaflets and helped direct agitation. Socialists in unions, like Harry Parker and Charles Sehl, pushed for a greater commitment from the CLU. Parker summed up the resurgence in socialist spirit: "The masters have taught us these sacred words: 'The voice of the people is the voice of God.' And we, too, can give expression to our thought as well as listen, by carrying this idea to the ballot box and voting in the Socialist Republic."[66] Combined with the absence of Frank Feeney's machine from the CLU, the general strike allowed the socialists to play a larger role in redirecting trade-union politics. Parker stated that in 1907 the CLU had "voted for City Hall thugs and criminals," including mayor Reyburn, who had brutally suppressed the general strike.[67]

The rising tide of Philadelphia radicalism blended with a much more extensive challenge to conservative unionism at the national level. After 1909, industrial workers, led by socialists or the IWW, engaged in mass strikes in such places as McKees Rocks and Newcastle, Pennsylvania; Lawrence, Massachusetts; and Little Falls, New York. Within the AFL, radicals in several unions banned involvement with the capitalist-dominated National Civic Federation, which ostensibly preached labor–capital harmony and reform but whose members rarely lived up to the ideal. Mounting dissatisfaction with conservative policies and the intensification of industrial conflict enabled socialist factions to topple leaders in the Tailors, the Machinists, the Hatters, the Patternmakers, and the Sheet Metal Workers. Left-led factions came close in others, including Samuel Gompers's own Cigarmakers International Union, where Philadelphia's Harry Parker narrowly missed election as president. Ongoing feuds between radicals and conservatives within the Electrical Workers and the Garment Workers appeared to portend a dramatic break with the labor movement of the past.[68]

Even the return of Frank Feeney to the CLU in 1911 barely slowed the growth of radicalism within Philadelphia labor. In the 1911 mayoral election, left-wing unionists in the CLU threw their support to Progressive candidate Rudolf Blankenburg, who swept to victory. The CLU congratulated union men and women who supported progressive and clean politics.[69] Radicals passed resolutions in the CLU promising aid to the McNamara brothers, who had been arrested for bombing the *Los Angeles Times* building, and endorsing the socialist New York *Call* as the only daily paper in the interest of trade unionism. Left-wing unionists also prompted the CLU to raise funds for the IWW-led Lawrence textile strike and to condemn U.S. intervention in Mexico.[70]

Furthermore, national developments filtered down to the local movement. Led by textile worker John Whitehead, machinist

Edward Keenan, and cigarmaker Harry Parker, the CLU, like many national unions, denounced cooperation with the National Civic Federation. Parker resolved that "it would be better for labor to have nothing to do with the Civic Federation, financed by capitalists who bitterly oppose their own employees organizing."[71] Meanwhile, socialists in the garment trades began a struggle for control of the Philadelphia locals. In the building trades, the rebel IBEW, openly espousing socialism and industrial unionism, organized a rival building trades council. The IWW won control of the meatcutters and the interracial longshoremen's unions, the latter conducting a militant strike that closed the city's port in 1913. In this surge of what labor historian David Montgomery calls the "new unionism," blacks, women, and unskilled industrial workers, together with radicals in the established unions, created a powerful challenge to craft-union conservatism.[72]

By 1913, then, the open shop drive against Philadelphia labor had actually strengthened the more radical wing of the CLU. Workers in many trades rebelled against union leaders who retreated into machine politics and craft-union exclusiveness. Socialists not only pushed the CLU to the left, but also helped elect one of their own, James H. Maurer, as president of the Pennsylvania Federation of Labor.[73] At the same time, women, blacks, and industrial workers demanded to be included in the labor movement.

The moderate craft-union course, which Social-Gospel Protestantism did so much to encourage, appeared to have lost its vitality. In November 1913, Presbyterian minister William B. Patterson, head of the local Interchurch Federation, took a delegation of prominent ministers to the CLU meeting hoping to restore Social-Gospel influence. He wanted organized labor to know that responsible labor activities had the support of such national Social-Gospel leaders as Charles MacFarland, Samuel Zane Batten, and Harry F. Ward. All of these fraternal delegates addressed the meeting, suggesting that unions give ministers a chance to abolish child labor, end substandard housing, and "teach the use of the union label in churches." About half of the gathering applauded the ministers.

At the end of the meeting, however, Episcopalian minister George Chalmers Richmond, a local Christian Socialist, rose to object to the distinguished guests. He claimed that many clergymen were hired by capitalists to fool labor, and singled out Reverend James B. Ely who ran the Lemon Hill tent meetings. Richmond told "of what a nice fat job the Rev. Mr. Ely had preaching to the laboring man every Sunday afternoon for a very large salary paid by a man who keeps his 10,000 employees in abject slavery." Half of the CLU members gave Richmond a rising vote of thanks for his speech and elected him as their fraternal delegate.[74]

The Philadelphia labor movement was deeply divided in 1913. Political perspectives placed a barrier between CLU factions. Entrenched craft unionists denounced socialism, industrial unionism, and mass strikes as "a reign of terror by the Industrial Workers of the World." This, they claimed, was "a prospect against which the moral and physical nostrils of the public majority insistently revolts." Harry Parker, as usual, spoke for the other side. Demanding increased militancy, he told the CLU "that Organized Capital has at all times used every endeavor to crush Organized Labor."[75] However, the continued stagnation of the labor movement benefitted neither side. Despite challenging craft-union leadership, the radicals were unable to sustain systematic growth. Unions continued to lose members, and dramatic strikes only temporarily halted declining conditions. In most cases, IWW and socialist-led victories were fleeting. It was in this context that craft unions launched their revival movement.

An Incalculable Chain of Influences

During 1912, the AFL, like the Philadelphia CLU, was beset with problems. The open shop movement had undermined areas once considered the stronghold of unionism. The growing incidence of industrial violence had shattered organized labor's claim to legitimacy. Frustrated with union stagnation and neglect, unorganized workers joined radical groups like the Industrial Workers of the World, while union members turned a receptive ear to socialism or syndicalism. Many unions experienced intense factionalism and internal rebellions. Dramatic victories seemed to strengthen only those elements outside the mainstream of the labor movement, while defeats weakened all of labor.

Yet, in April 1912, craft unionists discovered a solution to their sagging spirits in the Labor Forward movement. Across the country in 1911–12, unionists had witnessed a Social-Gospel revival movement sponsored by the Federal Council of Churches of Christ in America called the Men and Religion Forward movement. Led by such pro-labor Protestants as Charles Stelzle, Raymond Robins, Harry F. Ward, and Charles MacFarland, the movement also recruited prominent union leaders like John Mitchell, James O'Connell, and Peter Brady. The revivals consisted of teams of six prominent Social-Gospel clergy and lay leaders who, with a tremendous prerevival press buildup, would conduct whirlwind eight-day campaigns in major cities and towns. The revivals exploited parades, mass meetings, and media (like motion pictures) to generate overall excitement. They then followed with small, more intense meetings where Men and Religion Forward speakers could encourage a personalized commitment to the Gospel.[76]

Although the principal Men and Religion Forward idea was to stimulate religion, it was heavily laced with social as well as moral messages. In addition to attacks on brothels, gambling, and vice, the campaign targeted the economic and social causes of sin, criticizing slum housing, child labor, and economic inequality. Raymond Robins, husband of Women's Trade Union League leader Margaret Dreier Robins and an ex-union-member himself, in particular addressed the concerns of workers. Both he and Stelzle cited the Federal Council of Churches' "social creed," which advocated labor organization and collective bargaining. They aroused "considerable enthusiasm" at special meetings held for trade unionists at which they envisioned a "square deal" for organized labor. Social-Gospel revivalists pointed to the cooperation of famous labor leaders like John Mitchell of the United Mine Workers and John Lennon of the Journeymen Tailors to hammer home their message to labor. It is telling that many of the prominent unionists they recruited were leaders who had been ousted by the labor factionalism of the period.[77]

Several labor leaders who participated in the Men and Religion Forward revivals felt that similar campaigns, drawing upon revival techniques and the support of the Social Gospel, could revitalize craft unionism. One, Minneapolis labor editor Tom Hamlin, suggested that his city's Trade and Labor Assembly sponsor a Labor Forward movement. In April 1912, about six months after the Minneapolis Men and Religion Forward campaign, a committee of more than 200 unionists launched a two-week long labor revival, which attracted organizers from many national unions, enlisted the support of local ministers and church clubs, and delivered a message that organized labor was not a menace but rather an "instrument for social uplift." The campaign successfully organized thousands of workers, boosted the union label, and portrayed craft unionism as a respectable alternative to the IWW and the Socialist Party of America. In fact, many church-based businessmen's clubs endorsed union labels and collective bargaining with AFL unions. As an added bonus, the Labor Forward movement revived the local labor movement and thus silenced socialist critics of the Minneapolis union leadership.[78]

National union leaders and the AFL executive council quickly adopted Labor Forward as a revitalization campaign. At a time when craft unionism was stalled, the revivals offered a new source of energy and legitimacy. AFL president Samuel Gompers, for one, felt that Labor Forward could "give a tremendous impetus" to organizing and "carry an incalculable chain of influences and results—both psychic and material." At the urging of labor leaders, both locally and nationally, the movement spread rapidly. Within a year, towns and cities as diverse as Topeka, Kansas; Syracuse, New York; Dallas, Texas; Erie, Pennsylvania; and Los Angeles, undertook campaigns. Over the next four years, Labor Forward constituted the major organizing tool of the AFL, as it reached well over 150 towns and cities.[79]

Undoubtedly, the revivals tapped an important reserve of craft-union sentiments. Wherever Labor Forward went, it stimulated a growth and spirit not witnessed since the era of the Knights of Labor. Utilizing music, parades, door-to-door canvassing, and balls that workers attended in their craft "uniforms," the revivals drew upon the experiences and culture of skilled, male workers. But Labor Forward also gave expression to the contradictions within craft unionism. On the one hand, the revivals celebrated working-class solidarity across gender, racial, and ethnic lines. Unions lowered dues and initiation fees to recruit less-skilled or ethnic coworkers. Skilled workers assisted the organizing efforts of female domestics and laundry workers, and special events attempted to bring all wage earners under the umbrella of organized labor. On the other hand, the revival gospel relied on Protestant values of sobriety, moderation, and the work ethic, often utilizing such male separatist mechanisms as smokers. Moreover, Labor Forward rested on a delicate adherence to craft exclusiveness rooted in the autonomy, independence, and respectability of the skilled, white male worker at a time when employers were undermining skill and unskilled workers were clamoring for inclusion.[80]

Faced with those contradictions, the revivals achieved mixed results. Spectacular organizing successes occurred contemporaneously to dismal failures. Revivals in St. Louis and Brooklyn never got underway. In Des Moines, the "rank and file was apathetic." But in Syracuse, union membership jumped by more than one-third, causing the "whole Central and Northern Sections of the state [to come] alive as they never were before to the spirit of unionism." Organized labor in Baltimore increased by over 13,000. Indeed, William Z. Foster, editor of *The Syndicalist* and future head of the Communist Party of America, was impressed with the power of Labor Forward, crediting the campaigns with revitalizing a labor movement he thought was moribund.[81]

One facet of Labor Forward in particular appealed to labor leaders. The revivals proved especially effective in solidifying and justifying craft unions at the expense of their radical critics. Labor Forward allowed such labor leaders as George Perkins of the Cigarmakers, James O'Connell of the Machinists, Hugh Frayne of the Sheet Metal Workers, John Lennon of the Tailors, and John Mitchell of the United Mine Workers to become active in a vibrant organizing campaign at a time when their leadership was under attack. In fact, O'Connell, Frayne, Mitchell, and Lennon had all been deposed by socialist-led factions criticizing their inactivity, and remained tied to labor only through AFL patronage. Perkins only narrowly survived a socialist challenge. Yet all five were active supporters of Labor Forward.[82]

Similar events also occurred at the local level. The success of the revivals in Minnesota preserved the leadership of state federation president E. G. Hall, and in Syracuse they bolstered the conservative regime of Central Labor Union leader Thomas Gafney. Moreover, they facilitated the elimination of radical insurgents from the labor movement. In Auburn, New York, Labor Forward organizing stalled an IWW challenge in local textile mills, and in several locales, trade-union revivals led to the expulsion of rebellious locals from the Electrical Workers.[83] This is not to suggest that Labor Forward was merely a manipulative crusade, orchestrated to undo a radical challenge. But its message, tone, and appeal helped revive and stimulate conservative craft-unionism at a time when it seemed to be losing control.

Moderate union leaders in Philadelphia attempted to utilize the revivals in the summer of 1913. The CLU appointed a committee of ten to "uplift the Labor Movement." Radical–conservative factionalism, however, destroyed the effort. Textile union leader John Whitehead tried to have Frank Feeney expelled from the CLU after political intriguer Martin Mulhall told a congressional investigation that Feeney had been in the pay of the National Association of Manufacturers. Mulhall also charged Feeney with undermining the printers' strike in 1906 and with sabotaging labor opposition to the Republican machine in 1905 and 1907. Although he was cleared of the charges, the investigation split the CLU. Meanwhile, the United Garment Workers began a long and bitter strike, during which they fought not only the employers but also radical insurgents within the union. Politics divided the building trades unions too as the rebel Electrical Workers established a rival building trades council by allying with opponents of Feeney.[84] Under these circumstances, the revival effort collapsed.

Six months later, however, Philadelphia unionists took advantage of AFL support to launch a second attempt. The CLU appointed a committee headed by Glass Workers business agent Joseph Richie. The committee established its headquarters at the Parkway Building and inaugurated the proposed six-month campaign with a mass meeting at the end of March 1914. Conditions were not conducive to success. During the winter, the CLU had divided over whether or not to seat fraternal delegates from Protestant churches and over the extent of support for the Garment Workers' strike. Nevertheless, this time the campaign produced results. Large meetings boosted union-label products while smaller craft-union smokers built trade solidarity. By May, the Labor Forward campaign had an organizing committee of 200 that appointed a Policy Committee, a Literature Committee, and an Executive group.[85]

More importantly, the revival began to heal the political factionalism within the CLU, in large part by winning over representatives from many left-wing unions. The arrival of Thomas Wilson, a national organizer from the Machinists, helped convert that union to the moderate Labor Forward gospel. Wilson appealed to all CLU delegates to "put aside all political differences and get down to business." Harry Parker also joined the campaign. "Men may have fixed ideas on the subjects of religion and politics as solutions to the labor question," Parker stated, but added that there was no better or more holy efforts being made than those coming from Labor Forward. Two old foes from the Cigarmakers, AFL president Samuel Gompers and Socialist Party of America leader J. Mahlon Barnes, joined hands at the Parkway Building. Gompers urged a "more united movement," and Barnes sought citywide support for the AFL convention.[86]

What gave the Philadelphia Labor Forward campaign its appeal was its ability to borrow and blend elements from Protestantism and traditional craft-union culture. Machinists Edward Keenan and Thomas Wilson suggested that the revival copy YMCA fund-raising techniques, and have a large dial that like a clock marks the number of newly organized members. John J. Boyle of the Molders sought to attach the campaign to Christian respectability by emphasizing the temperance issue in meetings. The Typographical Union stressed the need of a periodic "awakening of this sort," for, as with religion, the importance of enthusiasm and devotion to duty was apparent. The Labor Forward committee followed up the efforts of individual trades by organizing personal door-to-door canvasses similar to the revival tactics of Billy Sunday.[87]

Traditional craft-union social mechanisms also regenerated spirits. Smokers mixed lively singing, humorous speeches, and joking sing-a-longs. Open, outdoor meetings, with special discounts on initiation fees, attempted to attract new members. Each week, the *Trades' Union News* carried short descriptions of various union socials, featuring the speeches and highlights of the entertainments. For example, during one week three Teamsters locals held socials for prospective members at Odd Fellows' Hall and the Waiters' Union Hall, where they conducted a "whirlwind campaign" to spread "the gospel of unionism to every member of their craft." Similarly, Garment Workers leader Thomas Quinn treated members to a variety show featuring solos by union members and refreshments that "created more harmony" among the ethnic groups that comprised the trade.[88]

Many elements used to revitalize union culture were taken directly from the Social-Gospel Men and Religion Forward campaign. The Labor Forward committee printed thousands of cards and pamphlets for mass distribution, and the use of motion pictures to draw attention to union-label products was particularly successful. Much like the earlier revival, prominent teams of organizers—in this case well-known and popular union leaders—descended upon the city. James O'Connell from the AFL Metal Trades Department, United Textile Workers organizer Sara Conboy, Teamsters president John Tobin, and Cigarmakers president George Perkins were just a few of the "flying squadron" of nationally known labor activists to join the organizing drive.[89]

Christianity provided much of the underlying imagery of labor's revival. James O'Connell told Labor Forward crowds that unionism stood "for the inculcation of the noblest Christian purposes . . . by infusing into human society a loftier morality than is known at the present time." The Cigarmakers and Garment Workers boosted union labels as "religious emblems," arguing that it was "a religious act" to buy goods to which union labels were attached, "an act blessed on earth and honored in heaven." Indeed, trade unionists drew upon the example of Jesus as a justification for the current crusade of organized labor. "Christ did not win the plaudits of successive eras of advancing civilization by teaching men to turn the passive cheek to continued blows," argued the *Trades' Union News*. Rather, "He gained the recognition of humanity by the militant inculcation of strong, severe, all-conquering purpose."[90]

In advancing their cause through connections to Social-Gospel Protestantism, Philadelphia's unionists were perhaps better situated than their counterparts in other cities. Philadelphia was not a major recipient of new immigrants from Southern and Eastern Europe; it had a moderately sized foreign-born population, most of which was from old-stock immigrant nationalities.[91] In addition, one of the new immigrant groups, the Italians, were somewhat alienated from their native Catholicism and thus less resistant to Labor Forward. Another group of new immigrants, Eastern European Jews, had labor-union traditions and were already favorably disposed toward unionism. For both Italians and Jews, the revivals' positive attraction lay in the festive atmosphere of Labor Forward and the downplaying of specifically religious rhetoric at certain meetings.[92]

Another factor in the revival's success lay in the composition of craft unionism. Many unions were still dominated by native, white, Protestants, or old-stock immigrants and their children. Even where non-Protestant immigrants comprised a significant portion of a trade, such as in the garment industry, the leadership remained old-stock. While one might expect such old-stock groups as the Irish Catholics to resist Labor Forward's connections to Protestantism, the role of the Irish in the building trades suggests otherwise. In these unions, the overwhelmingly Catholic leaders provided the staunchest support for the efforts to draw on Protestant culture to "uplift the Labor Movement," especially because the conservative message of Labor Forward blended so well with their own social and political needs as well as with the antisocialism of the Catholic Church.[93]

The revival thus allowed the city's trade unions to make unprecedented gains. Many reported impressive increases in membership; the Upholsterers gained 200 new recruits, the Electrical Workers 175, and the Teamsters between 300 and 400. The Lace Workers, Elevator Constructors, Asbestos Workers, and Brewery Workers claimed to be 100 percent organized and ready to assist the rest. Overall, the CLU asserted that Philadelphia unions grew by 15,000 members at a total cost of only $815 used in the campaign.[94] Improvements were not limited to membership lists. The United Textile Workers, for instance, forced the huge Dobson's mills to improve working conditions. Metal workers, whose union had been stymied at Philadelphia's Navy Yard, gained higher wages and union recognition during Labor Forward. The Printers reestablished control in several daily papers, and many unions obtained union recognition for the first time since the open shop movement began in 1904. The revival succeeded so well that the AFL granted special financial assistance to the CLU to carry the movement through 1915.[95]

Nowhere was the revival of the Philadelphia labor movement more evident than at the parade ushering in the AFL convention in November 1914. The CLU orchestrated a 75,000-person lineup with floats, costumes, lights, bands, and prominent marshals. Printers' apprentices attended in "devil" costumes, reflecting the popular term used in the shop to describe them. The women in the Garment Workers rode in coaches, reflecting the male chauvinism of the craft-union culture. More than 10,000 Carpenters donned white coveralls and built floats depicting every phase of their craft. The Musicians' Union amassed more than 3,000 band members to provide the music. Sheet Metal Workers organizer James Ryan remarked on the turnaround in the city's labor movement: "It certainly was surprising to the majority of delegates that Philadelphia could muster that many men in line—it certainly was a surprise to me."[96]

The parade also exhibited the new conservative foundation on which organized labor's revival rested. The CLU chose Frank Feeney to head the parade as grand marshall. While two socialists —Cigarmaker George Ullrich and Machinist Edward Keenan—

were appointed as aides, most of the parade leaders were from the conservative faction. The featured speaker was James O'Connell, the recently ousted head of the Machinists, who was a staunch opponent of socialism.

Indeed, Labor Forward proved to be an ideal mechanism for limiting socialist influence in the local labor movement. The increased activity destroyed the remaining support for the rebel Electrical Workers and solidified the Building Trades Council under Feeney's leadership. Similarly, the revival crushed the socialist opposition in the United Garment Workers (UGW). The left-wing Amalgamated Clothing Workers, which split from the UGW in 1914, acknowledged the dominance of the conservative "Bible-house gang" in Philadelphia, despite the Amalgamated's power in many other major clothing industry cities.[97] In other cases, Labor Forward provided the means for the inclusion of socialists under the umbrella of moderate craft unionism. Such socialists as Edward Keenan, Harry Parker, and I. W. Bisbing ceased criticism of the CLU and joined the revival. Keenan actually became the secretary of the Labor Forward committee while Bisbing and Parker continually spoke for union growth and labor unity.[98]

In addition, Labor Forward offered enough inducements to other workers to silence their criticism of its Protestantism and its emphasis on skilled, male craftsmen. After early successes in healing craft-union factionalism, the revival turned to organizing women, blacks, and unskilled immigrants in certain trades. In particular, the CLU targeted waitresses, women in the textile and clothing industries, and blacks and immigrants who were laborers or unskilled workers in the Navy Yard. The CLU also elected Garment Worker Isabela Toner as a trustee. But even here, positive actions veiled antiradical motives. Organizing in the clothing industry helped offset the challenge of the Amalgamated Clothing Workers. Moreover, the CLU established dual unions of longshoremen and meatcutters to undermine interracial and interethnic industrial unions that were affiliated with the IWW.[99]

Within a year of the inauguration of the Labor Forward movement, the radical challenge to Philadelphia unions dissipated.

The CLU swung its votes back to the political machine in the local elections of 1915, and supported Wilsonian liberalism in the national elections of 1916. In part, this reflected the disillusionment with Progressive mayor Rudolf Blankenburg, who proved to be no friend of labor. He had appointed Morris Cooke, a disciple of efficiency expert Frederick W. Taylor, as superintendent of public works; Cooke promptly took nearly all city contracts away from union firms. In a relatively weak union city, such actions were devastating. In national politics, the Democrats made enough overtures to labor to obtain AFL backing, but the CLU was unable to overcome the long-time Republican allegiances of most Philadelphia workers.[100]

The trade-union revival had succeeded beyond the most sanguine expectations of its supporters. The organizing drive had added as many as 20,000 workers to union rolls by the fall of 1915. Women, blacks, and unskilled workers played a larger role than at any time since the Knights of Labor, although they remained under the domination of white, male, craft workers. The campaign also set the stage for a further expansion of unionism during World War I, in part by encouraging craft unions to make room for industrial components within their jurisdiction. More to the point, the legitimacy labor had sought in its adoption of Protestantism was actually realized through its support of the war effort after 1917. In Philadelphia, as elsewhere, Labor Forward had contributed to that legitimacy by revitalizing craft unionism and assuaging some of its most severe critics. By 1916, local unions had muted dissenting voices, despite the fact that it continued to represent only a small percentage of the workforce. To a large extent, this was the result of the trade-union revival.

The Advancement of the Workingman

In March 1911, when the socialists were attempting to take control of the CLU, one delegate spoke of his fears to the *Trades' Union News*: "It is very apparent to every trade unionist that there must be a fight for control between the labor men who are for the advancement of the workingman and the Socialist." Continuing, he noted the various successes of organized labor—increased pay, shorter hours, sanitary conditions, and protective legislation. Moreover, "if the truth be known," he stated, "it was not done with the help of the Socialists." At the time, many may have accused him of a false confidence when he challenged the radicals: "So let the issue come; we must lick the Socialist, or lose all we have gained."[101] Yet, within three short years, craft unionists in the city found the means to "lick the socialists."

However, the Labor Forward movement could not have succeeded if it was only a manipulated crusade to silence radical critics of craft unionism; neither was religion the "opiate of the masses." Instead, it is more important to see Protestantism as a complex social force, especially when interacting with the contradictions inherent in the labor movement of the early twentieth century. Throughout the Progressive Era, Protestantism extended the social conscience and the genuine concern about inequality among workers and nonworkers alike. The achievements to which opponents of socialism pointed were important and, in no small part, had resulted from the alliance of craft unionism and the Social Gospel. They fulfilled many long-standing goals of workers, both union and nonunion. Although craft unionism lost some of its vitality during the open shop movement, it remained a vital force, moving in the direction of an urban liberalism with strong working-class roots.[102]

Moreover, Social-Gospel Protestants were not prepared to abandon the unions. Despite the bombs planted by the McNamara brothers, the militancy of the Philadelphia general strike, and the violence associated with mass uprisings of industrial workers throughout the country, liberal clergy in the Federal Council of Churches continued their support for moderate trade unionism.[103] During their revival efforts in 1911–12, in fact, the Federal Council unwittingly provided the AFL with an ideal revitalization mechanism at a time when craft unionism was being challenged from above and below. Once again, the blending of the messages, mechanisms, and institutional support of Protestantism with respectable craft unionism enabled skilled, male workers to organize, rebuild, and reassert their social and political voice.

The course of a revitalized craft unionism, however, had different implications for other segments of the working class. Much of the craft-union culture was objectionable to women, blacks, and immigrants. In addition, trade unionists separated themselves from socialism and more militant forms of industrial organizing, although it is far from clear that less skilled workers were more inclined in that direction. Still, Labor Forward blended well with the growth of Wilsonian liberalism in ways that helped narrow trade-union political choices. The merging of Social-Gospel Protestantism and labor evangelism ensured a moderate course for organized labor in a period of turmoil and challenge.

7

Epilogue: The Salvation of Their Own Souls

SHORTLY after the massive parade in November 1914 that signalled the revitalization of the local labor movement, Philadelphians prepared for another huge pageant, a Billy Sunday revival. Protestant congregations and their prominent supporters raised over $50,000 to build a tabernacle on Logan Square and support Sunday's entourage during the eleven-week crusade. By the end of March 1915, the evangelist had surpassed the Labor Forward movement in converts. Upwards of 25,000 persons had signed a Sunday pledge card, taken a vow of sobriety, and "hit the sawdust trail" to win more souls for Christ. The converts were men and women from all walks of life. A delegation of 200 wage earners from the Lawton Machine Works, clerks from the Franklin National Bank, a small crowd from the Viavi Company, and a throng of more than 10,000 from the Baldwin Locomotive Works all supplied "trail hitters." Even the Central Labor Union welcomed a Sunday disciple.[1]

The messages of Sunday's revival clashed with the ideas that had motivated the Labor Forward campaign. The evangelist stressed the individual rather than the social causes of poverty, preached piety and hard work instead of union organization, and even went out of his way to build his tabernacle with nonunion labor. Amid the wave of strikes and labor militancy that followed Labor Forward, Sunday arrived in Philadelphia as the agent of "a league to enforce peace." The *Public Ledger* charged that the Citizen's Committee that financed Sunday's revival was made up of millionaires who were "willing to pay him for strikebreaking."[2]

The closeness of Sunday's crusade and the Labor Forward Movement demonstrates just how fleeting a friend religion was for trade unions. In fact, the staunchest supporters of Protestant fraternal delegates in the CLU, the building trades workers, felt the brunt of Sunday's anti-unionism. The contradictions that attended labor's alliance with social Christianity were heightened when Protestants retreated to a pietistic fundamentalism. Indeed, the Sunday revival announced the resurgence of a conservative, nativistic evangelicalism that had formerly rested just slightly beneath the surface of Philadelphia Protestantism. Organized labor found little to applaud in the new developments.

Billy Sunday did not arrive in Philadelphia through divine providence. A Citizen's Committee of forty-four prominent Philadelphians carefully planned the campaign and sent several local ministers to convince the evangelist to make the city his next stop. The committee included twelve captains of industry, an equal number of bankers, four eminent corporate lawyers, three city officials, and the president of the Chamber of Commerce, among others. Nearly all the large industrial corporations, including the Baldwin Locomotive Works, Cramp's Shipyard, Midvale Steel, and both the Reading and Pennsylvania Railroads were represented.

The committee's composition told much about its objectives. Baldwin's president Alba Johnson, for one, had "decided that what the country needed was a moral awakening. Purity, modesty, contentment and thrift," were crumbling before the working class's obsession with material things. But when questioned about labor agitation, he clearly revealed why the committee would go to such lengths to finance the revival. "You know," Johnson asserted, "the widespread Social Unrest is largely due to the workingman's envy of those who make a little more money than he does. Now Billy Sunday makes people look to the salvation of their own souls; and when a man is looking after his own soul's good, he forgets his selfish desire to become rich. Instead of agitating for a raise in wages, he turns and helps some poorer brother."[3]

The Sunday revival wreaked havoc within the labor movement. The Citizen's Committee built the tabernacle with non-union labor, prompting the Building Trades Council to "condemn the 'Sunday' movement as unfair to organized labor." Similarly, many of the trades that relied on sociable public drinking—bartenders, waiters, coopers, brewers, cigarmakers—objected to Sunday's attack on the saloons, which were considered by many to be the workingman's club. They especially denounced the hypocrisy of the wealthy backers of Sunday who quietly consumed alcoholic beverages in the privacy of their homes and elite clubs. But even more importantly, at a time when unions were holding weekly meetings and socials in an attempt to enlist new members, Sunday's lavish and well-financed meetings were competing for the time and attention of the city's wage earners.[4]

The crusade divided the loyalties of many workers and splintered an ethnically and culturally heterogenous labor movement. For example, William Crawford, a wood lather who had suffered several bouts with alcoholism, was advised by union president W. J. McSorley to hit the saw-dust trail with Billy Sunday. But Crawford was also a member of the Building Trades Council, which had condemned the revival. Others, like printer and Central Labor Union official Ernest Kraft, supported Sunday's efforts to convert the middle class despite the anti-union message. He cavalierly dismissed the factory Bible classes formed by Sunday's assistants and the large worker delegations that had reserved seats in the tabernacle by stating that "most of those places are not organized." He added, however, that Sunday was doing "a fine work."[5]

An even more pervasive byproduct of the Sunday revival was the reemergence of nativistic sentiments in Philadelphia. Social-Gospel Christianity, while never entirely free from cultural prejudices, had promoted a tolerant, ecumenical spirit that had downplayed and truly suppressed nativism. During the revival, however, a mysterious Episcopalian clergyman, H. C. Stone, organized a paramilitary organization that expressed zealous anti-Catholic and anti-immigrant emotions. The Stone Men's League actively recruited among the Protestant working class and set a nativistic tone that lasted throughout World War I and the immediate postwar period. In particular, their anti-Irish and anti-German nativism was destructive to organized labor in Philadelphia, but the Stone Men's League also singled out radicalism for special denunciation.[6]

The Sunday revival disrupted more than trade unions; it also coincided with a growing schism between liberal and fundamental tendencies in Philadelphia and, more generally, within American Protestantism. Although the two groups had managed to coexist peacefully in the buoyant atmosphere of the Progressive Era, the militant conflict that characterized American industry after 1910 heightened conservative dissatisfaction with the Social Gospel. The publication and widespread distribution of *The Fundamentals*, a series of twelve paperback volumes written by conservative evangelists and financed by a California oil millionaire between 1910 and 1915, provided the theological underpinnings of the fundamentalist backlash. In particular, conservatives attacked the environmentalism of the Social-Gospel advocates and argued for more attention to the individualistic, spiritual messages of the Bible instead of materialistic social concerns.[7]

One of the Protestant clergymen who served as a barometer of this change was James B. Ely. This local Presbyterian evangelist, who had spearheaded the summer tent meetings for workers, scorned the militant actions of city unions. He and fellow Presbyterian minister George H. Bickley organized the delegation sent to convince Billy Sunday to come to Philadelphia. While Ely was ambivalent about unions during the early years of his evangelistic work, his turn to more fundamentalist solutions for social unrest worsened the division within the Presbyterian Church. In fact, conservatives in the church were already in the process of forcing Charles Stelzle out of his influential position as head of the Presbyterian Department of Church and Labor charging that he was too disposed toward socialism. In Philadelphia, Bickley and Ely took issue with the local Presbyterian Social-Gospel leader, William B. Patterson, charging that he had become too involved with labor-management relationships which were questions "of economics, not of religion."[8]

Sunday's Philadelphia revival spurred other conservative reactions to Social-Gospel liberalism, both in churches and in secular institutions. University of Pennsylvania provost Edgar Smith and trustee George Wharton Pepper, both active supporters of the Sunday campaign, objected to economics professor Scott Nearing's challenge to Sunday to preach about the poverty of the masses and the callous exploitation of the capitalists. Nearing also attempted to counter Sunday's appearance in the city by inviting AFL president Samuel Gompers to address crowds of University students. When the University denied Gompers access to its facilities, Nearing, a professor of ten years' experience, took his classes off campus to hear the labor leader. University officials, citing Nearing's socialistic and atheistic tendencies, dismissed the professor two months later.[9]

In the Protestant Episcopal Church, Sunday's revival also helped fuel internal strife. In November 1914, Episcopalian minister George Chalmers Richmond denounced the conservatism of Philadelphia's clergy at a Central Labor Union (CLU) meeting. Then, during the Labor Forward movement, he incurred the wrath of the local Episcopalian bishop, Philip Mercer Rhinelander, by offering United Textile Workers organizer Sara Conboy his pulpit to address his largely working-class congregation. Rhinelander banned the service, but Richmond retaliated by denouncing the Sunday revival and criticizing Rhinelander's support for both the evangelist and the nativistic Stone Men's League, prompting the Church to excommunicate Richmond.[10] Consequently, two of the major Social-Gospel congregations in Philadelphia, the Episcopalians and the Presbyterians, began attacks on liberalism coinciding with the Billy Sunday revival, while the preeminent Social-Gospel Baptist in the city, Samuel Zane Batten, retreated to a conservative nativism around the same time. Finally, evangelical conservatism undercut the liberal, pro-union activism of the YM and YWCAs.[11]

The liberal–fundamentalist split within Protestantism had ironic implications for organized labor. Left-wing unionists from the textile and metal trades, composed mainly of old-stock immigrants and native-born Protestants, attempted to get the CLU to condemn the Episcopal Church's ban on the sermon of Sara

Conboy, but they were backed by the Irish Catholic leaders of the building trades unions. This occurred despite a growing anti-Irish sentiment within American Protestantism, which was linked to Ireland's pro-German sympathies in the European war. Similarly, the CLU offered no criticism of the firing of Nearing or the excommunication of Richmond, despite the efforts of both in behalf of organized labor.

The conservative attack on the Social Gospel reopened the political divisions in the CLU that had been mended by the Labor Forward movement. When conservatives regained control of the city's religious bodies, radicals and new-stock immigrants resumed their criticism of both Protestantism and moderate craft-union methods. But by 1916, the left-wing of the Philadelphia labor movement was losing ground as nativism, patriotism, and antiradicalism became increasingly fashionable and respectable. In 1918, the conservative building trades unions demonstrated their new dominance. They launched a new labor weekly, the *Progressive Labor World*, which condemned radicalism and militancy in the labor movement as the outgrowth of Bolshevism.[12]

All of these developments—nativism, anti-unionism, the declining influence of the Social Gospel, and labor movement factionalism—cannot, of course, be attributed solely to Billy Sunday and the rise of fundamentalism. But the convergence of the evangelist's crusade and the rising tide of anti-unionism in the city was not merely coincidental. The new conservatism of Philadelphia Protestants, evinced in the Stone Men's League, the Nearing and Richmond cases, the ousting of Stelzle, and the retreat from liberalism, shows just how dynamic and ambiguous a force religion proved to be throughout the half-century of labor strife following the Civil War. As the period ended, Philadelphia unionists again found themselves outcasts, targets of a new "American Plan," objects of police and government surveillance, and pariahs in the eyes of the dominant religious culture.

A new configuration of religious influences shaped organized labor in the post–World War I era. This is not to suggest that Protestantism was completely abandoned or became synonymous with reaction. Old Progressives like Gifford Pinchot and Robert

LaFollette sustained a liberal Christian support for trade unionism. At the local level, Social-Gospel Protestants gained control of the YWCAs and made them neighborhood centers for CIO organizing and New Deal political activity. However, in the main, the CIO had a different religious character, one rooted in the Catholic corporatism and liberal Judaism that informed the consciousness of a newly empowered urban, ethnic working class.[13] Religious sentiments were not absent from the struggle of organized labor in the 1930s, but—as was true for the period from the Civil War to World War I—they were constantly evolving.

Conclusion: The Uses of Religion

THE story of labor's interaction with Christianity is filled with irony. In 1885, the conservative Philadelphia YMCA began its successful missionary activities in Kensington's factories at just the point when the Knights of Labor's millennialism predicted an alternative political and economic system. A decade later, immigrant bakers, many of whom had ties to socialism, participated in meetings to abolish Sunday labor at the Baptist Temple of Russell Conwell, the city's most famous proponent of the Gospel of Wealth. In 1915, two citywide revivals consumed the evenings of Philadelphia's wage earners. In the first, trade unionists emphasized their close association with Social-Gospel Christianity and liberal reform; in the second, businessmen sponsored Billy Sunday's message of individual salvation and political reaction. Yet, by all accounts, many workers—even trade unionists—attended both, in some cases with no apparent reservations.

Far from being curious anomalies, these seemingly contradictory events are central to the story of labor's relationship to the dominant religious culture of the Gilded Age and Progressive Era. They suggest that popular religious sentiment was an extremely complex force that helped people adapt to the new realities of industrial society. These contradictions also reveal how churches and Christian voluntary organizations were dynamic institutions, capable of supporting a variety of political and economic positions. Finally, such events as the 1915 revivals demonstrated the dilemmas facing Philadelphia trade unionists when they sought to be included in a liberal social order.

The history of Philadelphia labor provides a number of other insights concerning working-class religiosity. First and perhaps foremost, it is clear that religious beliefs preceded political commitments; the Christianity of Philadelphia's workers cannot be reduced to economic interests alone. Certainly, the pro-labor message of a Charles Stelzle was self-affirming and gratifying, but many of those same workers were also likely to sit through religious services critical of the way labor conducted its daily affairs. Protestant trade unionists must surely have blanched at statements made by the likes of Dwight Moody and Billy Sunday, but labor clung to popular Christianity, and church membership still offered succor for many unionists. Similarly, Catholic workers found the city's Protestant denominations far more sympathetic to organized labor in the Progressive Era. They understood the importance of cooperating with—and even defending—the Protestant proponents of liberal reform. But few gave up their Catholicism.

Secondly, the popular Christianity of organized labor interacted with the formal religion of the mainstream churches; they were not simply parallel phenomena. Indeed, much of what Christian clergy and lay people thought about social justice they learned from trade unionists. This was particularly true of ministers like Stelzle and A. J. Arkin, who discovered social Christianity while they were members of organized labor. But it was also true for Methodists reading the columns of labor activists in *Zion's Herald*, for Presbyterians and Baptists confronting congregations transformed by middle-class urban flight, and by Social-Gospel-inspired reformers pursuing ideals of Christian charity in settlements or the YM and YWCAs. The popular millennialism of the labor movement frequently challenged Christians to adhere to the implications of their creeds and condemn unfair privilege or exploitative relationships.

The interaction of churches and organized labor transformed both sides, however. When mainstream religious institutions proved they were flexible enough to respond to new ideas of social justice, trade unionists sought alliances with liberal Christians. The labor movement's religiosity did not decline after 1900; rather, it changed its character and expression.

In the era of the Knights of Labor, the dominant religious culture gave little thought to labor reform or economic justice. It allowed no role for collective, working-class activism. For the Knights, then, religious sentiments had to be cast in a popular, almost sect-like mold. Labor rejected the more traditional gauges of religious expression, such as church attendance or participation in religious organizations, for a popular Christianity linked to scriptural inspiration, the fellowship of true believers (sister and brother Knights), and a vision of an alternative social and political order based on producer cooperation and brotherhood.

Working-class moral criticism of capitalist social relations, however, jarred the social conscience of the mainstream churches. The depression of the 1890s further eroded the individualistic self-righteousness of the dominant religious culture, as did the new theological developments and the advance of science. Religious organizations faced a crisis. Many church leaders feared they were in danger of permanently losing touch with the masses and turned to an aggressive strategy of assisting the poor in an effort to expand their influence. As expressed in the Social Gospel, activists in both churches and voluntary organizations slowly developed new attitudes toward the efforts of workers to help themselves, particularly through trade unions. By the early twentieth century, many Christians were prepared to accept some forms of collective action and positive state intervention in the economy, provided that certain rules were followed; to summarize Charles Stelzle's admonition, organized labor must cease the "slugging," the "boycotting," and the consorting with Socialists—"the Pharisees of the labor movement."[1]

In exchange for trade unionism's acceptance of these strictures, Social-Gospel Christians, especially Protestants, supported a tremendous expansion in labor legislation. Laws governing female and child labor, workmen's compensation, factory safety and sanitation, and even the hours and wages of labor gained a grudging but significant middle-class approval. In cities like Philadelphia, ordinances protected union wages and working conditions on municipal construction and printing. At the national level, prominent Social-Gospel reformers assisted labor in obtaining the passage of the Clayton Act and the plethora of social-reform laws that comprised Wilsonian liberalism.[2]

In the more approving milieu of Progressive-Era urban liberalism, organized labor's Christian sentiments took on a different character. Many trade unionists, particularly the white, male skilled workers who benefitted from legislation protecting their labor markets, were pleased with the political support they received from Social-Gospel Protestants. Liberal Christians did not wholly denounce strikes, and at public ceremonies, liberal Protestants shared the platform with representatives of trade unions and countenanced the labor movement's objectives as typifying a true Christianity. In return, respectable craft unionism, whose bargaining power was being safeguarded, contributed to a public culture affirming the essentially mainstream character of organized labor.

The acceptance of respectable trade unionism into the social order, however, diminished the autonomy and vitality of the labor movement's religiosity. Organized labor ceased to rely on premillennial predictions of doom or to exhort members with postmillennial prophecies. Labor's gain in public stature and the achievements in the political arena precluded such idioms. Instead, the religious sensibilities of trade unionists became more church-like: the intensity of their devotion to scripture and popular religious inspiration abated; they established more formal connections to mainstream churches; and they became more accepting of the existing social order. These religious sentiments, calculated to enhance the institution's standing in American public culture, did not necessarily represent more secular behavior. Rather they delineated a different, more limited type of emotional commitment, one that some historians suggest characterized popular participation in a whole range of activities at the turn of the century.[3]

A third point suggested by church–labor interaction in Philadelphia concerns the political results of that interaction. The embattled but millennialistic Knights of Labor tended to be inclusive, aiming to build a vibrant movement culture. The Knights' popular religious expression, uncoupled from sectarianism and creeds, attracted Irish Catholics, German radicals, and women mobilized in defense of domestic ideals. The vaguely defined but powerfully appealing vision of an alternative social and political order rooted in a "labor republicanism" briefly united culturally differentiated groups of workers in a class-based movement. But millennialism was not conducive to compromise or political coalition building. An employer counterattack, aided by middle-class fears of boycotts and political radicalism, halted the forward march of the Knights and bared the cultural and ideological tensions of a heterogeneous rank and file.[4] Many workers jettisoned the inclusive but risky class-based strategies for surer, if more limited, tactics for advancing their interests.

Those tactics found expression in the American Federation of Labor's more calculated religious sentiments, a Christianity which tended to be *exclusive*. To function in the political mainstream, the AFL accepted the dominant culture's racial, ethnic, and gender-based proscriptions, rejected certain militant tactics, and severed the most obvious connections with socialism. Although the AFL's political initiatives amounted to something less than a class-wide program, this was not necessarily apparent to workers in the Progressive Era. The rapid growth of trade unionism between 1898 and 1904 and the vast expansion of social-welfare activism after 1900 promised material benefits and a steady growth of working-class power. If, in the end, the AFL's alliance with Social-Gospel Christianity amounted to a particularistic and defensive strategy, it also provided moments when trade unionism could step outside its narrow perspectives and achieve legislative gains that benefitted blacks, women, and new immigrants. Links to mainstream churches and the dominant religious culture enabled labor to establish political alliances that resulted in the flourishing of urban liberalism.

A fourth conclusion revolves around the importance of Protestantism, as opposed to Catholicism, as a rallying point for organized labor in the Progressive Era. Despite the growing Catholicism of the working class and regardless of the social conscience expressed in Pope Leo XIII's encyclical, *Rerum Novarum* (1891), Catholicism could not legitimate organized labor in the dominant culture. In part, the resurgence of nativist anti-Catholicism following the identification of the church with the Knights of Labor cautioned Catholic priests against outspoken positions on social questions. Also contributing to the conservatism of the church was an attitude of immigrant defensiveness, spawning a "notably nonideological" American Catholic social thought. Emerging Catholic social theorists like John Ryan and Peter Dietz were in the minority. Concerned about respectability and religious orthodoxy in a Protestant-dominated society, American Catholicism was particularly attractive to exsocialist converts who valued the Catholic religion "primarily as an ideological weapon against social change."[5]

Catholicism, then, was unable to lend legitimacy to labor struggles or offer a meaningful program for political reform; the church remained suspicious of state intervention and social reform. To maximize political clout, union leaders consequently turned for assistance to the entrenched, mainstream religious liberals—the Social-Gospel Protestants. While Catholic union leaders privately opted for the defensive, traditional posture of their ethnic churches, publicly they sought and built alliances with Protestants. In return for clergy support, Catholic unionists paid respect to the dominant religious culture and recognized its power. The fact that Protestantism's message to labor included antisocialism made Catholic acceptance somewhat easier. Thus, the heavily represented Catholics in the Central Labor Union chose Protestant ministers as fraternal delegates. When socialists objected to the seating of ministers at CLU meetings, Catholics became the clergymen's most vocal defenders.

To what extent was Christianity merely a tool of conservative craft-union leaders and moderate Social-Gospel ministers seeking to undermine a vibrant rank-and-file socialism? Obviously, both groups hoped to weaken working-class radicalism, and the readiness with which Catholic union leaders adopted Protestant mechanisms and support lends weight to this interpretation. Such an analysis, however, ignores the sincerity with which Social-

Gospel ministers aided trade unions at a time when many Christians were denouncing them. Similarly, it discounts the appeal that accommodation to the dominant culture held for many immigrants, especially with the emergence of urban liberalism.[6] Indeed, the American Catholic Church was at that time turning to many Protestant traits—revivalism, temperance, lay initiative—suggesting that Catholic union leaders may have been attempting simply to Americanize their movement through an alliance with Social-Gospel Christians. Because Protestantism bolstered the leadership of moderate Catholic trade unionists does not mean their cooperation was artificial or manipulated.

Rather than attribute a large degree of manipulation to craft unionists and middle-class Protestants, it seems more appropriate to recognize the importance of Christianity in American culture. The ideals of liberal Protestantism complemented a wide spectrum of political and class positions. Similarly, its ambiguous messages were filtered through a variety of experiences. Contact with new conditions dramatically altered the original purposes of both reformers and trade unionists. As the social outlook of a settlement worker, a minister, or a YWCA staff member changed, so too did the attitudes of female garment workers, semiskilled factory operatives, and skilled union workers. In the balance, Christianity continually shifted in the labor turmoil between the Civil War and World War I, encouraging alternatively organized resistance and patient passivity.

The constant flux of Christianity, however, should not diminish its persistence within the mainstream of American culture. If the swings in Protestantism between social and fundamentalist tendencies seemed large, in actuality they never deviated far from the center. Especially because Protestants still hoped to speak for the majority of the population, they had to offer some comfort for the working class. Christians could not blindly condemn wage earners and expect to convert them to their ideal of a Christian America. At the other end, because Protestantism relied on the assistance of the wealthy, it had to stand for order, continuity, and stability despite the forces pressing for a greater social vision from the churches.

Within those parameters, the labor movement gained from its

Christianity. In fact, adherence to the ideals, values, and moderation of Protestantism made organized labor a recognized force for social uplift in the Progressive Era. But this achievement was not without costs. Trade unionists obligingly distanced themselves from socialism and industrial unionism. The rise of Social-Gospel Protestantism and labor evangelism bolstered those elements steering a moderate course for labor during a peak of radical strength in working-class circles. Craft unionists organized vigorously and diligently pursued their objectives, but the range of their goals and appeal was more constricted than it otherwise might have been. It was this complexity and this ambiguity that Protestantism bequeathed to the Progressive-Era labor movement.

Notes

Introduction

1. Samuel Gompers, "Labor Forward Movement," *American Federationist*, Oct. 1912, pp. 828–31. For an overview of the Labor Forward Movement, see Elizabeth and Kenneth Fones-Wolf, "Trade-Union Evangelism: Religion and the AFL in the Labor Forward Movement, 1912–16," in Michael H. Frisch and Daniel J. Walkowitz, eds., *Working-Class America: Essays on Labor, Community, and American Society* (Urbana: University of Illinois Press, 1983), pp. 153–84.

2. See the excellent summary of the writings of Marx, Durkheim, and Weber on religion in Anthony Giddens, *Capitalism and Modern Social Theory: An Analysis of the Writings of Marx, Durkheim, and Max Weber* (New York: Cambridge University Press, 1971), pp. 205–23.

3. Paul E. Johnson, *A Shopkeeper's Millenium: Society and Revivals in Rochester, New York, 1815–1837* (New York: Hill and Wang, 1978). Johnson made explicit use of Durkheim as a model, but Alan Dawley has suggested that his framework owes just as much to Marx. See Alan Dawley, "Death and Rebirth of the American Mill Town," *Labour/Le Travailleur* no. 8/9 (Autumn/Spring 1981/82): 144–45.

4. See, among others, Anthony F. C. Wallace, *Rockdale: The Growth of an American Village in the Early Industrial Revolution* (New York: Alfred A. Knopf, 1978); Bruce Laurie, *Working People of Philadelphia, 1800–1850* (Philadelphia: Temple University Press, 1980), ch. 2; Jonathan Prude, *The Coming of Industrial Order: Town and Factory Life in Rural Massachusetts, 1810–1860* (New York: Cambridge University Press, 1983), ch. 4; Sean Wilentz, *Chants Democratic: New York City and the Rise of the American Working Class, 1788–1850* (New York: Oxford University Press, 1984), pp. 77–87, 305–12; Paul G. Faler, *Mechanics and Manufacturers in the Early Industrial Revolution: Lynn, Massachusetts, 1786–1860* (Albany: State University of New York Press, 1981); Roy Rosenzweig, *Eight Hours for What We Will: Work and Leisure in an Industrial City 1870–1920* (New York: Cambridge Uni-

versity Press, 1983), ch. 4; Francis G. Couvares, *The Remaking of Pittsburgh: Class and Culture in an Industrializing City, 1877–1919* (Albany: State University of New York Press, 1984), ch. 4.

Lumping all of these excellent works together, unfortunately, does injustice to the sophistication and complexity of the arguments presented in each. However, all have the tendency to present religion as principally serving the interests of capitalism.

5. Richard Oestreicher, *Solidarity and Fragmentation: Working People and Class Consciousness in Detroit, 1875–1900* (Urbana: University of Illinois Press, 1986), ch. 2; Laurie, *Working People*, chs. 6, 9; John Bodnar, *The Transplanted: A History of Immigrants in Urban America* (Bloomington: Indiana University Press, 1985), ch. 6; Rosenzweig, *Eight Hours for What We Will*, pp. 27–32; Amy Bridges, *A City in the Republic: Antebellum New York and the Origins of Machine Politics* (Ithaca, N.Y.: Cornell University Press, 1984), ch. 3.

6. Mary H. Blewett, *Men, Women, and Work: Class, Gender, and Protest in the New England Shoe Industry, 1780–1910* (Urbana: University of Illinois Press, 1988), offers the fullest and most sophisticated exploration of this theme. But, see also Alice Kessler-Harris, *Out to Work: A History of Wage-Earning Women in the United States* (New York: Oxford University Press, 1982), ch. 4, and Christine Stansell, *City of Women: Sex and Class in New York, 1789–1860* (Urbana: University of Illinois Press, 1987), ch. 7.

7. The work and advice of Bruce Nelson has been of enormous help here. See his " 'We Can't Get Them to Do Aggressive Work': Chicago's Anarchists and the Eight-Hour Movement," *International Labor and Working-Class History* no. 29 (Spring 1986): 1–13. Also see my "Religion and Trade-Union Politics in the United States, 1880–1920," *International Labor and Working-Class History* no. 34 (Fall 1988): 39–55.

8. Paul J. Kleppner, *The Cross of Culture: A Social Analysis of Midwestern Politics, 1850–1890* (New York: The Free Press, 1970); Richard Jensen, *The Winning of the Midwest: Social and Political Conflict, 1888–1896* (Chicago: University of Chicago Press, 1971); Bridges, *City in the Republic*, ch. 3; Bodnar, *The Transplanted*, ch. 3; Gwendolyn Mink, *Old Labor and New Immigrants in American Political Development: Union, Party, and State, 1875–1920* (Ithaca, N.Y.: Cornell University Press, 1986); Oestreicher, *Solidarity and Fragmentation*, ch. 2.

9. Herbert G. Gutman, *Work, Culture, and Society in Industrializing America: Essays in American Working-Class and Social History* (New York: Vintage Books, 1976), ch. 2.

10. British labor historians have advanced this point much farther than their American counterparts. See, among others, Eileen Yeo, "Christianity in the Chartist Struggle, 1838–1842," *Past and Present* no. 91

(Dec. 1981): 109–39; Stephen Yeo, *Religion and Voluntary Organizations in Crisis* (London: Croom Helm, 1976); Stephen Yeo, "A New Life: The Religion of Socialism in Britain, 1883–1896," *History Workshop* no. 4 (Autumn 1977): 5–56; Patrick Joyce, *Work, Society, and Politics: The Culture of the Factory in Later Victorian England* (New Brunswick, N.J.: Rutgers University Press, 1980); James Obelkevich, *Religion and Rural Society: South Lindsey, 1825–1875* (Oxford: Oxford University Press, 1976).

Some recent examples of American historians working with that same sophistication include Jama Lazerow, "Religion and Labor Reform in Antebellum America: The World of William Field Young," *American Quarterly* 38 (Summer 1986): 265–86; Teresa Murphy, "Religious Authority and Labor Protest Among Antebellum Working People," unpublished paper presented at the American Historical Association convention, Dec. 28, 1986; Mark S. Schantz, "Missionaries and Mills: Religion in the Rhode Island Countryside," unpublished paper presented at the Society for Historians of the Early American Republic meeting, 1987; and Bruce C. Nelson, "Revival and Upheaval: Irreligion and Chicago's Working Class in 1886," unpublished paper presented to the Chicago Area Labor History Group, Newberry Library, Dec. 10, 1987. The latter three papers were kindly shared by the authors.

11. Gutman, *Work, Culture, and Society*, pp. 113–15; Liston Pope, *Millhands and Preachers: A Study of Gastonia* (New Haven, Conn.: Yale University Press, 1942), p. 86; Henry F. May, *Protestant Churches and Industrial America* (New York: Octagon Books, 1963), pp. 231–35; and Paul Carter, *The Spiritual Crisis of the Gilded Age* (DeKalb: Northern Illinois University Press, 1971), pp. 138–45.

12. Gutman, *Work, Culture, and Society*, pp. 107–8; Eric J. Hobsbawm, *The Workers: Worlds of Labor* (New York: Pantheon, 1984), pp. 31–42. For examples of labor historians influenced by this view, see Warren Van Tine, *The Making of the Labor Bureaucrat: Union Leadership in the United States, 1870–1920* (Amherst: University of Massachusetts Press, 1973), ch. 2; and Michael J. Cassity, "Modernization and Social Crisis: The Knights of Labor and a Midwest Community, 1885–1886," *Journal of American History* 66 (June 1979): 41–61.

13. The key work here was Marc Karson's *American Labor Unions and Politics, 1900–1918* (Boston: Beacon Press, 1965), ch. 7.

14. William G. McLoughlin, *Revivals, Awakenings, and Reform: An Essay on Religion and Social Change in America, 1607–1977* (Chicago: University of Chicago Press, 1978), p. 10.

15. Robert M. Crunden, *Ministers of Reform: The Progressives' Achievement in American Civilization, 1889–1920* (Urbana: University of Illinois Press, 1984); Kathryn Kish Sklar, "Hull House in the 1890s: A Community of Women Reformers," *Signs* 10 (Summer 1985): 658–

77; Paula Baker, "The Domestication of Politics: Women and American Political Society, 1780–1920," *American Historical Review* 89 (June 1984): 639–47.

16. See chapter 2.

17. The classic statement of the church and sect varieties of religious experience is found in Ernst Troeltsch, *The Social Teaching of the Christian Churches*, 2 vols. (London: Allen & Unwin, 1930). Particularly useful in my thinking about these categories was N. J. Demerath, III, *Social Class in American Protestantism* (Chicago: Rand McNally, 1965); Liston Pope, *Millhands and Preachers*; and Stephen A. Marini, *Radical Sects in Revolutionary New England* (Cambridge: Harvard University Press, 1982).

18. Demerath's analysis of church-type and sect-type religious behavior along a continuum seemed particularly appropriate to a discussion of the labor movement's uses of religion.

19. See my "Religion and Trade-Union Politics," for a more elaborate exploration of this.

20. Sam Bass Warner, Jr., "If All the World Were Philadelphia: A Scaffolding for Urban History, 1774–1930," *American Historical Review* 74 (Oct. 1968): 26–43.

Chapter 1

1. For information on Cooke, see Gladys L. Palmer, *Union Tactics and Economic Change: A Case Study of Three Philadelphia Textile Unions* (Philadelphia: University of Pennsylvania Press, 1932), pp. 141–45; for Collins, see U.S. Industrial Commission, *Report on the Relations and Conditions of Capital and Labor Employed in Manufactures and General Business*, 19 vols. (Washington, D.C.: GPO, 1902), vol. 14, pp. 306–10 (hereafter cited as USIC, *Report* [1902]); for Keenan, see U.S. Commission on Industrial Relations, *Final Report and Testimony*, 11 vols. (Washington, D.C.: GPO, 1916), vol. 3, pp. 2877–83 (hereafter cited as USCIR, *Final Report* [1916]); and for a description of the setting that Lucinda Hall entered, see Susan Levine, *Labor's True Woman: Carpet Weavers, Industrialization, and Labor Reform in the Gilded Age* (Philadelphia: Temple University Press, 1984).

2. For descriptions of the changes in the textile, shoe, and metal industries, see Levine, *Labor's True Woman*, ch. 2; Augusta Emile Galster, *The Labor Movement in the Shoe Industry with Special Reference to Philadelphia* (New York: Ronald Press, 1924); David Montgomery, *Workers' Control in America: Studies on the History of Work, Technology, and Labor Struggles* (New York: Cambridge University Press, 1979), ch. 3.

3. An excellent discussion of the uneven transformation of Phila-

delphia's economy is in Bruce Laurie and Mark Schmitz, "Manufacture and Productivity: The Making of an Industrial Base, Philadelphia, 1850–1880," in Theodore Hershberg, ed., *Philadelphia: Work, Space, Family, and Group Experience in the Nineteenth Century* (New York: Oxford University Press, 1981), ch. 2. See also Philip Scranton and Walter Licht, *Work Sights: Industrial Philadelphia, 1890–1950* (Philadelphia: Temple University Press, 1986).

4. Bruce Laurie, Theodore Hershberg, and George Alter, "Immigrants and Industry: The Philadelphia Experience, 1850–1880," in Hershberg, ed., *Philadelphia*, ch. 3; Andrew Dawson, "The Paradox of Dynamic Technological Change and the Labor Aristocracy in the United States, 1880–1914," *Labor History* 20 (Summer 1979): 325–51.

5. Lorin Blodget, *The Census of Industrial Employment, Wages, and Social Condition, in Philadelphia, in 1870* (Philadelphia: Social Science Association, 1872).

6. See, for example, Robert Ellis Thompson, *Hard Times and What to Learn from Them: A Plain Talk with the Working People* (Philadelphia: Edward Stern & Co., 1877).

7. David M. Gordon, Richard Edwards, and Michael Reich, *Segmented Work, Divided Workers: The Historical Transformation of Labor in the United States* (London: Cambridge University Press, 1982), pp. 94–106; Rendigs Fels, *American Business Cycles, 1865–1897* (Chapel Hill: University of North Carolina Press, 1959), ch. 5.

8. Laurie and Schmitz, "Manufacture and Productivity," pp. 43–88; Richard C. Edwards, *Contested Terrain: The Transformation of the Workplace in the Twentieth Century* (New York: Basic Books, 1979), ch. 3.

9. Alfred C. Chandler, *The Visible Hand: The Managerial Revolution in American Business* (Cambridge: Harvard University Press, 1977), pp. 320–36; Daniel Nelson, *Managers and Workers: The Origins of the New Factory System in the United States, 1880–1920* (Madison: University of Wisconsin Press, 1975).

10. Much of this is detailed in Nelson, *Managers and Workers*, pp. 17–25; Dan Clawson, *Bureaucracy and the Labor Process: The Transformation of U.S. Industry, 1860–1920* (New York: Monthly Review Press, 1980), pp. 167–201; and Chandler, *Visible Hand*, ch. 8. See also David A. Hounshell, *From the American System to Mass Production, 1800–1932* (Baltimore, Md.: Johns Hopkins University Press, 1984).

11. Chandler, *Visible Hand*, ch. 8, provides the best and most concise overview of mass production technology; see also Nathan Rosenberg, *Technology and the American Economy* (New York: Harper and Row, 1972); and Hounshell, *From the American System*.

12. Gordon, Edwards, and Reich, *Segmented Work*, pp. 113–27; Laurie and Schmitz, "Manufacture and Productivity," pp. 82–88.

13. Caroline Golab, *Immigrant Destinations* (Philadelphia: Temple University Press, 1977), pp. 29–30; Rosara Lucy Pasero, "Ethnicity in the Men's Ready-Made Clothing Industry, 1880–1950: The Italian Experience in Philadelphia," unpub. Ph.D. diss., University of Pennsylvania, 1978, pp. 240–42; Laurie and Schmitz, "Manufacture and Productivity," table 1, p. 45, and table 4, p. 50.

14. For the importance of flexibility, as opposed to efficiency, in textile production see Philip Scranton, *Proprietary Capitalism: The Textile Manufacture at Philadelphia, 1800–1885* (New York: Cambridge University Press, 1984), pp. 319–37.

15. For an excellent description of inside contracting at Baldwin's, see Clawson, *Bureaucracy and the Labor Process*, ch. 3.

16. Laurie, Hershberg, and Alter, "Immigrants and Industry," pp. 103–5; Raphael Samuel, "Workshop of the World: Steam Power and Hand Technology in Mid-Victorian Britain," *History Workshop* no. 3 (Spring 1977): 6–72; Dawson, "Paradox of Dynamic Change," pp. 330–36.

17. John B. Jentz, "Skilled Workers and Industrialization: Chicago's German Cabinetmakers and Machinists, 1880–1900," in Harmut Keil and John B. Jentz, eds. *German Workers in Industrial Chicago, 1850–1910: A Comparative Perspective* (DeKalb: Northern Illinois University Press, 1983), pp. 73–85; Laurie, Hershberg, and Alter, "Immigrants and Industry," pp. 108–16.

18. U.S. Bureau of the Census, *Twelfth Census of the United States (1900): Vol. 8, Statistics of Manufactures*, pp. 784–91 (hereafter cited as USBC, *Twelfth Census* [1900]); Pennsylvania Secretary of Internal Affairs, *Annual Report*, vol. 22 (1894), pt. 3, sec. B (hereafter cited as PaSIA, *Annual Report*); Eudice Glassberg, "Work, Wages and the Cost of Living: Ethnic Differences and the Poverty Line, Philadelphia, 1880," *Pennsylvania History* 46 (Jan. 1979): 39.

19. PaSIA, *Annual Report*, vol. 15 (1887), pt. 3, pp. 4H–13H.

20. U.S. Bureau of the Census, *Occupations at the Twelfth Census: Special Report* (Washington, D.C.: 1904), pp. 672–79 (hereafter cited as USBC, *Occupations* [1900]): Golab, *Immigrant Destinations*, pp. 179–92; Frank A. Craig, *A Study of the Housing and Social Conditions in Selected Districts of Philadelphia* (Philadelphia: Henry Phipps Institute, 1916), p. 72; PaSIA, *Annual Report*, vol. 15 (1887), pt. 3, p. H9.

21. Barbara Mary Klaczynska, "Working Women in Philadelphia—1900–1930," unpub. Ph.D. diss., Temple University, 1975, pp. 14–42; Esther Louise Little and William Joseph Henry Cotton, *Budgets of Families and Individuals of Kensington, Philadelphia* (Lancaster, Pa.: New Era Printing Co., 1920), table 4, p. 15. This was also true of other cities. See, for example, Olivier Zunz, *The Changing Face of Inequality: Urbanization, Industrial Development, and Immigrants in Detroit, 1880–1920* (Chicago: University of Chicago Press, 1982), pp. 232–37.

22. USIC, *Report* (1902), vol. 7, p. 950; Albert Rees, *Real Wages in Manufacturing, 1890–1914* (Princeton, N.J.: Princeton University Press, 1961), pp. 102–3; John F. Sutherland, "Housing the Poor in the City of Homes: Philadelphia at the Turn of the Century," in Allen F. Davis and Mark H. Haller, eds., *The Peoples of Philadelphia: A History of Ethnic Groups and Lower-Class Life, 1790–1940* (Philadelphia: Temple University Press, 1973), pp. 182–83.

23. Sutherland, "Housing the Poor," pp. 186–87; Glassberg, "Poverty Line," pp. 56–58.

24. Joseph H. Willits, *Philadelphia Unemployment, with Special Reference to the Textile Industries* (Philadelphia: Dept. of Public Works, 1915), p. 17. On the frequent unemployment of workers in the industrial economy, see Alexander Keyssar, *Out of Work: The First Century of Unemployment in Massachusetts* (New York: Cambridge University Press, 1986).

25. Clarence D. Long, *Wages and Earnings in the United States, 1860–1890* (Princeton, N.J.: Princeton University Press, 1960), pp. 65–72; Dawson, "Paradox of Dynamic Change," pp. 325–51.

26. Some fascinating but impressionistic evidence of the danger of industrial employment can be found in the chapter "Hazardous Pay," in Dennis J. Clark, *The Irish Relations: Trials of an Immigrant Tradition* (Rutherford, N.J.: Farleigh Dickinson University Press, 1982).

27. *Public Ledger* (Philadelphia), June 1, 12, 14, 18, 1872.

28. *Public Ledger*, June 13, 14, 18, 19, 22, 29, 1872.

29. Laurie and Schmitz, "Manufacture and Productivity," tables 3, 4, 7 and 9; USBC, *Twelfth Census* (1900), vol. 8, pp. 786–87. Small shops accounted for 82 percent of the firms in 1900, but only 26 percent of the workforce. Many were repair or custom shops, but paid only slightly higher wages than factories.

30. Jentz, "Skilled Workers," pp. 74–78; Steven J. Ross, *Workers on the Edge: Work, Leisure, and Politics in Industrializing Cincinnati, 1788–1890* (New York: Columbia University Press, 1985), pp. 100–104.

31. Ross, *Workers on the Edge*, pp. 100–104; USBC, *Twelfth Census* (1900), vol. 8, pp. 786–89; Laurie, Hershberg, and Alter, "Immigrants and Industry," table 12, p. 108.

32. Galster, *Labor Movement*, pp. 137, 185–87; David Bensman, *The Practice of Solidarity: American Hat Finishers in the Nineteenth Century* (Urbana: University of Illinois Press, 1985), pp. 191–99; Charles Hardy and Roman Czybriwsky, "The Stetson Hat Company and Benevolent Feudalism," *Pennsylvania Heritage* 7 (Spring 1981): 14–19; Pasero, "Ethnicity in Men's Clothing"; USIC, *Report* (1902), vol. 14, p. 266.

33. David Brody, *Steelworkers in America: The Nonunion Era* (New York: Harper & Row, 1960), ch. 1; John William Bennett, "Iron Workers

in Woods Run and Johnstown: The Union Era, 1865–1895," unpub. Ph. D. diss., University of Pittsburgh, 1977, pp. 1–75.

34. Gerald G. Eggert, *Steelmasters and Labor Reform, 1886–1923* (Pittsburgh, Pa.: University of Pittsburgh Press, 1981), ch. 1; Hermann Schlueter, *The Brewing Industry and the Brewery Workers' Movement in America* (New York: Burt Franklin, 1970; orig. pub. 1910), pp. 92–94.

35. Katherine Stone, "The Origins of Job Structures in the Steel Industry," in Richard C. Edwards, Michael Reich, and David M. Gordon, eds., *Labor Market Segmentation* (Lexington, Mass.: Lexington Books, 1975); Golab, *Immigrant Destinations*, app. E, p. 179.

36. John Bodnar, Roger Simon, and Michael P. Weber, *Lives of Their Own: Blacks, Italians, and Poles in Pittsburgh, 1900–1960* (Urbana: University of Illinois Press, 1982), ch. 3; Hershberg et al., "A Tale of Three Cities: Blacks, Immigrants, and Opportunity in Philadelphia, 1850–1880, 1930, 1970," in Hershberg, ed., *Philadelphia*. For a compelling investigation of the impact of racism on job opportunities, see Herbert Hill, "Race, Ethnicity, and Organized Labor: The Opposition to Affirmative Action," *New Politics* 1 [new series] (Winter 1987): 31–82.

37. Andrea Graziosi, "Common Laborers, Unskilled Workers, 1890–1915," *Labor History* 22 (Fall 1981): 512–44.

38. Dawson, "Paradox of Dynamic Change," p. 330.

39. USBC, *Occupations* (1900), pp. 674–75; Jentz, "Skilled Workers," pp. 78–82; Laurie, Hershberg, and Alter, "Immigrants and Industry," pp. 108–11; USBC, *Thirteenth Census of the United States* (1910): *Volume 8, Manufactures* (Washington, D.C.: GPO, 1914), pp. 1348–57.

40. Clawson, *Bureaucracy and the Labor Process*, ch. 3.

41. Nathan Rosenberg, "Technological Change in the Machine Tool Industry, 1840–1910," *Journal of Economic History* 23 (1963): 414–43; Daniel Nelson, *Frederick W. Taylor and the Rise of Scientific Management* (Madison: University of Wisconsin Press, 1980), pp. 4–13; Wayne Roberts, "Toronto Workers and the Second Industrial Revolution, 1889–1914," *Labour/Le Travailleur* no. 6 (Autumn 1980): 49–72.

42. United Labor League, "Minutes," Jan. 12, 1896, Mar. 22, 1896, and *passim*, United Labor League microfilm, UAC (hereafter ULL, "Minutes"; *Machinists' Monthly Journal*, Jan. 1907, pp. 73–74. See also Montgomery, *Workers' Control*, ch. 3; and Ken Fones-Wolf, "Mass Strikes, Corporate Strategies: The Baldwin Locomotive Works and the Philadelphia General Strike of 1910," *Pennsylvania Magazine of History and Biography* 110 (July 1986): 447–57.

43. Palmer, *Union Tactics*, pp. 5–15, 24–25, 52–54.

44. George E. Barnett, "The Printers: A Study in American Trade Unionism," *American Economic Association Quarterly*, 3d Ser., vol. 10 (1909); John Seybold, *The Philadelphia Printing Industry: A Case Study* (Philadelphia: University of Pennsylvania Press, 1949).

45. For fascinating testimonies on this, see Jean Seder, *Voices of*

Kensington: Vanishing Mills, Vanishing Neighborhoods (Ardmore, Pa.: Whitmore Publishing Co., 1982).

46. For the classic statement, see Harry Braveman, *Labor and Monopoly Capital: The Degradation of Work in the Twentieth Century* (New York: Monthly Review Press, 1974); but also see Gordon, Edwards, and Reich, *Segmented Work*, ch. 4.

47. Bruce Laurie, *Working People of Philadelphia, 1800–1850* (Philadelphia: Temple University Press, 1980), pp. 33–84.

For more on the categories used to analyze working-class cultures here, see Alan Dawley and Paul Faler, "Working-Class Culture and Politics in the Industrial Revolution: Sources of Loyalism and Rebellion," *Journal of Social History* 9 (Summer 1976): 466–80; Gareth Stedman Jones, "Working-Class Culture and Working-Class Politics in London, 1870–1900: Notes on the Remaking of a Working Class," *Journal of Social History* 7 (Summer 1974): 460–508; Eric J. Hobsbawm, *The Workers: Worlds of Labor* (New York: Pantheon Books, 1984), pp. 176–213; and Raymond Williams, *Problems in Materialism and Culture* (London: Verso Books, 1980), pp. 31–49.

48. See, in particular, Herbert G. Gutman, *Work, Culture, and Society in Industrializing America: Essays in American Working-Class and Social History* (New York: Vintage Books, 1976), chs. 1 and 2; and "Interview with Herbert Gutman," *Radical History Review* no. 27 (1983): 208–11.

49. Susan G. Davis, *Parades and Power: Street Theatre in Nineteenth-Century Philadelphia* (Philadelphia: Temple University Press, 1986); Roy Rosenzweig, *Eight Hours for What We Will: Workers and Leisure in an Industrial City, 1870–1920* (New York: Cambridge University Press, 1983), ch. 6. A recent exploration of this culture is found in Elliott J. Gorn, "'Good-Bye Boys, I Die a True American': Homicide, Nativism, and Working-Class Culture in Antebellum New York," *Journal of American History* 74 (Sept. 1987): 388–410.

50. Clark, *The Irish Relations*, ch. 11; W. E. B. Du Bois, *The Philadelphia Negro: A Social Study* (New York: Benjamin Blom, 1967; orig. pub. 1899), pp. 277–82; Arthur M. Burton, *The Value of a Principle as Illustrated in the History of the Law and Order Society* (Philadelphia, 1886), pp. 2–7, pamphlet in the Urban Archives Center, Temple University, Philadelphia, Pa. (hereafter UAC).

51. William Z. Foster, *Pages from a Worker's Life* (New York: International Publishers, 1939), pp. 15–18; *Philadelphia Inquirer*, Jan. 5, 1896; Sutherland, "Housing the Poor," pp. 175–201.

52. David Montgomery, "The Shuttle and the Cross: Weavers and Artisans in the Kensington Riots of 1844," *Journal of Social History* 5 (Summer 1972): 411–46; Dale Beryl Light, "Class, Ethnicity, and the Urban Ecology in a Nineteenth-Century City: Philadelphia's Irish, 1840–1890," unpub. Ph. D. diss., University of Pennsylvania, 1979, pp.

193–94; Dennis J. Clark, "Urban Blacks and Irishmen: Brothers in Prejudice," in Miriam Ershkowitz and Joseph Zikmund, eds., *Black Politics in Philadelphia* (New York: Basic Books, 1973), pp. 22–24.

53. Susan G. Davis, "The Popular Uses of Public Space in Philadelphia, 1800–1850," unpub. paper presented to the American Studies Association biennial meeting, Philadelphia, Nov. 5, 1983; Christine Stansell, *City of Women: Sex and Class in New York, 1789–1860* (New York: Alfred A. Knopf, 1986), ch. 10; Ellen Ross, "Survival Networks: Women's Neighborhood Sharing in London Before World War One," *History Workshop* no. 15 (Spring 1983): 4–27; Mary Kingsbury Simkhovitch, *The City Worker's World in America* (New York: Macmillan, 1917), pp. 85–86.

54. Rosenzweig, *Eight Hours for What We Will*, pp. 57–64; John M. Kingsdale, "The 'Poor man's Club': Social Functions of the Urban Working-Class Saloon," *American Quarterly* 25 (1973): 472–89. For an excellent, albeit unfriendly, description of saloons in Philadelphia, see *The Lighthouse: Report of Five Years' Work* (Philadelphia, 1900), and *The Lighthouse, The Needs of a Neighborhood: Tenth Annual Report* (Philadelphia, 1905), both pamphlets in UAC.

55. Foster, *Pages*, pp. 16–17; Du Bois, *Philadelphia Negro*, pp. 383–84; D. C. Gibboney, *Why the "Gang" Seeks to Legislate the Law and Order Society of Philadelphia Out of Existence* (Philadelphia, n.d.), pamphlet in UAC; Stedman Jones, "Working-Class Culture," pp. 460–508. For the Catholic Church's opposition to Protestant reformers, see *Catholic Standard* (Philadelphia), Jan. 26, 1872, Jan. 17, 1885, July 16, 1887.

56. The most recent description of this tendency is in John S. Gilkeson, Jr., *Middle-Class Providence, 1820–1940* (Princeton, N.J.: Princeton University Press, 1986), ch. 3. See also Eric Foner, *Free Soil, Free Labor, Free Men: The Ideology of the Republican Party Before the Civil War* (London: Oxford University Press, 1970).

57. Sam Bass Warner, Jr., *The Private City: Philadelphia in Three Periods of Its Growth* (Philadelphia: University of Pennsylvania Press, 1968), pp. 52–53; Alan M. Burstein, "Immigrants and Residential Mobility: The Irish and Germans in Philadelphia, 1850–1880," in Hershberg, ed., *Philadelphia*, p. 178; Hershberg et al., "The Journey to Work: An Empirical Investigation of Work, Residence, and Transportation, Philadelphia, 1850 and 1880," in Hershberg, ed., *Philadelphia*. For strategies in obtaining homes in other cities, see Bodnar, Simon, and Weber, *Lives of Their Own*, ch. 6 (on Pittsburgh); Zunz, *Changing Face of Inequality*, pp. 170–72 (on Detroit); and David Hogan, *Class and Reform: School and Society in Chicago, 1880–1930* (Philadelphia: University of Pennsylvania Press, 1985), ch. 3.

58. Joseph I. Doran, *The Operations of Our Building Associations* (Philadelphia: Social Science Association, 1876), pp. 18–19; U.S. Com-

missioner of Labor, *Ninth Annual Report, 1893: Building and Loan Associations* (Washington, D.C.: GPO, 1894), pp. 238–51; PaSIA, *Annual Report*, vol. 21 (1893), pt. 3, pp. 32A, 492A.

59. Burk quoted in *Papers on Building Associations* (Philadelphia: Social Science Association, 1877), p. 1; USIC, *Report* (1902), vol. 14, pp. 217, 595.

60. USCIR, *Final Report* (1916), vol. 4, p. 3037; *The Union* (Philadelphia), Sept. 7, 1889; *The Workingman* (Philadelphia), Aug. 29, 1882; USIC, *Report* (1902), vol. 14, p. 596. For the importance of home ownership to labor militance, see Linda Schneider, "The Citizen Striker: Workers' Ideology in the Homestead Strike of 1892," *Labor History* 23 (Winter 1982): 47–66.

61. *Report of the General Committee for the Relief of Unemployed Odd Fellows During the Winter of 1873–74* (Philadelphia, 1874), p. 5, pamphlet in UAC. See the excellent discussion of fraternal orders in Brian Greenberg, *Worker and Community: Response to Industrialization in a Nineteenth-Century American City, Albany, New York, 1850–1884* (Albany: State University of New York Press, 1985), ch. 5.

62. *Third Annual Report of the Home for Free and Accepted Masons* (Philadelphia, 1887); *Souvenir Commemorating the Dedication of the Odd Fellows' Temple, Philadelphia, May 21, 1895* (Philadelphia, 1895); *Souvenir for the Dedication of the New Home, Philadelphia Lodge No. 54, Loyal Order of Moose* (Philadelphia, 1887), all pamphlets in UAC; *Public Ledger*, July 5, 1876, Sept. 18, 1876, Oct. 13, 1891.

63. *Third Annual Report of the Masons*; *Souvenir, Odd Fellows' Temple*; *Souvenir, Loyal Order of Moose*; *Programme: Masonic Ceremonies at the Laying of the Corner Stone of the Goethe Monument, November 14, 1887* (Philadelphia, 1887), pamphlet in UAC. Names were checked against Gopsill's city directories for occupations.

64. *Third Annual Report of the Masons*, pp. 7–8; *Souvenir, Odd Fellows' Temple*, pp. 17–19, 92; Greenberg, *Worker and Community*, p. 97.

65. Samuel Gompers, *Seventy Years of Life and Labor*. 2 vols. (New York: Augustus M. Kelley, 1967; orig. pub. 1925), vol. 1, pp. 43–48; *Cigar Makers' Official Journal*, June 15, 1910, p. 10.

66. *Souvenir, Loyal Order of Moose; New Era* (Philadelphia), June 4, Sept. 6, 1902.

67. General Membership Meeting, "Minutes," 1909–14 volume, Box 2, American Federation of Musicians, Local 77 Records, UAC; *Typographical Journal*, Mar. 1903, p. 276.

68. Foster, *Pages from a Worker's Life*, pp. 16–17; Du Bois, *Philadelphia Negro*, pp. 383–84; Testimony of Theodore Justice, USIC, *Report* (1902), vol. 14, p. 384; the "S" Company of the Republican Invincibles, "Minutebook," 1884–1890, UAC. For the success of the Republican formula in attracting working-class support, see James L.

Huston, "A Political Response to Industrialism: The Republican Embrace of Protectionist Labor Doctrine," *Journal of American History* 70 (June 1983): 35–57.

69. Francis G. Couvares, *The Remaking of Pittsburgh: Class and Culture in an Industrializing City, 1877–1919* (Albany: State University of New York Press, 1984), ch. 3.

70. Mary P. Ryan, *Cradle of the Middle Class: The Family in Oneida County, New York, 1790–1865* (New York: Cambridge University Press, 1981); Ruth Bordin, *Woman and Temperance: The Quest for Power and Liberty, 1873–1900* (Philadelphia: Temple University Press, 1981), ch. 6; Barbara Leslie Epstein, *The Politics of Domesticity: Women, Evangelism, and Temperance in Nineteenth-Century America* (Middletown, Conn.: Wesleyan University Press, 1981); Paula Baker, "The Domestication of Politics: Women and American Political Society, 1780–1920," *American Historical Review* 89 (June 1984): 620–47.

71. *Fifteenth Annual Financial Report of the Eighteenth Street M.E. Church* (Philadelphia, 1889), pamphlet in UAC; YMCA, "Membership Records Book," 1894–1903, Box 7, Germantown YMCA Records, UAC; Philadelphia County Sabbath School Association, *Eleventh Annual Report* (Philadelphia, 1904), pamphlet in UAC. Factory paternalism and religion are examined in British society in Patrick Joyce, *Work, Society and Politics: The Culture of the Factory in Later Victorian England* (New Brunswick, N.J.: Rutgers University Press, 1980), pp. 179–87; Sunday schools are the subject of Thomas Walter Laqueur's *Religion and Respectability: Sunday Schools and Working Class Culture, 1780–1850* (New Haven, Conn.: Yale University Press, 1976); and the pervasive presence of religious institutions in the urban landscape is analyzed in Stephen Yeo, *Religion and Voluntary Organizations in Crisis* (London: Croom Helm, 1976).

72. *Catholic Standard*, Mar. 15, 1884; Mar. 14, 1885; Jay Dolan, *Catholic Revivalism: The American Experience, 1830–1900* (Notre Dame, Ind.: University of Notre Dame Press, 1978); Colleen McDannell, *The Christian Home in Victorian America* (Bloomington: Indiana University Press, 1986).

73. Philadelphia Typographical Union, Local 2, "Minutes," Oct. 7, 1882, in Philadelphia Typographical Union Records, Historical Society of Pennsylvania, Philadelphia, Pa. (hereafter cited as PTU, "Minutes"); *The Trades* (Philadelphia), June 21, 1879; ULL, "Minutes," Aug. 23, 1892; *The Union* (Philadelphia), Sept. 7, 1889. See also Davis, *Parades and Power*, ch. 5, for the importance of parades as a medium of communication.

74. *The Union*, Sept. 7, 1889; ULL, "Minutes," Aug. 8, 1897; *Eastern Laborer* (Philadelphia), Sept. 14, 1907.

75. *The Trades*, July 12, 1879.

76. *Eastern Laborer*, July 6, 1907; *Trades' Union News*, Aug. 18,

1904; Operative Plasterers Union, Local 8, "Minutes," June 23, 1890, Box 2, Operative Plasterers Union, Local 8 Records, UAC; PTU, "Minutes," Apr. 17, 1886; United Brotherhood of Carpenters and Joiners of America (UBCJA), Local 8, "Minutes," June 4, 1900, Box 1, UBCJA, Local 8 Records, UAC.

77. Mari Jo Buhle, *Women and American Socialism, 1870–1920* (Urbana: University of Illinois Press, 1983), pp. 14–20; Susan Levine, *Labor's True Woman*, ch. 2; *Trades' Union News*, July 7, 1904; Elizabeth Jameson, "Imperfect Unions: Class and Gender in Cripple Creek, 1894–1904," in Milton Cantor and Bruce Laurie, eds., *Class, Sex, and the Woman Worker* (Westport, Conn.: Greenwood Press, 1977), pp. 166–202.

78. Testimony of Denis Hayes, in USIC, *Report* (1902), vol. 7, p. 103.

79. Julie Blodgett, "Fountain of Power: The Origins of the Knights of Labor in Philadelphia, 1869–1874," unpub. paper presented at the Knights of Labor centennial conference, Chicago, 1979, pp. 13–15; Terence V. Powderly, *The Path I Trod: The Autobiography of Terence V. Powderly* (New York: Columbia University Press, 1940), pp. 61–66.

80. Testimony of No. 29, "Workingmen's Returns," PaSIA, *Annual Report*, vol. 15 (1887), pt. 3, p. H21; *The Trades*, Apr. 18, 1879, Jan. 24, 1880; *Cigar Makers' Official Journal*, Dec. 1900, p. 5; *New Era*, Jan. 4, 1902.

81. *New Era*, Dec. 21, 1901; *The Trades*, Apr. 5, 1879, Jan. 17, 1880; *Philadelphia Labor*, Nov. 25, 1893.

82. *Public Ledger*, Aug. 14, 1877, Sept. 31, 1877; ULL, "Minutes," Sept. 24, 1893, Nov. 25, 1894. Similar controversies over public facilities are recounted in Rosenzweig, *Eight Hours for What We Will*, chs. 5 and 6.

83. *The Trades*, Apr. 17, 1880; *Philadelphia Labor*, Nov. 25, 1893; Social Democratic Workingmen's Party of Philadelphia, "Minutes," July 1877, in Manuscript Division, Library of Congress, Washington, D.C.; *Unionism, Industrial and Political: The Philadelphia Street Car Strike and General Strike* (Philadelphia: Socialist Party of Philadelphia, 1910).

84. Greenberg, *Worker and Community*, ch. 3. Valuable insights into the cooperative movement in Philadelphia can be gleaned from the Thomas Phillips Papers, reel 6, *American Bureau of Industrial Research: Records of the Early Labor Movement* (Frederick, Md.: University Publications of America, 1986), originals in the State Historical Society of Wisconsin, Madison, Wisconsin.

85. *New Era*, Aug. 9, 1902; *The People*, Sept. 5, 1875; *The Trades*, Jan. 17, 1880; *Philadelphia Labor*, Nov. 25, 1893. See ULL, "Minutes," from 1897–99 for the tensions caused by the devotion of many unionists to maintaining a newspaper.

86. *The Trades*, Feb. 28, 1880.

87. Couvares, *Remaking of Pittsburgh*, ch. 2; Richard Jules Oestreicher, *Solidarity and Fragmentation: Working People and Class Consciousness in Detroit, 1875–1900* (Urbana: University of Illinois Press, 1986), ch. 3; Steven J. Ross, *Workers on the Edge: Work, Leisure, and Politics in Industrializing Cincinnati, 1788–1890* (New York: Columbia University Press, 1985).

88. *Industrial Republic* (Philadelphia), Aug. 1, 1891; *The Trades*, Mar. 29, July 12, 1879; as quoted in Philip S. Foner, *We the Other People* (Urbana: University of Illinois Press, 1976), p. 97.

89. *Fincher's Trades' Review* (Philadelphia), Feb. 2, 1864, as quoted in Gutman, *Work, Culture, and Society*, p. 93; *The People*, Sept. 5, 1875.

90. Testimony of John Jarrett, in U.S. Senate Committee Upon the Relations Between Labor and Capital, *Report*, 4 vols. (Washington, D.C.: GPO, 1885), vol. 1, p. 1160. For more on the declining connection between Protestantism and republicanism in the dominant culture, see J. F. Maclear, "The Republic and the Millenium," in Elwyn A. Smith, ed., *The Religion of the Republic* (Philadelphia: Fortress Press, 1971), pp. 183–216; and Sean Wilentz, "On Class and Politics in Jacksonian America," *Reviews in American History* 10 (Dec. 1982): 55.

91. *The Workingman*, Aug. 29, 1882.

92. Response of No. 3, "Workingmen's Returns," PaSIA, *Annual Report* (1887), pt. 3, p. 16H.

93. *The Workingman*, Aug. 29, 1882; Testimony of Tobias Hall, in USCIR, *Final Report* (1916), vol. 4, pp. 3035–42.

94. For the best study of the role of irreligion in the labor movement, see Bruce C. Nelson, *Beyond the Martyrs: A Social History of Chicago's Anarchists* (New Brunswick, N.J.: Rutgers University Press, 1988), pp. 165–70.

Chapter 2

1. Russell H. Conwell, *Acres of Diamonds*, as quoted in Henry F. May, *Protestant Churches and Industrial America* (New York: Octagon Books, 1963), pp. 199–200.

2. Clyde Kenneth Nelson, "The Social Ideas of Russell H. Conwell," unpub. Ph.D. diss., University of Pennsylvania, 1968, ch. 6; Lyman Abbott, "The Baptist Temple, Philadelphia," *The Outlook*, Feb. 22, 1896, p. 349; Edmund K. Aldon, "The Temple, Philadelphia," *Christian Union*, Mar. 18, 1893.

3. George M. Fredrickson, *The Inner Civil War: Northern Intellectuals and the Crisis of Union* (New York: Harper and Row, 1965), ch. 7; Anthony F. C. Wallace, *Rockdale: The Growth of an American Village in the Early Industrial Revolution* (New York: Alfred A. Knopf, 1978), ch. 9; Alan Dawley and Paul Faler, "Working-Class Culture and Politics in the Industrial Revolution: Sources of Loyalism and Rebellion," *Journal of Social History* 9 (Summer 1976): 466–80.

4. May, *Protestant Churches*, p. 42; Charles Howard Hopkins, *The Rise of the Social Gospel in American Protestantism* (New Haven, Conn.: Yale University Press, 1967), pp. 14–23.

5. *A Fruitful Church: A Brief History of the Several Churches and Sabbath Schools That Have Been the Outgrowth of the Historic First Presbyterian Church* (Philadelphia, n.p., 1892), pp. 39–49; Robert G. Torbet, "A Social History of the Philadelphia Baptist Association: 1707–1940," unpub. Ph.D. diss., University of Pennsylvania, 1940, p. 204.

6. John Higham, *Strangers in the Land: Patterns of American Nativism, 1860–1925* (New York: Atheneum, 1977), pp. 35–67; Robert Wiebe, *The Search for Order, 1877–1920* (New York: Hill and Wang, 1967), pp. 44–75; Robert Ellis Thompson, *Hard Times and What to Learn from Them: A Plain Talk with the Working People* (Philadelphia: Edward Stern & Co., 1877).

7. Dwight L. Moody, quoted in Marion L. Bell, *Crusade in the City: Revivalism in Nineteenth-Century Philadelphia* (Lewisburg, Pa.: Bucknell University Press, 1977), p. 249. See also Sandra Sizer, "Politics and Apolitical Religion: The Great Urban Revivals of the Nineteenth Century," *Church History* 48 (Mar. 1979): 81–98; Edwin Scott Gaustad, *A Religious History of America* (New York: Harper and Row, 1966), p. 149; Melvin Easterday Dieter, *The Holiness Revival of the Nineteenth Century* (Metuchen, N.J.: Scarecrow Press, 1980), ch. 3. Historian William G. McLoughlin characterized this phase of American religion as a "nativistic response to the rising cultural distortion that was building up to the 'new light' of the Social Gospel and liberal Protestantism," in *Revivals, Awakenings, and Reform: An Essay on Religion and Social Change in America, 1607–1977* (Chicago: University of Chicago Press, 1978), pp. 142–44.

8. Home Missionary Society of Philadelphia, *Sixty-Eighth Annual Report* (Philadelphia, 1903), p. 17; Thompson, *Hard Times and What to Learn from Them*, pp. 23–41; Philadelphia Society for Organizing Charity, *Twenty-Sixth Annual Report* (Philadelphia, 1904), pp. 13–14. This same point is made in George M. Marsden, *Fundamentalism and American Culture: The Shaping of Twentieth-Century Evangelicalism, 1870–1925* (New York: Oxford University Press, 1980), pp. 80–85.

9. William Williams Keen, *The Bi-Centennial Celebration of the Founding of the First Baptist Church of the City of Philadelphia* (Philadelphia: American Baptist Publication Society, 1899), pp. 96–99; *A Directory of the Charitable, Social Improvement, Educational, and Religious Associations and Churches of Philadelphia* (Philadelphia: Civic Club, 1903), pp. 658, 663; *Catholic Standard* (Philadelphia), Jan. 26, Mar. 15, 1884, Apr. 4, Sept. 12, 1885.

10. Alfred Nevin, *History of the Presbytery of Philadelphia and of the Philadelphia Central* (Philadelphia: W. S. Fortescue & Co., 1888), pp. 118–20, 144–50; Torbet, "Philadelphia Baptist Association," p. 204;

Who's Who in Philadelphia in Wartime (Philadelphia: Stafford's National News Service, 1920), p. 25.

11. John Martin Ritter, *One Man and His God* (Philadelphia, n.p., 1969), p.4.

12. Information on Philadelphia's business and political leaders can be gleaned from John N. Ingham, *Biographical Dictionary of American Business Leaders*, 3 vols. (Westport, Conn.: Greenwood Press, 1983); Melvin G. Holli and Peter d'A. Jones, *Biographical Dictionary of American Mayors, 1820–1980: Big City Mayors* (Westport, Conn.: Greenwood Press, 1981). See also data on more modest careers in Philip Scranton, *Proprietary Capitalism: The Textile Manufacture at Philadelphia, 1800–1885* (New York: Cambridge University Press, 1984).

13. For a description of the capitalistic uses of free moral agency in another city, see Paul Johnson, *A Shopkeeper's Millenium: Society and Revivals in Rochester, New York, 1815–1837* (New York: Hill and Wang, 1978), ch. 6. See also Torbet, "Philadelphia Baptist Association"; Nevin, *History of the Presbytery*; and Ritter, *One Man and His God*, for descriptions of similar social perspectives of Philadelphia Christian capitalists in this era.

14. For the antebellum influence of Christian paternalism, see Wallace, *Rockdale*, ch. 7. Also, see the excellent description of paternalism in England in Patrick Joyce, *Work, Society, and Politics: The Culture of the Factory in Later Victorian England* (New Brunswick, N.J.: Rutgers University Press, 1980).

15. Pennsylvania Secretary of Internal Affairs, *Annual Report: Part III: Industrial Statistics* (Harrisburg, 1888), pp. 28E–35E (hereafter cited as PaSIA, *Annual Report*, vol. 15 [1888] pt. 3); Pennsylvania Commissioner of Labor and Industry, *Second Annual Report* (Harrisburg, 1915), pp. 3–43 (hereafter cited as PaCLI, *Second Annual Report*).

16. *Ibid.* See also *Privileges of the Employees of the Miller Lock Company* (1917), pamphlet in Urban Archives Center, Temple University, Philadelphia, Pa. (hereafter UAC), for the extent of programs in some Philadelphia plants.

17. PaCLI, *Second Annual Report*, pp. 41–42.

18. U.S. Industrial Commission, *Report on the Relations and Conditions of Capital and Labor Employed in Manufactures and General Business*, 19 vols. (Washington, D.C.: GPO, 1902), vol. 14, pp. 281, 353, 385 (hereafter cited as USIC, *Report* [1902]); Barbara Mary Klaczynska, "Working Women in Philadelphia—1900–1930," unpub. Ph.D. diss., Temple University, 1975, pp. 7–8.

19. "John B. Stetson," in *Prominent and Progressive Pennsylvanians of the Nineteenth Century*, 3 vols. (Philadelphia: Record Publishing Co., 1898) vol. 1, p. 439; USIC, *Report* (1902), vol. 14, p. 416.

20. USIC, *Report* (1902), vol. 14, pp. 269–70, 281.

21. PaSIA, *Annual Report*, vol. 15 (1888) pt. 3, pp. B5, B15; *Trades'*

Union News (Philadelphia), Mar. 2, 1905, Jan. 17, 1907.

22. Klaczynska, "Working Women," p. 8; USIC, *Report* (1902), vol. 14, p. 281; *New Era* (Philadelphia), Dec. 21, 1901.

23. U.S. Commission on Industrial Relations, *Final Report and Testimony*, 11 vols. (Washington, D.C.: GPO, 1916), vol. 3, p. 2823 (hereafter cited as USCIR, *Final Report* [1916]).

24. Victoria de Grazia, *The Culture of Consent: Mass Organization of Leisure in Fascist Italy* (New York: Cambridge University Press, 1981), p. 60.

25. Roy Rosenzweig, *Eight Hours for What We Will: Workers and Leisure in an Industrial City, 1870–1920* (New York: Cambridge University Press, 1983), pp. 35–40; Susan G. Davis, "The Popular Uses of Public Space in Philadelphia, 1800–1850," unpub. paper presented at the American Studies Association biennial meeting, Philadelphia, Nov. 5, 1983.

26. For Catholic antipathy to Sabbatarianism, see *Catholic Standard*, Jan. 17, 1885, June 11, 1887.

27. *The Tocsin* (Philadelphia), July 31, 1886; J. Thomas Jable, "Sport, Amusements, and the Pennsylvania Blue Laws, 1682–1973," unpub. Ph.D. diss., Pennsylvania State University, 1974, pp. 78–92.

28. Earl Clifford Kaylor, "The Prohibition Movement in Pennsylvania, 1865–1920," unpub. Ph.D. diss., Pennsylvania State University, 1963, pp. 74–80; Barbara Leslie Epstein, *The Politics of Domesticity: Women, Evangelism, and Temperance in Nineteenth-Century America* (Middletown, Conn.: Wesleyan University Press, 1981), pp. 137–42; Ruth Bordin, *Woman and Temperance: The Quest for Power and Liberty, 1873–1900* (Philadelphia: Temple University Press, 1981), ch. 6.

29. *The Workingman* (Philadelphia), Aug. 29, 1882.

30. Frank M. Goodchild, "The Social Evil in Philadelphia," *Arena*, Mar. 1896, pp. 579–80; Arthur M. Burton, *The Value of a Principle As Illustrated in the History of the Law and Order Society of Philadelphia* (Philadelphia, 1886), pp. 2–3, pamphlet in UAC.

31. *The Philadelphia Inquirer*, June 25, 1872.

32. David J. Pivar, "Theocratic Businessmen and Philadelphia Municipal Reform, 1870–1900," *Pennsylvania History* 33 (July 1966): 289–307; Kaylor, "Prohibition Movement," pp. 203–8; D. Clarence Gibboney, *Why the "Gang" Seeks to Legislate the Law and Order Society of Philadelphia Out of Existence* (Philadelphia, n.d.), pp. 10–11, pamphlet in UAC; Burton, *Value of a Principle*, p. 8.

33. Kaylor, "Prohibition Movement," pp. 145–46, 242–46; Burton, *Value of a Principle*, pp. 2–6. Similar parallels can also be found in *The Presbyterian* (Philadelphia), July 14, 28, 1887, June 5, Oct. 23, 30, 1886.

34. Samuel Lane Loomis quoted in Jable, "Pennsylvania Blue Laws," p. 108; *The Presbyterian*, July 28, 1877.

35. On the ward politics, see *The Tocsin*, Oct. 15, 1887. On the

constant complaint that mayors were obligated to the liquor interests and immigrant "ward heelers," see Gibboney, *Why the "Gang" Seeks*, pp. 4–5.

36. *Public Ledger* (Philadelphia), Aug. 14, Sept. 31, 1877.

37. U.S. Senate Committee Upon the Relations Between Capital and Labor, *Report*, 4 vols. (Washington, D.C.: GPO, 1885) vol. 1, p. 39 (hereafter cited as USSC, *Report* [1885]); Jable, "Pennsylvania Blue Laws," p. 134.

38. *The Tocsin*, Dec. 31, 1887; USSC, *Report* (1885), vol. 1, p. 50; Robert C. Ogden, *Pew Rents and the New Testament: Can They Be Reconciled?* (New York: Fleming H. Revell Co., 1892), p. 33; Presbyterian Church of Philadelphia, *Missions and Evangelization in Our Own City* (Philadelphia, 1904), pp. 2–3.

39. *The Trades* (Philadelphia), Aug. 16, 1879; *The Tocsin*, Oct. 9, June 26, 1886. For a sampling of the outrage against labor boycotts, see *Public Opinion*, May 1, 1886, pp. 47–52.

40. *Public Ledger*, June 5, 1880; quote drawn from United Labor League, "Minutes," June 22, July 5, 1895, microfilm in UAC (hereafter ULL, "Minutes"); Judith Lazarus Goldberg, "Strikes, Organizing, and Change: The Knights of Labor in Philadelphia, 1869–1890," unpub. Ph.D. diss., New York University, 1985, pp. 105–7.

41. ULL, "Minutes," Jan. 8, 1899.

42. Elizabeth N. Biddle, *Mission Work in Great Cities: A Paper Read Before the Conference of Churchwomen of the Diocese of Pennsylvania, January 8, 1886* (Philadelphia, n.p. 1886), pp. 2–3, pamphlet in UAC.

43. Home Missionary Society, *Sixty-Ninth Annual Report* (Philadelphia, 1904), p. 17. The rise of Protestant child saving organizations is explored with thought-provoking insight in David John Hogan, *Class and Reform: School and Society in Chicago, 1880–1930* (Philadelphia: University of Pennsylvania Press, 1985), ch. 3.

44. Philadelphia Society for Organizing Charity, *Twenty-Sixth Annual Report*, p. 13; Home Missionary Society, *Sixty-Eighth Annual Report*, p. 18.

45. Home Missionary Society, *Sixty-Eighth Annual Report*, p. 18; Testimony of Charles Cramp, USIC, *Report* (1902), vol. 14, p. 416; Testimony of Alba B. Johnson of the Baldwin Locomotive Works, USCIR, *Final Report* (1916), vol. 3, p. 2828.

46. Testimony of Charles J. Harrah of Midvale Steel, USIC, *Report* (1902), vol. 14, p. 353; Edward Meredith Fee, *The Origin and Growth of Vocational Industrial Education in Philadelphia to 1917* (Philadelphia: Westbrook Publishing Co., 1938), pp. 146–50.

47. *Trades' Union News*, Dec. 15, 1904; Testimony of Johnson, USCIR, *Final Report* (1916), vol. 3, p. 2834.

48. *Trades' Union News*, Dec. 15, 1904; Fee, *Origin and Growth*,

pp. 162–70. See also, Central Labor Union, "Minutes," Jan. 8, 1911, microfilm in UAC; and ULL, "Minutes," Sept. 10, 1893, for examples of the tension between organized labor and the YM and YWCAs.

49. *Trades' Union News*, Mar. 2, 1905; Clement H. Congdon, *History of the Master Builders' Exchange of the City of Philadelphia from 1886 to 1893* (Philadelphia: Sunshine Publishing Co., 1893), pp. 22–23; Bricklayers' Company of Philadelphia, "Minutebook," Apr. 11, 1910, Historical Society of Pennsylvania, Philadelphia, Pa.; Elizabeth Ann Fones-Wolf, "Industrial Education and the Decline of AFL Voluntarism, 1881–1917," unpub. M.A. thesis, University of Maryland, 1979, esp. ch. 1.

50. *The Trades*, June 21, 1879; *New Era* (Philadelphia), Dec. 21, 1901.

51. J. Lynn Barnard, *Factory Legislation in Pennsylvania: Its History and Administration* (Philadelphia: University of Pennsylvania Press, 1907), pp. 53–57, 86–91; ULL, "Minutes," Jan. 13, 27, 1895.

52. Raymond Calkins, *Substitutes for the Saloon* (Boston: Houghton Mifflin Co., 1901), pp. 376–80.

53. E. P. Thompson, *Whigs and Hunters: The Origins of the Black Act* (New York: Pantheon Books, 1975), pp. 268, 263.

54. Alice Kessler-Harris, *Out to Work: A History of Wage-Earning Women in the United States* (New York: Oxford University Press, 1982), ch. 6, explores some of the problems and contradictions facing advocates of the "family wage" especially when most working-class families still relied on the "family economy."

55. On Catholicism's opposing attitudes on children and the Sabbath, see Colleen McDannell, *The Christian Home in Victorian America, 1840–1900* (Bloomington: Indiana University Press, 1986), pp. 64–65, 91–99. For Philadelphia, see *Catholic Standard*, Mar. 15, 1884, Sept. 12, 1885.

56. For a critique of the male construction of the working class, see Joan W. Scott, "On Language, Gender, and Working-Class History," *International Labor and Working-Class History* no. 31 (Spring 1987): 1–13; Christine Stansell, *City of Women: Sex and Class in New York, 1789–1860* (New York: Alfred A. Knopf, 1986).

57. *Evening Bulletin* (Philadelphia), June 13, 1872.

58. Leon Fink, *Workingmen's Democracy: The Knights of Labor and American Politics, 1886–1896* (Urbana: University of Illinois Press, 1983), p. 8; Herbert G. Gutman, *Work, Culture, and Society in Industrializing America: Essays in American Working-Class and Social History* (New York: Vintage Books, 1976), ch. 2. For the background of Philadelphia's Gilded-Age politics, see Pivar, "Theocratic Businessmen," pp. 289–307; John D. Steward, "Philadelphia's Politics in the Gilded Age," unpub. Ph.D. diss., St. John's University, 1973; Howard Frank Gillette,

Jr., "Corrupt and Contented: Philadelphia's Political Machine, 1865–1887," unpub. Ph.D. diss., Yale University, 1970.

59. Gillette, "Corrupt and Contented," pp. 222–58; Nathaniel Burt and Wallace E. Davies, "The Iron Age, 1876–1905," in Russell Weigley, ed., *Philadelphia: A 300-Year History* (New York: W. W. Norton, 1982), pp. 496–98; George Vickers, *The Fall of Bossism: A History of the Committee of One Hundred* (Philadelphia: A.C. Bryson, 1883).

60. On King, see Holli and Jones, *Big City Mayors*, pp. 197, 347–48; Burt and Davies, "The Iron Age," pp. 496–98.

61. Torbet, "Philadelphia Baptist Association," pp. 194–95; Gillette, "Corrupt and Contented," pp. 222–58.

62. Edward P. Allinson and Boies Penrose, *Philadelphia, 1681–1887: A History of Municipal Development* (Philadelphia: Allen, Lane & Scott, 1887), pp. 262–72; Gillette, "Corrupt and Contented," ch. 8; Steward, "Philadelphia's Politics," pp. 224–26.

63. William H. Issel, "Modernization in Philadelphia School Reform, 1882–1905," *Pennsylvania Magazine of History and Biography* 94 (July 1970): 358–83, quote on p. 372. A different perspective is offered in Burt and Davies, "The Iron Age," pp. 498–99.

64. On Smith, see Holli and Jones, *Big City Mayors*, pp. 335–36. A list of the Committee is in Appendix II of Gillette, "Corrupt and Contented." For more on the anti-labor activities of those mentioned, see the Metal Manufacturers' Association of Philadelphia, "Minutes," 1904–15, in Box 2, UAC; and Scranton, *Proprietary Capitalism*.

65. Gillette, "Corrupt and Contented," pp. 244–49. A similar analysis of the urban reform impulse is found in Zane L. Miller, *Boss Cox's Cincinnati: Urban Politics in the Progressive Era* (New York: Oxford University Press, 1968).

66. Dennis J. Clark, *The Irish Relations: Trials of an Immigrant Tradition* (Rutherford, N.J.: Farleigh Dickinson University Press, 1982), ch. 6; Joseph Jackson, *Manual of the Mechanics' Lien Law Applying to the City and County of Philadelphia* (Philadelphia, 1872).

67. The *Catholic Standard*, between 1884 and 1887, offers ample proof of the Church's support for workers resisting Protestant-led repressive cultural associations.

68. *The Tocsin*, Oct. 8, 1887. Burton, *Value of a Principle*, gives a good sample of the moralistic tone of the Protestant establishment.

69. An excellent summary of the characteristic values and language of the Knights of Labor can be found in Gregory S. Kealey and Bryan D. Palmer, *Dreaming of What Might Be: The Knights of Labor in Ontario, 1880–1900* (New York: Cambridge University Press, 1982), ch. 8.

70. Walter Rauschenbusch, *Christianizing the Social Order* (New York: Macmillan, 1914), p. 456.

Chapter 3

1. U.S. Senate Committee Upon the Relations Between Labor and Capital, *Report*, 4 vols. (Washington, D.C.: GPO, 1885), vol. 1, pp. 49–50 (hereafter cited as USSC, *Report* [1885]).

2. *The Trades* (Philadelphia), Mar. 29, 1879. The pathbreaking work in this area was Herbert G. Gutman, "Protestantism and the American Labor Movement: The Christian Spirit in the Gilded Age," *American Historical Review* 52 (1966): 74–101.

3. Marion L. Bell, *Crusade in the City: Revivalism in Nineteenth-Century Philadelphia* (Lewisburg, Pa.: Bucknell University Press, 1977), p. 254; Philadelphia County Sabbath School Association, *Eleventh Annual Report* (Philadelphia, 1904), pamphlet in the Urban Archives Center, Temple University, Philadelphia, Pa. (hereafter UAC); *A Fruitful Church: A Brief History of the Several Churches and Sabbath Schools That Have Been the Outgrowth of the Historic First Presbyterian Church* (Philadelphia, n.p., 1892).

4. *Journal of United Labor*, Oct. 15, 1881, p. 160 (hereafter *JUL*); Ernest Hamlin Abbott, *Religious Life in America: A Record of Personal Observation* (New York: The Outlook Co., 1903), pp. 22–23.

5. Abbott, *Religious Life*, pp. 15–16; *The Trades*, May 10, 1879; Jarrett testimony, in U.S. Senate Committee, *Report* (1885), vol. 1, p. 1160.

6. David Montgomery, *Beyond Equality: Labor and the Radical Republicans, 1862–1872* (New York: Alfred A. Knopf, 1967), ch. 4; David Roediger, "Ira Steward and the Anti-Slavery Origins of American Eight-Hour Theory," *Labor History* 27 (Summer 1986): 410–26.

7. *Co-Operative Tract, No. 1* (Philadelphia, n.d.), pamphlet in the State Historical Society of Wisconsin, Madison (hereafter SHSW). For the pervasiveness of cooperatives of all sorts in Philadelphia, see the Thomas Phillips Papers, reel 6, *American Bureau of Industrial Research: Records of the Early Labor Movement* (Frederick, Md.: University Publications of America, 1986), originals in SHSW (hereafter cited as Phillips Papers).

8. Ray Boston, *British Chartists in America, 1839–1900* (Totowa, N.J.: Rowman & Littlefield, 1971); Gareth Stedman Jones, *Languages of Class: Studies in English Working Class History, 1832–1982* (New York: Cambridge University Press, 1983), ch. 3; Eileen Yeo, "Christianity in Chartist Struggle, 1838–1842," *Past and Present* no. 91 (May 1981): 109–39.

9. For Shedden, see Bruce Laurie, *Working People of Philadelphia, 1800–1850* (Philadelphia: Temple University Press, 1980), pp. 180, 192–93; and International Workingmen's Association Papers, "Section 26 Minutebook," SHSW (hereafter cited as IWA, "Section 26 Minutebook"). For Phillips, see "Autobiographical Sketch," Phillips Papers; Montgomery, *Beyond Equality*, pp. 221–22; *Constitution and By-Laws*

of the Union Co-Operative General Trading and Manufacturing Association No. 1 of Philadelphia (Philadelphia: J. C. Fincher, 1865); *The Industrial Republic* (Philadelphia: n.p., 1891); and IWA, "Section 26 Minutebook." The "commonwealth ethic" attached to cooperatives is described in Brian Greenberg, *Worker and Community: Response to Industrialization in a Nineteenth-Century American City, Albany, New York, 1850–1884* (Albany: State University of New York Press, 1985), ch. 3.

10. Montgomery, *Beyond Equality*, pp. 202–3. The influence of small-town orthodoxy on labor is described in autobiographical novels by two important nineteenth-century labor leaders. See Frank Keyes Foster, *Evolution of a Trade Unionist* (Worcester, Mass., 1901); and Martin Foran, *The Other Side: A Social Study Based on Fact* (Washington, D.C.: Gray & Clarkson, 1886).

11. *JUL*, June 15, 1880, p. 24. For the broad sweep of labor's political program, see Jonathan Grossman, *William Sylvis: Pioneer of American Labor* (New York: Columbia University Press, 1945).

12. *The Trades*, Apr. 12, 1879; *The Tocsin* (Philadelphia), Sept. 4, 1886.

13. E. P. Thompson, *The Making of the English Working Class* (New York: Vintage Books, 1966), pp. 375–400; Standish Meacham, *A Life Apart: The English Working Class, 1890–1914* (Cambridge: Harvard University Press, 1977), pp. 199–200; Bell, *Crusade in the City*, pp. 235–37.

14. Dennis J. Clark, "The Philadelphia Irish: Persistent Presence," in Allen F. Davis and Mark H. Haller, eds., *The Peoples of Philadelphia* (Philadelphia: Temple University Press, 1973), pp. 139–40; Laurie, *Working People*, pp. 148–51.

15. Joseph George, Jr., "Philadelphia's *Catholic Herald:* The Civil War Years," *Pennsylvania Magazine of History and Biography* 103 (Apr. 1979): 196–221; Philip S. Foner, *History of the Labor Movement in the United States*, 7 vols. (New York: International Publishers, 1947), Vol. I, chs. 16 and 17.

16. Dennis J. Clark, *The Irish Relations: Trials of an Immigrant Tradition* (Rutherford, N.J.: Fairleigh Dickinson University Press, 1982), ch. 7; George, "*Catholic Herald*," pp. 218–21; Eric Foner, *Politics and Ideology in the Age of the Civil War* (New York: Oxford University Press, 1980), ch. 8.

17. For Kilgore's importance, see IWA, "Section 26 Minutebook"; coverage of the June 1872 eight-hour strikes in the Philadelphia *Public Ledger*; and his presence in the labor movement of the late 1870s in *The Trades*.

18. *Catholic Standard*, Jan. 19, 1884; Clark, "The Philadelphia Irish," pp. 139–41; Colleen McDannell, *The Christian Home in Vic-*

torian America, 1840–1900 (Bloomington: Indiana University Press, 1986), pp. 72–76.

19. Clark, *Irish Relations*, ch. 8; *The Trades*, Oct. 25, Nov. 8, 1879, Jan. 17, 24, Apr. 3, 1880.

20. *The Trades*, Apr. 17, 1880; Dale Beryl Light, Jr., "Class, Ethnicity, and the Urban Ecology in a Nineteenth-Century City: Philadelphia's Irish, 1840–1890," unpub. Ph.D. diss., University of Pennsylvania, 1979, ch. 7; Foner, *Politics and Ideology*, pp. 180–87.

21. *Catholic Standard*, Mar. 29, 1884, Jan. 31, Dec. 26, 1885.

22. *Catholic Standard*, Mar. 15, Apr. 12, 1884, Jan. 31, May 9, Sept. 12, Dec. 26, 1885.

23. Bruce C. Levine, "Immigrant Workers, 'Equal Rights,' and Anti-Slavery: The Germans of Newark, New Jersey," *Labor History* 25 (Winter 1984): 26–52; Bruce C. Levine, "Free Soil, Free Labor, Freimaenner: German Chicago in the Civil War Era," in Hartmut Keil and John B. Jentz, eds., *German Workers in Industrial Chicago* (DeKalb: Northern Illinois University Press, 1983), pp. 52–69. Also see Hartmut Keil, ed., *German Workers' Culture in the United States 1850 to 1920* (Washington, D.C.: Smithsonian Institution Press, 1988).

24. Edgar Barclay Cale, *The Organization of Labor in Philadelphia, 1850–1870* (Philadelphia: University of Pennsylvania Press, 1940), pp. 42–59; James C. Sylvis, *The Life, Speeches, Labors, and Essays of William H. Sylvis* (Philadelphia: Claxton, Remsel, and Hafflefinger, 1872), p. 41.

25. Jay P. Dolan, *The Immigrant Church: New York's Irish and German Catholics, 1815–1865* (Baltimore, Md.: Johns Hopkins University Press, 1975), chs. 7, 8; Fred W. Meuser, "Facing the Twentieth Century," in E. Clifford Nelson, ed., *The Lutherans in North America* (Philadelphia: Fortress Press, 1975), pp. 385–86.

26. Bruce C. Nelson, *Beyond the Martyrs: A Social History of Chicago's Anarchists* (New Brunswick, N.J.: Rutgers University Press, 1988), pp. 165–170; Laurie, *Working People*, p. 187.

27. *Philadelphia Inquirer*, June 11, 25, 1872; *Evening Bulletin*, June 13, 18, 22, 1872. See also Ken Fones-Wolf and Elliott Shore, "The German Press and Working-Class Politics in Gilded-Age Philadelphia," unpub. paper presented at the Max Kade Institute conference on the German-American Press, Madison, Wisconsin, Oct. 9, 1987.

28. B. Hubert to Isaac Rhen, Sept. 27, 1872, Hubert to John Shedden, Nov. 7, 1872, IWA Papers, Section 26 correspondence, reel 2; Social Democratic Workingmen's Party, Philadelphia Branch, "Minutes," May 1, 29, 1877, in Manuscripts Division, Library of Congress, Washington, D.C. For background, see Paul Buhle, *Marxism in the United States: Remapping the History of the American Left* (London: Verso Books, 1987), ch. 1.

29. Bruce Laurie, Theodore Hershberg, and George Alter, "Immigrants and Industry: The Philadelphia Experience, 1850–1880," in Hershberg, ed., *Philadelphia: Work, Space, Family, and Group Experience in the Nineteenth Century* (New York: Oxford University Press, 1981), ch. 2; Fones-Wolf and Shore, "German Press."

30. Cale, *Organization of Labor*, ch. 6. For the overwhelming importance of racism in the working class generally, see Herbert Hill, "Race, Ethnicity and Organized Labor: The Opposition to Affirmative Action," *New Politics* 1 [new series] (Winter 1987): 31–82.

31. W. E. B. Du Bois, *The Philadelphia Negro: A Social Study* (New York: Benjamin Blom, 1967; orig. pub. 1899), pp. 126–31.

32. *Fincher's Trades' Review*, Feb. 2, 1864; *JUL*, July 1883, p. 527, June 15, 1880, p. 24; *Philadelphia Labor*, Nov. 25, 1893.

33. Susan Levine, *Labor's True Woman: Carpet Weavers, Industrialization, and Labor Reform in the Gilded Age* (Philadelphia: Temple University Press, 1984), ch. 2; Augusta Emile Galster, *The Labor Movement in the Shoe Industry with Special Reference to Philadelphia* (New York: Ronald Press, 1924), ch. 4; Steven J. Ross, *Workers on the Edge: Work, Leisure, and Politics in Industrializing Cincinnati, 1788–1890* (New York: Columbia University Press, 1985), pp. 100–4.

34. Quote from *Public Ledger*, June 18, 1872; see also *Die Tageblatt*, June 10–24, 1872.

35. *The Toiler*, Aug. 1, 8, 1874, as quoted in Foner, *History of the Labor Movement*, p. 442.

36. *Minutes of the Ninety-First Session of the Philadelphia Conference of the Methodist Episcopal Church* (Philadelphia, 1878), pp. 28–32.

37. Robert G. Torbet, "A Social History of the Philadelphia Baptist Association: 1707–1940," unpub. Ph.D. diss., University of Pennsylvania, 1944, p. 205; Robert Ellis Thompson, *Hard Times and What to Learn from Them: A Plain Talk with the Working People* (Philadelphia: Edward Stern & Co., 1877).

38. *The Presbyterian* (Philadelphia), Aug. 18, 1877; Philip English Mackey, "Law and Order, 1877: Philadelphia's Response to the Railroad Riots," *Pennsylvania Magazine of History and Biography* 96 (Apr. 1972): 183–202.

39. *Public Ledger*, Dec. 17, 1879; *The Trades*, Mar. 29, 1879.

40. William Ashmead Schaeffer, "Something of Interest to the Lutheran Church in Philadelphia," *Lutheran Church Review*, Jan. 1892, pp. 71–72; William P. White and William H. Scott, *The Presbyterian Church in Philadelphia* (Philadelphia: Allen, Lane, & Scott, 1895), p. xix.

41. For this typology, I drew extensively on Ernst Troeltsch, *The Social Teaching of the Christian Churches*, 2 vols. (New York: Macmillan, 1931); Liston Pope, *Millhands and Preachers: A Study of Gas-*

tonia (New Haven, Conn.: Yale University Press, 1942); and N. J. Demerath, III, *Social Class in American Protestantism* (Chicago: Rand McNally, 1965). See also my elaboration on this point in "Religion and Trade-Union Politics in the U.S., 1880–1920," *International Labor and Working Class History* no. 34 (Fall 1988): 39–55. For a Philadelphia clergyman who witnessed the same type of working-class religious commitment, see Reverend Edwin S. Lane (an Episcopalian) to Bernard Newman, Oct. 6, 1915, in the Housing Association of the Delaware Valley Records, Box 13, folder 175, in UAC. Lane wrote that "religious idealism is as prevalent among those living in low grade houses as among the upper classes. In fact religion itself makes more of an appeal to the former than to the latter. For spiritual results I would take the less economically fixed almost every time."

42. Clifford Geertz, *The Interpretation of Cultures: Selected Essays* (New York: Basic Books, 1973), pp. 94–98; Paul A. Carter, *The Spiritual Crisis in the Gilded Age* (DeKalb: Northern Illinois University Press, 1971), pp. 138–45; Gutman, "Protestantism and the Labor Movement."

43. *JUL*, Feb. 1883, pp. 397–98; Apr. 1883, pp. 437–38; May 1883, pp. 457–58; June 1883, pp. 485–86; and July 1883, pp. 513–14, offers biographical sketches of national leaders including Gilbert Rockwood, Richard Griffiths, Daniel McLoughlin, Terence Powderly, and Frederick Turner.

44. Robert E. Weir, "The Knights of Labor in Ritual: A Culture of Fraternalism," unpub. paper, University of Massachusetts-Amherst, 1987, in author's possession.

45. *The Trades*, July 12, Oct. 25, Nov. 8, 1879.

46. *The Trades*, Jan. 17, 1880, Oct. 25, 1879.

47. *The Trades*, Apr. 5, 1879.

48. *The Trades*, Oct. 29, 1879, Apr. 17, 1880.

49. *JUL*, Feb. 1884, pp. 646, 649; Mar. 25, 1886, p. 2031.

50. *John Swinton's Paper* (New York), Oct. 14, 1883; *JUL*, Nov. 25, 1886, p. 2207.

51. *JUL*, Apr. 25, 1886, p. 2054. For Waters quotes, see *The Tocsin*, Oct. 2, Sept. 4, 1886.

52. *John Swinton's Paper*, Sept. 25, 1886.

53. *The Tocsin*, Sept. 4, Oct. 30, 1886; *Catholic Standard*, Feb. 28, 1885.

54. See, in particular, the minutes of Philadelphia Typographical Union, Local 2, May 17, June 21, 1884, in Philadelphia Typographical Union Records, Historical Society of Pennsylvania, Philadelphia, Pa. (hereafter cited as PTU, "Minutes").

55. Judith Lazarus Goldberg, "Strikes, Organizing, and Change: The Knights of Labor in Philadelphia, 1869–1890," unpub. Ph.D. diss., New York University, 1985, pp. 89–90; *The Trades*, Mar. 6, Apr. 3, 17, 1880.

56. Goldberg, "Strikes," ch. 4; PTU, "Minutes," Mar. 17, 1883.

For similar analyses, see Richard Oestreicher, *Solidarity and Fragmentation: Working People and Class Consciousness in Detroit, 1875–1900* (Urbana: University of Illinois Press, 1986), ch. 4; Bruce Laurie, *Artisans into Workers: Labor in Nineteenth-Century America* (New York: The Noonday Press, 1989), ch. 5.

57. Susan Levine, "Labor's True Woman: Domesticity and Equal Rights in the Knights of Labor," *Journal of American History* 70 (Sept. 1983): 323–39; Barbara Leslie Epstein, *The Politics of Domesticity: Women, Evangelism, and Temperance in Nineteenth-Century America* (Middletown, Conn.: Wesleyan University Press, 1981).

58. Goldberg, "Strikes," pp. 131–38, 415–18.

59. *JUL*, Jan. 10, 1885, as quoted in Goldberg, "Strikes," p. 420. Note the conflicting analyses of the poem and the strike in Levine, *Labor's True Woman*, ch. 5 and Goldberg, "Strikes," pp. 138–63.

60. Goldberg, "Strikes," pp. 138–63; Levine, *Labor's True Woman*, ch. 5; Jonathan Garlock, *Guide to the Local Assemblies of the Knights of Labor* (Westport, Conn.: Greenwood Press, 1982), pp. 453–55.

61. *The Tocsin*, Jan. 29, 1887; *JUL*, Mar. 25, 1886, p. 2031; PTU, "Minutes," Aug. 16, 1884.

62. *The Tocsin*, July 31, 1886.

63. Garlock, *Guide*, pp. 453–59; Galster, *Labor Movement*, ch. 4; PTU, "Minutes," July 19, Sept. 20, 1884, Feb. 21, Mar. 21, 1885; *The Tocsin*, Sept. 25, 1886.

64. U.S. Commissioner of Labor, *Third Annual Report: Strikes and Lockouts* (Washington, D.C.: GPO, 1887), pp. 528–67; U.S. Commissioner of Labor, *Tenth Annual Report* (Washington, D.C.: GPO, 1894), pp. 538–65; Goldberg, "Strikes," ch. 9; David Montgomery, "Strikes in Nineteenth-Century America," *Social Science History* 4 (Feb. 1980): 81–104.

65. *The Tocsin*, Feb. 28, 1885, June 12, July 31, Aug. 7, 1886, Apr. 9, 1887.

66. *The Tocsin*, Aug. 14, 1886.

67. See the especially fine analysis of Knights of Labor politics in Leon Fink, *Workingmen's Democracy: The Knights of Labor and American Politics* (Urbana: University of Illinois Press, 1983); and Goldberg, "Strikes," ch. 10.

68. The results of Philadelphia elections are in *Smull's Legislative Handbook* (Philadelphia, n.p., 1887), pp. 433–35.

69. Galster, *Labor Movement*, pp. 64–73; Philip Scranton, *Proprietary Capitalism: The Textile Manufacture at Philadelphia, 1800–1885* (New York: Cambridge University Press, 1984), pp. 382–86; Levine, "Their Own Sphere," pp. 144–52; Clement H. Congdon, *History of the Master Builder's Exchange of the City of Philadelphia from 1886 to 1893* (Philadelphia: Sunshine Publishing Co., 1893), pp. 20–34, 94–97.

70. Levine, "Their Own Sphere," pp. 149–51; Goldberg, "Strikes," ch. 6; *The Tocsin*, Aug. 14, Sept. 4, 18, 1886; PTU, "Minutes," July 17, 1886.

71. *The Tocsin*, Aug. 7, Sept. 11, Oct. 30, 1886, Apr. 23, Oct. 29, 1887.

72. The impact of the violence at Haymarket has been explored in several works, most recently in Paul Avrich, *Haymarket* (Princeton, N.J.: Princeton University Press, 1985). For a sampling of opinion regarding boycotts, see *Public Opinion*, May 1, 1886, pp. 47–50. For the importance of the boycott, see Michael A. Gordon, "The Labor Boycott in New York City, 1880–1886," *Labor History* 16 (1975): 184–229.

73. *The Nation*, May 27, 1886, p. 440; *The Tocsin*, Feb. 5, 1887. For the complex interaction of the Knights and the Catholic Church, see Henry J. Browne, *The Catholic Church and the Knights of Labor* (Washington, D.C.: Catholic University of America Press, 1949).

74. Joseph W. McIntyre to Terence Powderly, Mar. 25, 1888, in the *Terence Vincent Powderly Papers*, microfilm ed., (Glen Rock, N.J.: Microfilming Corporation of America, 1975), reel 25. The correspondence generally in 1886–87 is filled with letters documenting the turmoil of the Knights–Church relationship. For the resurgence of the Order of United American Mechanics, see John Higham, *Strangers in the Land: Patterns of American Nativism, 1860–1925* (New York: Atheneum, 1977), pp. 52–63.

75. PTU, "Minutes," July 17, Oct. 16, 1886. An excellent, brief analysis of the episode can also be found in Stuart B. Kaufman, ed., *The Samuel Gompers Papers, Volume 2: The Early Years of the American Federation of Labor, 1887–90* (Urbana: University of Illinois Press, 1987), pp. 25–26.

76. *The Tocsin*, Dec. 4, 11, 25, 1886.

77. *The Tocsin*, Oct. 15, 1887; Fones-Wolf and Shore, "The German Press," pp. 15–18.

78. John Devlin to Terence Powderly, Aug. 14, 1889, Powderly Papers, reel 31; Samuel Gompers to John Kirchner, Oct. 1, 1889, in Samuel Gompers *Letterbooks*, microfilm ed., reel 3, Manuscripts Division, Library of Congress, Washington, D.C.

79. Fink, *Workingmen's Democracy*, ch. 2.

Chapter 4

1. *New Era* (Philadelphia), Dec. 21, 1901.

2. Charles Stelzle, *American Social and Religious Conditions* (New York: Fleming H. Revell, 1912), p. 167. For the evangelical origins of the Social Gospel, see Ferenc M. Szasz, *The Divided Mind of Protestant America, 1880–1930* (University: University of Alabama Press, 1982), pp. 30–46; Robert T. Handy, *A Christian America: Protestant Hopes*

and Historical Realities (New York: Oxford University Press, 1984), ch. 6.

3. *The Tocsin* (Philadelphia), Sept. 4, Oct. 30, Nov. 6, 1886; Alfred H. Love to Terence V. Powderly, Mar. 2, 1887, in *Terence Vincent Powderly Papers*, microfilm ed. (Glen Rock, N.J.: Microfilming Corporation of New Jersey, 1975), reel 21, [hereafter cited as Powderly Papers].

4. Henriette A. Keyser, *Bishop Potter: The People's Friend* (New York: Thomas Whittaker, Inc., 1910), pp. 18–19; Henry F. May, *Protestant Churches and Industrial America* (New York: Octagon Books, 1963), pp. 182–95; Jacob Henry Dorn, *Washington Gladden: Prophet of the Social Gospel* (Columbus: Ohio State University Press, 1966).

5. See letters to Terence Powderly from A. A. Beaton, Dec. 26, 1887, Jay F. Hendrix, Dec. 26, 1887, John O'Keefe, Dec. 27, 1887, Thomas Neasham, Jan. 5, 1888, John Costello, Jan. 8, 1888, and A. M. Church, Jan. 9, 1888, Powderly Papers, reel 24.

6. William R. Hutchinson, *The Modernist Impulse in American Protestantism* (Cambridge: Harvard University Press, 1976), ch. 3; Szasz, *Divided Mind*, pp. 30–41; Grant Wacker, "The Holy Spirit and the Spirit of the Age in American Protestantism, 1880–1910," *Journal of American History* 72 (June 1985): 45–48.

7. Jay P. Dolan, *The American Catholic Experience: A History from Colonial Times to the Present* (New York: Doubleday, 1985), ch. 12.

8. Philadelphia Protestant Episcopal City Mission, *Twenty-Fourth Annual Report* (Philadelphia, 1894), pp. 8–10; Stelzle, *American Social and Religious Conditions*, p. 176. These points are emphasized in Ferenc M. Szasz, "Protestantism and the Search for Stability: Liberal and Conservative Quests for a Christian America, 1875–1925," in Jerry Israel, ed., *Building the Organizational Society* (New York: The Free Press, 1972), pp. 88–102; Handy, *Christian America*, pp. 134–36; George M. Marsden, *Fundamentalism and American Culture: The Shaping of Twentieth-Century Evangelicalism, 1870–1925* (New York: Oxford University Press, 1980), pp. 80–85.

9. A cursory look through *A Directory of the Charitable, Social Improvement, Educational, and Religious Associations and Churches of Philadelphia* (Philadelphia: Civic Club, 1903), provides ample evidence of these developments.

10. See, for instance, the attacks on the YMCA and the Lighthouse, a Kensington settlement, in the *Catholic Standard and Times*, July 8, Aug. 5, 1911. For contrasting views of the Social Gospel in the settlement, see Allen F. Davis, *Spearheads for Reform: The Social Settlements and the Progressive Movement, 1890–1914* (New York: Oxford University Press, 1967), and Richard N. Juliani, "The Settlement House and the

Italian Family," unpub. paper presented at the tenth annual conference of the American Italian Historical Association, Toronto, Oct. 1977, in the Urban Archives Center, Temple University, Philadelphia, Pa. (hereafter UAC).

The distinction between the social control and social justice thrusts of urban moral reform in this era is made in Paul Boyer, *Urban Masses and Moral Order in America, 1820–1920* (Cambridge: Harvard University Press, 1978), pp. 175–87; and in Arthur S. Link and Richard L. McCormick, *Progressivism* (Arlington Heights, Ill.: Harlan Davidson, 1983), ch. 3.

11. *Public Ledger* (Philadelphia), Feb. 7, 1893; Harlan B. Phillips, "A War on Philadelphia's Slums: Walter Vrooman and the Conference of Moral Workers, 1893," *Pennsylvania Magazine of History and Biography* 70 (Jan. 1952): 47–62. For more on Vrooman, see Ross E. Paulson, *Radicalism and Reform: The Vrooman Family and American Social Thought, 1837–1937* (Lexington: University of Kentucky Press, 1968).

12. *A Brief History of the Movement to Abolish the Slums of Philadelphia and Provide Decent Homes for the Poor* (Philadelphia, 1893), pp. 12–15, pamphlet in UAC.

13. Phillips, "War on Slums," pp. 48–54.

14. Philadelphia Typographical Union, "Minutes," May 21, 1893, in Philadelphia Typographical Union Records, Historical Society of Pennsylvania, Philadelphia, Pa. (hereafter PTU, "Minutes"); *North American* (Philadelphia), Mar. 27, 1893; *Brief History*, pp. 10–11; United Labor League, "Minutes," Mar. 12, 1893, microfilm in UAC (hereafter ULL, "Minutes"); Paulson, *Radicalism and Reform*, pp. 95–96.

15. Operative Plasterers Mutual Protective Union, "Minutebook," Mar. 21, 1893, in UAC; PTU, "Minutes," May 21, 1893.

16. *Public Ledger*, Feb. 25, 1893; Phillips, "War on Slums," pp. 58–60.

17. Phillips, "War on Slums," pp. 58–60.

18. For labor's rejection of Jews and Italians, see ULL, "Minutes," Mar. 26, 1893; PTU, "Minutes," Feb. 18, 1894; Plasterers, "Minutebook," Aug. 29, 1893; Edwin Fenton, "Italians in the Labor Movement," *Pennsylvania History* 26 (1959): 133–48. Bruce Laurie, in *Artisans Into Workers: Labor in Nineteenth-Century America* (New York: The Noonday Press, 1989), calls this the "prudential unionism" of the American Federation of Labor. See chapter 6. The point about the nativist resurgence in the American working class between the collapse of the Knights and the depression of the 1890s is explored in Mike Davis, "Why the U.S. Working Class is Different," *New Left Review* no. 123 (Sept.–Oct. 1980): 33–35, although I believe he overstates its impact and duration.

19. ULL, "Minutes," Dec. 24, 1893. For the impact of the depression on working-class agitation and unemployment demonstrations, see

Alexander Keyssar, *Out of Work: The First Century of Unemployment in Massachusetts* (New York: Cambridge University Press, 1986), especially chs. 7 and 9; Philip S. Foner, *History of the Labor Movement in the United States*: 8 vols. (New York: International Publishers, 1975), vol. 2, ch. 16.

20. Protestant Episcopal City Mission, *Twenty-Fourth Annual Report*, pp. 13, 40–43, 75–76; May, *Protestant Churches*, pp. 182–87 generally concedes that the Episcopal Church was the leader in the early Social Gospel. For Helen Devereux, see ULL, "Minutes," generally for the 1890s, and Lucy Perkins Carner, *The Settlement Way in Philadelphia* (Philadelphia, 1964), pamphlet in UAC.

21. William Williams Keen, *The Bi-Centennial Celebration of the Founding of the First Baptist Church of the City of Philadelphia* (Philadelphia: American Baptist Publishing Society, 1899), pp. 108–118; Lawrence B. Davis, *Immigrants, Baptists, and the Protestant Mind in America* (Urbana: University of Illinois Press, 1973), pp. 138–42.

22. Robert G. Torbet, "A Social History of the Philadelphia Baptist Association: 1707–1940," unpub. Ph.D. diss., University of Pennsylvania, 1944, pp. 201–17; Clyde Kenneth Nelson, "The Social Ideas of Russell H. Conwell," unpub. Ph.D. diss., University of Pennsylvania, 1968, pp. 210–16.

23. Compare, for instance, the change in tone of the *Catholic Standard*'s coverage of labor between Dec. 26, 1885 (before Haymarket), and Oct. 15, 1887. In Philadelphia, at least, the situation only worsened. In the early twentieth century, the *Catholic Standard and Times* characterized strikes as "wicked and wanton" (Sept. 23, 1911). Note also that Catholic clergy were conspicuously absent in interaction with Philadelphia's labor bodies from the 1890s through the 1910s, to judge from the minutes of those bodies as well as the local labor press. Protestants appear in those sources on a regular basis.

See, in addition, Philip S. Benjamin, *The Philadelphia Quakers in the Industrial Age, 1865–1920* (Philadelphia: Temple University Press, 1976), pp. 89–90, 162–63; Dolan, *American Catholic Experience*, ch. 12; James Edmund Roohan, *American Catholics and the Social Question, 1865–1900* (New York: Arno Press, 1976), ch. 11; and *The History of the Archdiocese of Philadelphia*, James F. Connelly, ed., (Philadelphia: Archdiocese of Philadelphia), pp. 286–95.

24. *The Lutheran*, Nov. 2, 1893, Dec. 3, 1903, Jan. 14, 1904; Fred W. Meuser, "Facing the Twentieth Century," in *The Lutherans in North America*, E. Clifford Nelson, ed. (Philadelphia: Fortress Press, 1975), pp. 385–86.

25. Edwin Heyl Delk, *Three Vital Problems* (Philadelphia: Lutheran Publishing Society, 1909), pp. 42, 62.

26. Presbytery of Philadelphia North, "Minutes," June 6, 1893, May 13, 1897, May 14, 1901, in Presbyterian Historical Society, Philadelphia,

Pa.; William P. White and William H. Scott, *The Presbyterian Church in Philadelphia* (Philadelphia: Allen, Lane, & Scott, 1895); Moseley H. Williams, "The New Era of Church Work in Philadelphia," *The Open Church*, Apr. 1897, pp. 53–75.

27. *New Era*, Nov. 1, 1902; *Eastern Laborer*, Apr. 20, 1907.

28. Clyde C. Griffen, "Rich Laymen and Early Social Christianity," *Church History* 36 (Mar. 1967): 45–65.

29. Samuel Wagenhals, "The Industrial Situation," *Lutheran Church Review*, Apr. 1895, pp. 149–50; May, *Protestant Churches*, pp. 108–9.

30. ULL, "Minutes," Feb. 11, 1894. I would like to thank Milton Cantor for pointing out to me this apparent contradiction.

31. John Gay's Sons' Carpet Mills, "Daybook," Dec. 16, 1893, Aug. 22, 1895, in Historical Society of Pennsylvania; Pennsylvania Secretary of Internal Affairs, *Annual Report: Vol. 23 Part III, Industrial Statistics* (Harrisburg, 1895), pp. 224–38 (hereafter cited as PaSIA, *Annual Report*, vol. 23, pt. III); ULL, "Minutes," Jan. 28, June 10, July 1, 8, Oct. 28, Dec. 23, 1894.

32. *Public Ledger*, Dec. 17–23, 1895; ULL, "Minutes," Jan. 13, July 28, Oct. 13, 1895. For one clergyman's response to the events of 1895, see Henry C. McCook, *The Rights and Wrongs of Motormen* (Philadelphia: Tabernacle Presbyterian Church, 1895), pamphlet in the Presbyterian Historical Society.

33. ULL, "Minutes," May 27, Dec. 23, 1894, Jan. 13, 1895.

34. PTU, "Minutes," Feb. 18, 1894; ULL, "Minutes," Mar. 11, Apr. 22, Oct. 28, 1894; David Bensman, *The Practice of Solidarity: American Hat Finishers in the Nineteenth Century* (Urbana: University of Illinois Press, 1985), p. 202; *Cigar Makers' Official Journal*, Sept. 15, 1906, p. 6; Nov. 15, 1906, pp. 6–7.

35. ULL, "Minutes," Jan. 13, May 12, June 22, 1895.

36. Carner, *Settlement Way in Philadelphia*, pp. 9–11; National Consumers' League, *Fourth Annual Report* (1903), p. 7, and *Seventh Annual Report* (1906), pp. 91–92, in Box A 5, National Consumers' League Papers, Manuscript Division, Library of Congress, Washington, D.C.; ULL, "Minutes," Feb. 14, 1897.

37. ULL, "Minutes," Apr. 28, May 26, 1895, Dec. 27, 1896.

38. ULL, "Minutes," Mar. 10, 24, 1895, Jan. 24, May 23, 1897. Similar reform movements in Detroit, Toledo, and other cities were enjoying success in capturing working-class movements. See Richard Oestreicher, *Solidarity and Fragmentation: Working People and Class Consciousness in Detroit, 1875–1900* (Urbana: University of Illinois Press, 1986), pp. 233–37; Gregory Zieren, "The Labor Boycott and Class Consciousness in Toledo, Ohio," in Charles Stephenson and Robert Asher, eds., *Life and Labor* (Albany: State University of New York Press, 1986), pp. 148–51.

39. Gompers to George Chance, Mar. 24, 1897, Samuel Gompers

Letterbooks, Manuscript Division, Library of Congress, Washington, D.C.; John Price Jackson, *Labor Laws of Pennsylvania* (Harrisburg: Pennsylvania Dept. of Labor and Industry, 1914).

40. ULL, "Minutes," Feb. 12, 1899. The many contradictory tendencies of the interplay of labor activism, employer initiatives, and state involvement are delineated in David Montgomery, *The Fall of the House of Labor: The Workplace, the State, and American Labor Activism, 1865–1925* (New York: Cambridge University Press, 1987), ch. 6.

41. *New Era*, Sept. 6, 1902.

42. *International Molders' Journal*, Apr. 1906, p. 272; *Trades' Union News* (Philadelphia), Jan. 12, 1905.

43. *Weekly Bulletin of the Clothing Trades*, Jan. 27, 1904; *New Era*, Dec. 21, 1901.

44. *Trades' Union News*, Oct. 20, Dec. 8, 29, 1904; ULL, "Minutes," Jan. 8, Feb. 12, 1899.

45. ULL, "Minutes," Aug. 22, 1897, Jan. 9, 1898, Mar. 12, 1899.

46. Building trades unions' opposition to the ULL can be traced back to April 12, 1892 (see ULL, "Minutes"). The growth of construction unions in this period is drawn from United Brotherhood of Carpenters and Joiners of America (UBCJA) Local 8, "Minutes," 1898–1902, in UBCJA Local 8 Records, UAC; Paperhangers Local 9, Records, Jewish Archives Center, Philadelphia, PA. The success of building trades unions in winning demands is detailed in ULL, "Minutes," Apr. 9, May 14, June 11, Aug. 27, 1899, Jan. 14, 1900.

47. Testimony of Denis Hayes, U.S. Industrial Commission, *Report on the Relations and Conditions of Capital and Labor Employed in Manufactures and General Business*, 19 vols. (Washington, D.C.: GPO, 1902), vol. 14, p. 103; Trades' Union News, June 16, July 7, 1904.

48. Contracts for the Molders and Foundrymen are in the Metal Manufacturers' Association of Philadelphia, Records, Box 2, UAC; for garment workers, see *Weekly Bulletin of the Clothing Trades*, Feb. 26, 1904; for the Printers, see *Typographical Journal*, July 1905, p. 49; for the building trades see Bricklayers' Company of Philadelphia, "Minutebook," Sept. 14, 1903, in Historical Society of Pennsylvania, Philadelphia; and Frank Feeney to Joseph Krauskopf, Dec. 15, 1903, in Rabbi Joseph Krauskopf Papers, UAC.

49. George H. Nash, "Charles Stelzle: Apostle to Labor," *Labor History* 11 (Spring, 1970): 151–74; *Labor Temple Bulletin*, Oct. 29, 1910, Feb. 17, 1912, in Labor Temple Records, Presbyterian Historical Society.

50. *Eastern Laborer* (Philadelphia), Oct. 19, 1907; *Trades' Union News*, Nov. 23, 1905.

51. Central Labor Union, "Minutes," Apr. 25, 1909, microfilm in UAC, originals in the Philadelphia Council, AFL-CIO Headquarters (hereafter CLU, "Minutes").

52. St. George's Church, *A Record of the Pastorate of Rev. A. J. Arkin* (Philadelphia, n.d.), unpaged pamphlet in UAC.

53. *Trades' Union News*, June 16, Nov. 10, 1904, Mar. 16, 1905; St. George's Church, *A Record*. For a good summary of the thinking behind such "uplift" mechanisms as playgrounds of the sort that involved Arkin, see Francis G. Couvares, *The Remaking of Pittsburgh: Class and Culture in an Industrializing City, 1877–1919* (Albany: State University of New York Press, 1984), ch. 7.

54. *Trades' Union News*, Sept. 1, 1904; *Five Years of Summer Services: Third Annual Report of the Second Presbyterian Church and Business Men's Committee* (Philadelphia, 1906), pp. 1–5, pamphlet in the Presbyterian Historical Society.

55. *Trades' Union News*, Nov. 17, Sept. 8, 1904; *Five Years*, p. 5.

56. *Trades' Union News*, Nov. 10, Dec. 29, 1904, Jan. 26, 1905, June 4, 1908. For the importance of collective bargaining as a panacea at this time, see Bruno Ramirez, *When Workers Fight: The Politics of Industrial Relations in the Progressive Era, 1898–1916* (Westport, Conn.: Greenwood Press, 1978).

57. Kemper Bocock, "The Social Question and the Christian Answer," *Sewanee Review*, Oct. 1902, pp. 454–57.

58. Freeman Otis Willey, *The Laborer and the Capitalist* (New York: Equitable Publishing Co., 1896), p. 12; Wilbur F. Crafts, *Practical Christian Sociology* (New York: Funk and Wagnals, 1895), pp. 171–73, 184.

59. Harry F. Ward, "The Labor Movement," in Harry F. Ward, ed., *Social Ministry: An Introduction to the Study and Practice of Social Service* (New York: Eaton and Mains, 1910), pp. 116–17; *Trades' Union News*, Sept. 26, 1906.

60. *Trades' Union News*, May 4, 1905, Sept. 17, 1908; *Eastern Laborer*, Oct. 19, 1907.

61. *Trades' Union News*, July 9, Sept. 3, 17, Dec. 17, 31, 1908, Jan. 21, Feb. 11, 1909.

62. *Public Ledger*, June 2, Aug. 17, 1903; Feeney to Krauskopf, Dec. 15, 1903, Krauskopf Papers. See also David Montgomery, "Strikes in Nineteenth-Century America," *Social Science History* 4 (Feb. 1980): 81–104; and David Montgomery, *Workers' Control in America: Studies in the History of Work, Technology, and Labor Struggles* (New York: Cambridge University Press, 1979), ch. 4.

63. *Trades' Union News*, Nov. 3, 1904.

64. *Trades' Union News*, Dec. 17, 31, 1908; *Eastern Laborer*, Apr. 27, 1907.

65. *The Lighthouse*, *The Needs of a Neighborhood: Tenth Annual Report* (1905), pp. 19–20, in pamphlet collection, UAC.

66. Graham Taylor, who also assisted with *The Survey*, entitled his 1913 book *Religion in Social Action* (New York: Dodd, Mead and Co., 1913). See, also, for a recent overview emphasizing the religious in-

put into Progressivism, Robert M. Crunden, *Ministers of Reform: The Progressives' Achievement in American Civilization, 1889–1920* (New York: Basic Books, 1982). The importance of this "new liberalism" is examined in Martin J. Sklar, *The Corporate Reconstruction of American Capitalism, 1890–1916: The Market, the Law, and Politics* (New York: Cambridge University Press, 1988).

67. The ongoing debate about the location and significance of the "labor aristocracy" in labor movements, both here and abroad, is summarized well in Eric J. Hobsbawm, *The Workers: Worlds of Labor* (New York: Pantheon Books, 1984), chs. 12–14. One of the most probing analyses of the consciousness of the American labor aristocracy is Andrew Dawson, "The Parameters of Craft Consciousness: The Social Outlook of the Skilled Worker, 1890–1920," in *American Labor and Immigration History, 1877–1920s: Recent European Research*, Dirk Hoerder, ed. (Urbana: University of Illinois Press, 1983), ch. 6.

Chapter 5

1. Philadelphia *Evening Bulletin*, Jan. 30, 1918; *Public Ledger* (Philadelphia), Jan. 31, 1918.

2. *Catholic Standard and Times*, Nov. 26, 1910. For more on the provincial character of the Philadelphia business elite, see E. Digby Baltzell, *The Philadelphia Gentlemen: The Making of a National Upper Class* (New York: Free Press, 1958); and Philip Scranton, *Proprietary Capitalism: The Textile Manufacture at Philadelphia* (New York: Cambridge University Press, 1984). Stephen Yeo, *Religion and Voluntary Organizations in Crisis* (London: Croom Helm, 1976), discusses the importance of provincialism in making voluntary associations function in such a way as to diminish class antagonisms.

3. College Settlement Association, *Twenty-Fifth Annual Report* (Philadelphia, 1914), p. 9.

4. Torrey Deborah Dickinson, "Redivided Lives: The Formation of the Working Class in Philadelphia, 1870–1945," unpub. Ph.D. diss., State University of New York at Binghamton, 1983), pp. 191–96. Of course, some settlement workers were more sympathetic to ethnic cultures, but these were probably in the minority. For more on the cultural pluralism of settlement workers, see Allen F. Davis, *Spearheads for Reform: The Social Settlements and the Progressive Movement, 1890–1914* (New York: Oxford University Press, 1967), ch. 5.

5. See the Pennsylvania Child Labor Association, "Minutes," 1905–1915, in the Urban Archives Center, Temple University, Philadelphia, Pa. (hereafter UAC), for the absence of contact with labor unions. For Mary Richmond's comments, see Paul Boyer, *Urban Masses and Moral Order, 1820–1920* (Cambridge: Harvard University Press, 1978), p. 156. For

a perceptive analysis of protective legislation, see Alice Kessler-Harris, *Out to Work: A History of Wage-Earning Women in the United States* (New York: Oxford University Press, 1982), ch. 7: and for its impact in one particular setting, see Mary H. Blewett, *Men, Women, and Work: Class, Gender, and Protest in the New England Shoe Industry, 1780–1910* (Urbana: University of Illinois Press, 1988), pp. 317–318.

6. *Catholic Standard and Times*, Aug. 5, 1911, Feb. 1, 1913.

7. *Catholic Standard and Times*, Feb. 4, Sept. 9, Dec. 16, 1911. Note the articles praising social reform in Britain and Belgium for their "stealing the thunder" of socialists; Sept. 16, Dec. 23, 1911, and the change in attitude concerning child labor legislation between Dec. 24, 1910 and Feb. 1, 1913.

8. Playgrounds Association of Philadelphia, *Why?* (Philadelphia, 1909), p. 10, pamphlet in UAC.

9. "Philadelphia Public Playgrounds Committee," *Survey*, Oct. 15, 1910, pp. 106–7; Public Playgrounds Commission, *Playgrounds for Philadelphia* (Philadelphia, 1910), p. 18, pamphlet in UAC. A thoughtful analysis of the thinking behind playgrounds and parks is in Roy Rosenzweig, "Middle-Class Parks and Working-Class Play: The Struggle Over Recreational Space in Worcester, Massachusetts, 1870–1910," *Radical History Review* 21 (1979): 31–48.

10. Philadelphia Society for Organizing Charity, *Thirty-Sixth Annual Report* (Philadelphia, 1914), pp. 10–11; *The Registration Bureau* (Philadelphia, n.d.), pamphlet in Box 1, Philadelphia–Camden Social Service Exchange Records, UAC. For a list of the agencies involved (almost all of which were older Protestant agencies), see J. P. Duffy to Womens Bible Readers Class, Feb. 24, 1911, in Box 1, *Ibid.*

11. "Men and Religion Forward Movement" survey, handwritten manuscript, Dec. 26, 1911, Box 20, University Settlements Records, UAC.

12. These points are made in Boyer, *Urban Masses*, pp. 175–87, but the dichotomy stressed by Boyer misses the earlier cooperation between "higher life" theology supporters like Torrey and Social-Gospel advocates. For a compelling discussion of these points, see Grant Wacker, "The Holy Spirit and the Spirit of the Age in American Protestantism, 1880–1910," *Journal of American History* 72 (June 1985): 45–62. For the messages of the revivals, see Torrey–Alexander Evangelistic Campaign, "Minutebook," 1905–6, in Box 7, Young Men's Christian Association Records, UAC (hereafter YMCA Records); John Reed, "Back of Billy Sunday," *Metropolitan Magazine*, May 1915, pp. 9–12, 66–72.

13. *Philadelphia Press*, Feb. 19, 1904.

14. Quoted in Dickinson, "Redivided Lives," p. 195. Francis G. Couvares, *The Remaking of Pittsburgh: Class and Culture in an Industrializing City, 1877–1919* (Albany: State University of New York

Press, 1984), ch. 7, makes the same point although I believe he overstates working-class opposition.

15. Rosenzweig, "Middle-Class Parks," pp. 31–48; Couvares, *Remaking of Pittsburgh*, ch. 7; David Glassberg, "Public Ritual and Cultural Hierarchy: Philadelphia's Civic Celebrations at the Turn of the Century," *Pennsylvania Magazine of History and Biography* 107 (July 1983): 421–48.

16. For Davies, see Lucy Perkins Carner, *The Settlement Way in Philadelphia* (Philadelphia, 1964), pp. 9–12, pamphlet in UAC. For Sanville, see Ken Fones-Wolf, "Contention and Christianity: Protestantism and the Labor Movement in Philadelphia, 1890–1920," in Vincent Mosco and Janet Wasko, eds., *Critical Communications Review*, 3d series (New York: Ablex Press, 1985); and Joseph M. Speakman, "Unwillingly to School: Child Labor and Its Reform in Pennsylvania in the Progressive Era," unpub. Ph.D. diss., Temple University, 1976, pp. 264–65.

17. Although there are many excellent works emphasizing the tensions in churches following the emergence of the Social Gospel, there have been few efforts to explore that tension within the vast array of Protestant voluntary associations. Stephen Yeo's *Religion and Voluntary Organizations in Crisis* does this for Reading, England.

18. Boyer, *Urban Masses*, pp. 108–20; Helen Bittar, "The Y.W.C.A. of the City of New York, 1870–1920," unpub. Ph.D. diss., New York University, 1979, pp. 3–4, 14–20; David I. Macleod, *Building Character in the American Boy: The Boy Scouts, YMCA, and Their Forerunners, 1870–1920* (Madison: University of Wisconsin Press, 1983), pp. 72–77.

19. YMCA of Philadelphia, *Fortieth Annual Report* (1895), p. 46; YWCA of Philadelphia, *Forty-First Annual Report* (1911), pp. 33–67; C. Howard Hopkins, *History of the Y.M.C.A. in North America* (New York: Association Press, 1951), p. 389.

20. See Scranton, *Proprietary Capitalism*, ch. 5; and the general testimonies on the paternalism of Philadelphia employers in U.S. Industrial Commission, *Report on the Relations and Conditions of Capital and Labor Employed in Manufactures and General Business*, 19 vols. (Washington, D.C.: GPO, 1902), vol. 14.

21. YMCA of Philadelphia, *Forty-First Annual Report* (1896), pp. 10–11; Kensington YMCA Board of Managers, "Minutes," Dec. 16, 1902, in Box 15, YMCA Records.

22. "Classbook of the Kensington YWCA," 1891–1900, Box 3, Kensington YWCA Records, UAC (hereafter YWCA-Kensington Records); Kensington YWCA Executive Committee, "Minutes," Apr. 2, 1895, Dec. 5, 1905, Box 1, YWCA-Kensington Records.

23. Hopkins, *History of the YMCA*, pp. 234–35; Pennsylvania Secretary of Internal Affairs, *Annual Report*, vol. 15, Pt. III: *Industrial Statistics* (Harrisburg, 1888), pp. B5, B15.

24. *Philadelphia Evening Times*, Jan. 13, 1911; *Public Ledger*, Jan. 18, 1911; Metropolitan YWCA Executive Committee, "Minutes," Dec. 31, 1917, Box 6, Metropolitan YWCA Records, supplementary accession #467, UAC (hereafter YWCA-Metropolitan Records #467).

25. Kensington YMCA Board of Managers, "Minutes," Mar. 7, 1899, Box 15, YMCA Records; YMCA of Philadelphia, *Forty-Eighth Annual Report* (1903), p. 5; YMCA of Philadelphia, *Fifty-Fourth Annual Report* (1909), p. 56.

26. Simms is quoted in Grace H. Wilson, *The Religious and Educational Philosophy of the Young Women's Christian Association*, Teachers' College Contributions to Education, no. 554 (New York: Columbia University Press, 1933), p. 29.

27. YMCA of Philadelphia, *Forty-Eighth Annual Report* (1903), pp. 27–28.

28. Emma Hays, "Report on Visitation of Young Women's Christian Association in Philadelphia and Germantown, July 10, 1913," typescript, Box 6, YWCA-Metropolitan Records #467.

29. See Central Labor Union, "Minutes," Jan. 8, 1911, microfilm in UAC, for evidence of the tension between unions and YMCA vocational training. The Kensington YMCA Board of Managers, "Minutes," Mar. 17, 1914, Box 16, YMCA Records, shows the refusal of the YMCA to host union meetings. *Faith and Works* (organ of the Philadelphia YWCA), Nov. 1897, p. 45, Apr. 1898, p. 24, offers just a few examples of the work-ethic ideology of the YWCA in Philadelphia. For the political uses of the work ethic in this time period, see Daniel T. Rodgers, *The Work Ethic in Industrial America, 1850–1920* (Chicago: University of Chicago Press, 1978).

30. YWCA of Philadelphia, *Fortieth Annual Report* (1910), p. 21; Metropolitan YWCA Executive Committee, "Minutes," Mar. 13, 1911, Box 6, YWCA-Metropolitan Records #467.

31. YMCA of Philadelphia, *Forty-Ninth Annual Report* (1904), pp. 36–37; YMCA of Philadelphia *Fifty-Fourth Annual Report* (1909), p. 6.

32. *Ibid.*; Kensington YMCA Board of Managers, "Minutes," Feb. 21, 1911, Box 16, YMCA Records; YMCA Shop Fellowship Meetings, "Minutes," Nov. 12, 1917, Box 15, YMCA Records.

33. *Monthly Bulletin of the Collins Y.W.C.A.* (Philadelphia), Oct. 1913, p. 4; *Philadelphia Press*, Dec. 4, 1912, in YWCA scrapbooks, Box 19, YWCA-Metropolitan Records.

34. YMCA of Philadelphia, *Fifty-Second Annual Report* (1907), p. 29.

35. Thomas M. Jacklin, "The Civic Awakening: Social Christianity and the Usable Past," *Mid-America* 64 (Fall 1981): 3–19; Richard L. McCormick, "The Discovery that Business Corrupts Politics: A Reappraisal of the Origins of Progressivism," *American Historical Review* 86 (Apr. 1981): 247–74.

36. Gustav Theodor Schwenning, "A History of the Industrial Work of the Young Men's Christian Association," unpub. Ph.D. diss., Clark University, 1925, pp. 184–88; Wilson, *Religious and Educational Philosophy*, pp. 15–46. For an interesting discussion of the emergence of collectivist thought, see James B. Gilbert, *Designing the Industrial State: The Intellectual Pursuit of Collectivism in America, 1880–1940* (Chicago: Quadrangle Books, 1972).

37. Scranton, *Proprietary Capitalism*, ch. 9; and Sam Bass Warner, Jr., *The Private City: Philadelphia in Three Periods of its Growth* (Philadelphia: University of Pennsylvania Press, 1968), ch. 5, provide interesting discussions of the parochial orientation of the Philadelphia elite.

38. Kensington YMCA Board of Managers, "Minutes," Jan. 22, 1907, Feb. 22, 1907, Box 15, YMCA Records; Hopkins, *History of the YMCA*, pp. 477–78.

39. *Eastern Laborer* (Philadelphia), Oct. 12, 19, 26, 1907. For more on the Metal Manufacturers' Association, see Ken Fones-Wolf, "Employer Unity and the Crisis of the Craftsman," *Pennsylvania Magazine of History and Biography* 107 (July 1983): 449–55, and forthcoming work from Howell John Harris, who was kind enough to share it with me.

40. Kensington YMCA Board of Managers, "Minutes," Oct. 15, 1907, Mar. 17, 1908, Jan. 19, 1909, Box 15, YMCA Records; Schwenning, "History," p. 187.

41. Charles Howard Hopkins, *The Rise of the Social Gospel in American Protestantism, 1865–1915* (New Haven: Yale University Press, 1940), pp. 306–9; *Trades' Union News* (Philadelphia), Dec. 10, 1908.

42. "What the Men and Religion Forward Movement Actually Accomplished," *Current Literature*, June 1912, pp. 673–75; William O. Easton, *The Church and Social Work* (Philadelphia, 1912), pamphlet in "Men and Religion Forward Movement" folder, unnumbered box, National Council of Churches of America Records, Presbyterian Historical Society, Philadelphia, Pa.

43. See, in YWCA scrapbooks, *Public Ledger*, Dec. 22, 1912; *North American*, Nov. 12, 1913; *The Record*, (Philadelphia), Mar. 9, 1913, Boxes 19 and 20, YWCA-Metropolitan Records.

44. *Catholic Standard and Times*, Jan. 14, 1911, Feb. 10, 1912, Feb. 8, May 3, Nov. 22, 1913. The large numbers of Italians and Jews entering working-class YWCAs became an issue in the dispute that splintered the Association after 1914; see also, note 52. Another, more skeptical perspective on immigrant women and Protestant social work is offered in Betty Boyd Caroli, ed., *The Italian Immigrant Woman in North America* (Toronto: Multicultural History Society of Ontario, 1978).

45. "Bulletin: Labor Forward Movement" [Philadelphia], attached to J. E. Roach letter to Samuel Gompers, Oct. 2, 1914, Reel 26, *The American Federation of Labor Records: The Samuel Gompers Era* (San-

ford, N.C.: Microfilming Corporation of America, 1979). On the Labor Forward Movement, see Elizabeth and Kenneth Fones-Wolf, "Trade Union Evangelism: Religion and the AFL in the Labor Forward Movement, 1912–1916," in Michael H. Frisch and Daniel J. Walkowitz, eds., *Working-Class America: Essays on Labor, Community, and American Society* (Urbana: University of Illinois Press, 1983), pp. 153–84.

46. Kensington YMCA Board of Managers, "Minutes," Mar. 17, 1914, Box 16, YMCA Records; Philadelphia YMCA Board of Directors, "Minutes," Dec. 16, 1914, Box 2, YMCA Records.

47. Metropolitan YWCA Executive Committee, "Minutes," Oct. 5, 1914, Oct. 29, 1917, Box 6, YWCA-Metropolitan Records #467. Dancing nevertheless continued at the Kensington YWCA until it was officially sanctioned in the 1920s. See also Kathy Peiss, *Cheap Amusements* (Philadelphia: Temple University Press, 1985), for the importance working-class women placed on their ability to control their leisure pursuits.

48. Metropolitan YWCA Executive Committee, "Minutes," Jan. 4, 25, 1916, Box 6, YWCA-Metropolitan Records #467; and *Public Ledger* as quoted in Donald Disbrow, "The Progressive Movement in Philadelphia, 1910–1916," unpub. Ph.D. diss., University of Rochester, 1956, pp. 209–10. For an amusing contemporary characterization of the Sunday campaign, see Reed, "Back of Billy Sunday."

49. Kensington YMCA Board of Managers, "Minutes," Mar. 20, 1917, Apr. 16, 1914, Box 16, YMCA Records; Hopkins, *History of the YMCA*, pp. 511–14.

50. Metropolitan YWCA Executive Committee, "Minutes," July 19, 1915, Sept. 13, 1915, Box 6, YWCA-Metropolitan Records #467; Kensington YWCA Executive Committee, "Minutes," Apr. 13, Oct. 12, 1915, Mar. 15, July 11, Dec. 6, 1916, Box 1, YWCA-Kensington Records.

51. Metropolitan YWCA Executive Committee, "Minutes," Nov. 6, Dec. 11, 18, 1916, Jan. 29, Mar. 5, 12, Apr. 10, 1917, Box 6, YWCA-Metropolitan Records, #467.

52. Metropolitan YWCA Executive Committee, "Minutes," May 8, 1916, May 21, July 24, 1917, in *Ibid.*; Kensington YWCA Executive Committee, "Minutes," June 20, 28, 1917, Box 1, YWCA-Kensington Records.

53. Metropolitan YWCA Executive Committee, "Minutes," Nov. 12, 26, 1917, Jan. 4, 21, 28, 1918, Box 6, YWCA-Metropolitan Records #467; "To the Board of Managers of the Young Women's Christian Association, Eighteenth and Arch Streets, Philadelphia, Pa.," undated petition, Box 9, YWCA-Metropolitan Records.

54. See *Public Ledger*, Feb. 13, 1918, Jan. 17,24, Dec. 18, 1919; *Philadelphia Inquirer*, Dec. 14, 1919; and trial materials in Box 9, YWCA-Metropolitan Records.

55. See, for example, Jill Conway, "Women Reformers and American

Culture, 1870–1930," *Journal of Social History* 5 (Winter 1971–72): 164–77; Estelle Freedman, "Separatism as Strategy: Female Institution Building and American Feminism, 1870–1930," *Feminist Studies* 5 (Fall 1979): 519; Nancy Schrom Dye, *As Equals and as Sisters: Feminism, the Labor Movement, and the Women's Trade Union League of New York* (Columbia: University of Missouri Press, 1980); Robin Miller Jacoby, "The Women's Trade Union League and American Feminism," *Feminist Studies* 3 (Fall 1975): 126–40.

56. Ethel M. Smith, "Applying Workers' Education: Report to the National Industrial Assembly of the Y.W.C.A.," typescript, circa 1927, Box 27, Germantown YWCA Records, UAC; Kensington YWCA Executive Committee, "Minutes," generally for the 1930s, in YWCA-Kensington Records.

57. *Catholic Standard and Times* Nov. 23, 1912, Mar. 15, 1913, Aug. 8, 1914. See also Marc Karson, *American Labor Unions and Politics, 1900–1918* (Boston: Beacon Press, 1965), ch. 7.

58. Disbrow, "Progressive Movement in Philadelphia," pp. 207–14.

59. *Public Ledger*, Dec. 18, 1919.

60. See, especially, Bruce C. Nelson, "Revival and Upheaval: Irreligion and Chicago's Working Class in 1886," unpub. paper presented to the Chicago Area Labor History Group, Dec. 10, 1987, through the kindness of Bruce Nelson; and chapter 6.

Chapter 6

1. *Trades' Union News*, Nov. 19, Oct. 22, 1914.

2. *Trades' Union News*, Sept. 1, 8, 1904.

3. *Trades' Union News*, Nov. 10, 17, Dec. 15, 1904; *Five Years of Summer Services: Third Annual Report of the Second Presbyterian Church and Business Men's Committee* (Philadelphia, 1906), p. 5, pamphlet in the Presbyterian Historical Society, Philadelphia, Pa.

4. Herbert G. Gutman, *Work, Culture, and Society in Industrializing America: Essays in American Working-Class and Social History* (New York: Vintage Books, 1976), ch. 2; John Reed, "Back of Billy Sunday," *Metropolitan Magazine*, May 1915, pp. 9–12.

5. U.S. Bureau of the Census, *Eleventh Census, 1890: Report on the Statistics of Churches* (Washington, D.C.: GPO, 1894), pp. 94–95; U.S. Bureau of the Census, *Twelfth Census, 1900, Special Reports: Religious Bodies* (Washington, D.C.: GPO, 1910), pp. 476–79; U.S. Bureau of the Census, *Thirteenth Census, 1910: Religious Bodies* (Washington, D.C.: GPO, 1919), pp. 468–71; Richard Jensen, *The Winning of the Midwest: Social and Political Conflict, 1888–1896* (Chicago: University of Chicago Press, 1971), p. 86.

6. Jean Seder, *Voices of Kensington: Vanishing Mills, Vanishing Neighborhoods* (Ardmore, Pa.: Whitmore Publishing Co., 1982), pp.

51–55. For an excellent exploration of the extent of popular Protestantism in another context, see Patrick Joyce, *Work, Society, and Politics: The Culture of the Factory in Later Victorian England* (New Brunswick, N.J.: Rutgers University Press, 1980), ch. 7.

7. Dennis J. Clark, "The Irish Catholics: A Postponed Perspective," in Randall Miller and Thomas Marzik, eds., *Immigrants and Religion in Urban America* (Philadelphia: Temple University Press, 1977), ch. 3; Joan Bland, *Hibernian Crusade: The Story of the Catholic Total Abstinence Union of America* (Washington, D.C.: Catholic University of America Press, 1951); Jay P. Dolan, *Catholic Revivalism: The American Experience, 1830–1900* (Notre Dame, Ind.: University of Notre Dame Press, 1978).

8. For the religion in many IWW songs, see Donald Winters, "The Soul of Solidarity: The Relationship Between the I.W.W. and American Religion in the Progressive Era," unpub. Ph.D. diss., University of Minnesota, 1981, ch. 3; and Philip S. Foner, *History of the Labor Movement in the United States: Vol. 4 The Industrial Workers of the World* (New York: International Publishers, 1965), ch. 6. For Socialist Sunday schools in Kensington, see *New Era*, Sept. 6, 1902; and for Socialist camp meetings, see James R. Green, *Grass-Roots Socialism: Radical Movements in the Southwest, 1895–1943* (Baton Rouge: Louisiana State University Press, 1978), pp. 151–62. For Debs's millennialist fervor, see Nick Salvatore, *Eugene V. Debs: Citizen and Socialist* (Urbana: University of Illinois Press, 1982).

9. Al Priddy, "The Workingman in His Own Church," *Literary Digest*, May 25, 1912, pp. 1105–6.

10. *Ibid.*, p. 1106.

11. *Trades' Union News*, Sept. 17, Nov. 5, Dec. 10, 1908; testimony of Denis Hayes, in U. S. Industrial Commission, *Report on the Relations and Conditions of Capital and Labor Employed in Manufactures and General Business*, 19 vols. (Washington, D.C.: GPO, 1902), vol. 7, p. 922 (hereafter cited as USIC, *Report*). For the importance of these cultural factors to a craft union outlook, see Francis G. Couvares, *The Remaking of Pittsburgh: Class and Culture in an Industrializing City, 1877–1919* (Albany: State University of New York Press, 1984), ch. 2; and Robert Q. Gray, *The Labour Aristocracy of Victorian Edinburgh* (Oxford: Oxford University Press, 1978), ch. 7.

12. Charles Stelzle, "How One Thousand Workingmen Spend Their Time," *The Outlook*, Apr. 4, 1914, pp. 763–64.

13. Mel Piehl, *Breaking Bread: The Catholic Worker and the Origins of Catholic Radicalism in America* (Philadelphia: Temple University Press, 1982), ch. 2; Joseph M. McShane, S.J., *"Sufficiently Radical": Catholicism, Progressivism, and the Bishops' Program of 1919* (Washington, D.C.: Catholic University of America Press, 1986), ch. 1.

14. See note 5, above. The evangelical–liturgical split is taken from

Jensen, *Winning of the Midwest*; and Paul Kleppner, *The Cross of Culture: A Social Analysis of Midwestern Politics, 1850–1900* (New York: Free Press, 1970).

15. *Iron Molders' Journal*, Apr. 1906, p. 272.

16. *International Bookbinder*, Dec. 1914, p. 646; USIC, *Report*, vol. 14, p. 303; *Trades' Union News*, Jan. 6, 1910, Dec. 14, 1911.

17. Testimony of Denis Hayes, USIC, *Report*, vol. 14, p. 103; David Brody, *Workers in Industrial America: Essays on the Twentieth-Century Struggle* (New York: Oxford University Press, 1980), pp. 21–32; James R. Green, *The World of the Worker: Labor in Twentieth-Century America* (New York: Hill and Wang, 1980), ch. 2.

18. *Cigar Makers' Official Journal*, Dec. 1900, p. 5; Paperhangers Local 9, "Minutes," Oct. 13, 1899, in Paperhangers Union Records, Jewish Archives Center, Philadelphia; Carpenters Local 8, "Minutes," 1898–1902, in United Brotherhood of Carpenters and Joiners of America, Local 8 Records, Urban Archives Center, Temple University, Philadelphia, Pa. (hereafter UAC).

19. "Secretary's Report, 1907," in Box 1, Metal Manufacturers' Association of Philadelphia Records, UAC, (hereafter MMAP Records); Gladys L. Palmer, *Union Tactics and Economic Change: A Case Study of Three Philadelphia Textile Unions* (Philadelphia: University of Pennsylvania Press, 1932), p. 16; John Seybold, *The Philadelphia Printing Industry: A Case Study* (Philadelphia: University of Pennsylvania Press, 1949), pp. 26–27; *Weekly Bulletin of the Clothing Trades*, Aug. 13, 1902. See also *Tenth Anniversary United Labor League of Philadelphia and Vicinity* [1889–1899] (Philadelphia, 1899), pamphlet in UAC; and *Trades' Union Directory, No. 1, of Philadelphia and Vicinity* (Philadelphia: H. B. Krefft, 1903).

20. *Weekly Bulletin of the Clothing Trades*, Feb. 26, 1904; Seybold, *Philadelphia Printing*, pp. 26–27; Ken Fones-Wolf, "Employer Unity and the Crisis of the Craftsman," *Pennsylvania Magazine of History and Biography* 107 (July 1983): 450.

21. *Granite Cutters' Journal*, May 1905, p. 7; Bricklayers' Company of Philadelphia, "Minutebook," Sept. 14, 1903, in Historical Society of Pennsylvania, Philadelphia, Pa.

22. Frank Feeney to Joseph Krauskopf, Dec. 15, 1903, in Joseph Krauskopf Papers, UAC; *Weekly Bulletin of the Clothing Trades*, Jan. 27, 1904; *Cigar Makers' Official Journal*, Dec. 1902, p. 6.

23. For legislative gains, see John Price Jackson, *Labor Laws of Pennsylvania* (Harrisburg: Pennsylvania Dept. of Labor and Industry, 1914). For city printing and construction, see Philadelphia Typographical Union, Local 2, "Minutes," Jan. 21, 1911, in Philadelphia Typographical Union Records, Historical Society of Pennsylvania, Philadelphia, Pa. (hereafter cited as PTU, "Minutes"); and United Labor League,

"Minutes" Sept. 10, 1899, microfilm at UAC (hereafter cited as ULL, "Minutes").

24. *Trades' Union News*, Jan. 6, 1910.

25. *New Era*, Sept. 6, 27, Nov. 1, 29, 1902; *Trades' Union News*, June 16, 1904.

26. This paragraph owes its analysis to McShane, "*Sufficiently Radical*," pp. 2–3.

27. Central Labor Union, "Minutes," 1908–1914 (hereafter cited as CLU, "Minutes"); *Trades' Union News*, Dec. 10, 1908.

28. Gray, *Labour Aristocracy*, ch. 7; Geoffrey Crossick, *An Artisan Elite in Victorian Society: Kentish London, 1840–1880* (London: Croom Helm, 1978), ch. 7; and Brian Palmer, *A Culture in Conflict: The Skilled Workers in Hamilton, Ontario, 1860–1914* (Toronto: McGill-Queen's University Press, 1979), ch. 2. All three argue for the importance of seeing respectability as the key to understanding the vitality and continuity of craft unionism.

29. "Circular Letter," Dec. 4, 1903; "Secretary's Report, 1907"; and Earl S. Sparks, "The Metal Manufacturers' Association of Philadelphia, 1903–1953," mimeograph; all in Box 1, MMAP Records.

30. *Weekly Bulletin of the Clothing Trades*, Feb. 26, Mar. 25, 1904.

31. *Typographical Journal*, Dec. 1905, pp. 675–76; John Gay's Sons' Carpet Mills, "Daybook," April 16, 1906, in Historical Society of Pennsylvania, Philadelphia, Pa. For a good overview of the open shop movement, see Philip S. Foner, *History of the Labor Movement in the United States, Vol. 3: The Policies and Practices of the American Federation of Labor, 1900–1909* (New York: International Publishers, 1964), ch. 2.

32. *Trades' Union News*, Oct. 4, 1906; Bricklayers' Company, "Minutebook," Oct. 11, Dec. 13, 1909.

33. Metal Manufacturers' Association of Philadelphia, "Minutes," Dec. 15, May 11, 1910, MMAP Records.

34. *Cigar Makers' Official Journal*, May 1902, pp. 10–11; Patricia A. Cooper, *Once a Cigar Maker: Men, Women, and Work Culture in American Cigar Factories, 1900–1919* (Urbana: University of Illinois Press, 1987), ch. 6; Metal Manufacturers' Association, "Minutes," Feb. 14, 1906, Box 2, MMAP Records; Lee Minton, *Flame and Heart: A History of the Glass Bottle Blowers Association of the United States and Canada* (Washington: Merkle Press, 1961), pp. 42–43; Harry Bates, *Bricklayers' Century of Craftsmanship: A History of the Bricklayers', Masons, and Plasterers International Union of America* (Washington, D.C.: Bricklayers', Masons, and Plasterers International Union of America, 1955), pp. 152–53; Bob Reckman, "Carpentry: The Craft and Trade," in Andrew Zimbalist, ed., *Case Studies on the Labor Process* (New York: Monthly Review Press, 1979), pp. 73–102.

35. Board of Directors, "Minutes," Dec. 19, 1906, Autocar Com-

pany Records, Historical Society of Pennsylvania. For the latter insight, I am particularly grateful to Howell John Harris who shared with me a draft of his forthcoming article on the Metal Manufacturers' Association.

36. Wayne Roberts, "Toronto Metal Workers and the Second Industrial Revolution, 1889–1914," *Labour/Le Travailleur* 6 (Autumn 1980): 49–72; Robert Max Jackson, *The Formation of Craft Labor Markets* (Orlando, Fla.: Academic Press, 1984), ch. 10.

37. Metal Manufacturers' Association, "Minutes," Mar. 13, 1906, Box 2, MMAP Records; U.S. Commission on Industrial Relations, *Final Report and Testimony*, 11 vols. (Washington, D.C.: GPO, 1916) vol. 3, pp. 2883–84 (hereafter cited as USCIR, *Final Report*).

38. *Trades' Union News*, Mar. 16, 1905. For more on the role of efficiency in the ideology of Progressivism, see Samuel Haber, *Efficiency and Uplift: Scientific Management in the Progressive Era, 1890–1920* (Chicago: University of Chicago Press, 1964); esp. pp. 108–110, for Philadelphia.

39. "Secretary's Report, 1907," Box 1, MMAP Records; USCIR, *Final Report*, vol. 3, p. 2917; PTU, "Minutes," June 19, 1910, PTU Records; *Typographical Journal*, Dec. 1906, p. 633.

40. *Weekly Bulletin of the Clothing Trades*, Oct. 7, 1904; Elden Lamar, *The Clothing Workers in Philadelphia: History of Their Struggles for Union and Security* (Philadelphia: Amalgamated Clothing Workers of America, 1940), pp. 50–53; *Eastern Laborer*, June 8, 1907.

41. *Machinists' Monthly Journal*, Nov. 1915, p. 1021; *Eastern Laborer*, June 15, 1907; *Amalgamated Sheet Metal Workers' Journal*, Mar. 15, 1914, pp. 85–86.

42. General membership meeting, "Minutes," Mar. 6, 1906, American Federation of Musicians Local 77 Records, UAC (hereafter cited as AFM #77 Records); Caroline Golab, *Immigrant Destinations* (Philadelphia: Temple University Press, 1977), p. 180; Testimony of Charles Harrah, USIC, *Report*, vol. 3, p. 353; W. E. B. Du Bois, *The Philadelphia Negro: A Social Study* (New York: Benjamin Blom, 1967), p. 323.

43. Lamar, *Clothing Workers*, p. 50; USIC, *Report*, vol. 14, pp. 261, 266; Donald Robinson, *Spotlight on a Union: The Story of the United Hatters, Cap, and Millinery Workers International Union* (New York: Dial Press, 1948), p. 80; General membership meeting, "Minutes," Feb. 5, 1907, Sept. 1, 1908, Jan. 5, 1909, AFM #77 Records; Palmer, *Union Tactics*, pp. 40–44.

44. Palmer, *Union Tactics*, pp. 56–59; Alice Kessler-Harris, *Out to Work: A History of Wage-Earning Women in the United States* (New York: Oxford University Press, 1982), pp. 158–59.

45. *Cigar Makers' Official Journal*, May 1901, p. 7; Cooper, *Once a Cigar Maker*, chs. 8–9; *Typographical Journal*, Aug. 1905, p. 179, Dec. 1905, pp. 675–76, Mar. 1907, p. 305.

46. Martha May, "Bread before Roses: American Workingmen,

Labor Unions, and the Family Wage," in Ruth Milkman, ed., *Women, Work, and Protest: A Century of U.S. Women's Labor History* (Boston: Routledge & Kegan Paul, 1985).

47. Andre Tridon, "The Workers' Only Hope: Direct Action," *Independent*, Jan. 2, 1913, p. 83.

48. Robert A. Christie, *Empire in Wood: A History of the Carpenters' Union* (Ithaca: Cornell University Press 1956), ch. 8; Christopher L. Tomlins, "AFL Unions in the 1930s: Their Performance in Historical Perspective," *Journal of American History* 65 (Mar. 1979): 1022–34. See also the excellent unpublished paper by Elizabeth Fones-Wolf, "Business Unionism, Rank-and-File Rebellion, and the Transformation of AFL Policy," unpublished paper in the author's possession.

49. Lloyd Ulman, *The Rise of the National Trade Union: The Development and Significance of Its Structure, Governing Institutions, and Economic Policies* (Cambridge: Harvard University Press, 1955), ch. 6; David Brody, "Career Leadership and American Trade Unionism," in Frederic Cople Jaher, ed., *The Age of Industrialism in America: Essays in Social Structure and Cultural Values* (New York: Free Press, 1968), pp. 288–300.

50. For an uncritical acceptance of Mulhall's charges, see Foner, *Policies and Practices*, pp. 145, 151. Although it appears plausible, especially since the AFL expelled Feeney for corruption in 1908, a CLU investigation cleared Feeney in 1913. The Printers Union, for one, staunchly defended Feeney; see PTU, "Minutes," July 18, 1913; CLU, "Minutes," July 27, Aug. 24, 1913.

51. PTU, "Minutes," Jan. 21, 1911; *Trades' Union News*, Feb. 7, 1907.

52. *Trades' Union News*, Oct. 4, 1906.

53. *Eastern Laborer*, Apr. 13, 1907; USIC, *Report*, vol. 14; *North American* (Philadelphia), Aug. 10, Sept. 15, 1908; Jackson, *Labor Laws*, pp. 270–75.

54. *Eastern Laborer*, May 18, 1907.

55. *Trades' Union News*, Feb. 4, 11, 1909; CLU, "Minutes," July 10, 1910; *Granite Cutters' Journal*, Oct. 1908, p. 7.

56. *Trades' Union News*, Oct. 18, Nov. 29, Dec. 6, 1906.

57. *Trades' Union News*, Sept. 10, Dec. 10, 1908.

58. *Trades' Union News*, Jan. 28, 1909.

59. See, in particular, Marc Karson, *American Labor Unions and Politics, 1900–1918* (Boston: Beacon Press, 1965) for the significance of Catholic antisocialism to the labor movement. This work's widespread acceptance has somewhat clouded the more subtle, but perhaps more prevalent, influence exerted by Protestantism. A close inspection of the Philadelphia labor press and the CLU "Minutes," 1908–1914, led me to the conclusions that I offer here.

60. Michael A. Mulcaire, *The International Brotherhood of Electri-*

cal Workers: A Study in Trade Union Structure and Functions (Washington, D.C.: Catholic University of America Press, 1923), pp. 9–10; James J. Reid to Samuel Gompers, May 18, 1910, Reel 25, in *American Federation of Labor Records: The Samuel Gompers Era* (Sanford, N.C.: Microfilming Corp. of America, 1979), (hereafter cited as *AFL Records*); W. J. McSorley to R. B. Jeffries, Feb. 5, 1912, in Lathers' Union, Local 58, Records, UAC (hereafter cited as Lathers' Local 58 Records).

61. Philip S. Foner, *Women and the American Labor Movement: From the First Trade Unions to the Present* (New York: Free Press, 1982), pp. 142–44; Barbara Mary Klaczynska, "Working Women in Philadelphia—1900–1930," unpub. Ph.D. diss., Temple University, 1975, pp. 240–43; Philadelphia *Evening Bulletin*, Jan. 18, Feb. 8, 1910.

62. Philip S. Foner, *History of the Labor Movement in the United States, Vol. 5: The AFL in the Progressive Era, 1910–1915* (New York: International Publishers, 1964), ch. 6, offers the best coverage of the Philadelphia general strike.

63. Foner, *The AFL*, pp. 146–49; Ken Fones-Wolf, "Mass Strikes, Corporate Strategies: Baldwin Locomotives and the Philadelphia General Strike of 1910," *Pennsylvania Magazine of History and Biography* 110 (Oct. 1986): 447–57.

64. Philadelphia *Public Ledger*, Mar. 7, 1910, as quoted in Foner, *The AFL*, pp. 154–55.

65. CLU, "Minutes," Mar. 13, 27, 1910.

66. Parker quoted in *Unionism, Industrial and Political: The Philadelphia Street Car Strike and General Strike* (Philadelphia: Socialist Party of Philadelphia, 1910), p. 16; Charles W. Ervin, *Homegrown Liberal: The Autobiography of Charles W. Ervin* (New York: Dodd, Mead & Co., 1954), pp. 39, 55–56; Elizabeth Gurley Flynn, *Rebel Girl: An Autobiography* (New York: International Publishers, 1955), pp. 122–23.

67. *Unionism, Industrial and Political*, pp. 10–11; CLU, "Minutes," Sept. 11, Nov. 13, Dec. 11, 1910.

68. David Montgomery, *Workers' Control in America: Studies in the History of Work, Technology, and Labor Struggles* (New York: Cambridge University Press, 1979), pp. 72–74, 93–95; Green, *World of the Worker*, ch. 3.

69. CLU, "Minutes," Nov. 26, 1911. Blankenburg, however, was not to meet the expectations of Progressive labor leaders.

70. CLU, "Minutes," Jan. 8, Mar. 12, May 7, 1911, Jan. 28, Mar. 24, 1912.

71. CLU, "Minutes," Mar. 12, 1911.

72. On the struggle in the UGW, see *Garment Worker*, Dec. 5, 1913; for the rival building trades council, see McSorley to Jeffries, Feb. 5, 1912, Lathers' Local 58 Records, and *Trades' Union News*, Apr. 10, 1913; for the IWW in the meatcutters, see CLU, "Minutes," July 27,

1913; and on the docks, see William Seraile, "Ben Fletcher, I.W.W. Organizer," *Pennsylvania History* 46 (July 1979): 213–32, and 1913 correspondence in Fred W. Taylor Papers, Historical Society of Pennsylvania. The division in the CLU along the lines mentioned is evinced in debates in "Minutes" on Mar. 12, 1911, Jan. 28, 1912, July 27, 1913; and in *Trades' Union News*, Mar. 9, 16, 23, 1911.

73. James H. Maurer, *It Can Be Done: The Autobiography of James Hudson Maurer* (New York: Rand School Press, 1938), pp. 166–67.

74. CLU, "Minutes," Nov. 9, 1913.

75. *Trades' Union News*, June 12, 1913; CLU, "Minutes," May 7, 1911.

76. "Campaigning with the Men and Religion Teams," *Survey*, Dec. 23, 1911; "What the Men and Religion Forward Movement Actually Accomplished," *Current Literature*, June 1913, p. 673; "The New Evangelism as Contrasted with the Old," *Current Literature*, Nov. 1911, p. 530.

77. *Ibid.*; Harry G. Lefever, "The Involvement of the Men and Religion Forward Movement in the Cause of Labor Justice," *Labor History* 14 (1973): 522; "Campaigning with a Men and Religion Forward Team," *Survey*, Feb. 3, 1912, p. 1678; "Men and Religion Forward Movement" folder, in National Council of Churches Records, Presbyterian Historical Society, Philadelphia, Pa.

78. Elizabeth and Kenneth Fones-Wolf, "Trade-Union Evangelism: Religion and the AFL in the Labor Forward Movement, 1912–1916," in Michael H. Frisch and Daniel J. Walkowitz, eds., *Working-Class America: Essays on Labor, Community, and American Society* (Urbana: University of Illinois Press, 1983), pp. 157–59.

79. *American Federationist*, Oct. 1912, pp. 828–31; Fones-Wolf, "Trade-Union Evangelism," pp. 160–62.

80. Fones-Wolf, "Trade-Union Evangelism," pp. 162–71.

81. Kenneth Fones-Wolf, "Revivalism and Craft Unionism in the Progressive Era: The Syracuse and Auburn Labor Forward Movements of 1913," *New York History* 63 (Oct. 1982): 389–416; Fones-Wolf, "Trade-Union Evangelism," pp. 175–78; *The Syndicalist*, May 1, 1913, p. 36.

82. Montgomery, *Workers' Control*, pp. 73–74; Ken Fones-Wolf, "Religion and Trade-Union Politics in the U.S., 1880–1920," *International Labor and Working Class History*, no. 34 (Fall 1988): 39–55.

83. *Trades' Union News*, July 10, 17, 24, 31, Aug. 7, 1913; CLU, "Minutes," July 27, Aug. 24, 1913; PTU, "Minutes," July 18, 1913; *Garment Worker*, Dec. 5, 1913, July 3, 1914; McSorley to Jeffries, Feb. 5, 1912, in Lathers' Local 58 Records.

84. CLU, "Minutes," Dec. 28, 1913, Jan. 11, Feb. 22, Mar. 8, 1914.

85. CLU, "Minutes," May 10, 24, 1914. Unfortunately the files of

Trades' Union News for the first nine months of 1914, which would have added some detail to the story, do not exist.

86. CLU, "Minutes," May 24, Aug. 9, 1914; *Trades' Union News*, Oct. 22, 1914.

87. *Machinists' Monthly Journal*, Aug. 1913, p. 779; *International Molders' Journal*, Dec. 1914, p. 997; PTU, "Minutes," July 18, Aug. 15, 1914.

88. *Coopers' International Journal*, Dec. 1914, p. 648, Jan. 1915, pp. 30–31; *Trades' Union News*, Nov. 5, 1914; *Garment Worker*, Feb. 12, 1915. Palmer, *A Culture in Conflict*, ch. 2, among others, suggests that the importance of social and cultural events in solidifying trade unionists should not be overlooked.

89. *Trades' Union News*, Dec. 17, 1914; CLU, "Minutes," Sept. 13, 1914.

90. *Trades' Union News*, Nov. 19, Dec. 24, 1914; *Cigar Makers' Official Journal*, Jan. 1915, p. 22; *Garment Worker*, Feb. 27, 1914. This represents a continuation of the power of Christianity for workers a generation after it had supposedly lost much of its influence. See, in particular, Gutman, *Work, Culture, and Society*, ch. 2; and Warren Van Tine, *The Making of the Labor Bureaucrat: Union Leadership in the United States, 1870–1920* (Amherst: University of Massachusetts Press, 1973).

91. Golab, *Immigrant Destinations*, chs. 1, 3; David Ward, *Cities and Immigrants: A Geography of Change in Nineteenth-Century America* (New York: Oxford University Press, 1971), pp. 76–77.

92. Lawrence B. Davis, *Immigrants, Baptists, and the Protestant Mind in America* (Urbana: University of Illinois Press, 1973), pp. 121–28; Rudolph J. Vecoli, "Cult and Occult in Italian-American Culture," in Miller and Marzik, *Immigrants and Religion*, ch. 2; Al Priddy, "Controlling the Passions of Men—In Lawrence," *Outlook*, Oct. 19, 1912, p. 343.

It is important to note, that while *The Catholic Standard and Times* was normally vigilant in warning away Catholics from any connection with Protestant-inspired reform, it was noticeably silent with regard to the Labor Forward Movement. *Catholic Standard and Times*, March 1914–January 1915.

93. Karson, *American Labor Unions and Politics*, ch. 8. Note that the major supporters for seating fraternal delegates from Protestant churches at CLU meetings from 1908 through 1914 frequently came from Irish Catholic building trades leaders. See, CLU, *Minutebook*, 1908–14.

94. "Bulletin: Labor Forward Movement," attached to J. E. Roach to Samuel Gompers, Oct. 2, 1914, Reel 26, *AFL Records*.

95. CLU, "Minutes," June 28, 1914; *Trades' Union News*, Apr. 1, 1915; *American Federationist*, Dec. 1915, p. 1066.

96. PTU, "Minutes," Oct. 17, 1914; *Trades' Union News*, Oct. 29, 1914; General membership meeting, "Minutes," Oct. 16, 1914, AFM #77 Records; *Amalgamated Sheet Metal Workers' Journal*, Dec. 15, 1914, p. 453.

97. For examples of the silencing of opposition to conservative craft union leaders, compare *Stone Cutters' Journal*, Jan. 1915, p. 5; *Amalgamated Sheet Metal Workers' Journal*, Apr. 15, 1914, p. 127, Jan. 15, 1915, p. 2; *Granite Cutters' Journal*, Sept. 1913, p. 13, Dec. 1914, p. 12; *Garment Worker*, July 3, 1914.

98. *Trades' Union News*, Oct. 22, 29, 1914.

99. *Trades' Union News*, Jan. 28, Feb. 4, 11, Mar. 4, 1915.

100. PTU, "Minutes," Feb. 20, 1914; *Trades' Union News*, Apr. 29, May 13, 27, July 29, Sept. 2, 1915.

101. *Trades' Union News*, Mar. 16, 1911.

102. See, for instance, Melvyn Dubofsky, "Abortive Reform: The Wilson Administration and Organized Labor, 1913–1920," in James E. Cronin and Carmen Sirianni, eds., *Work, Community, and Power: The Experience of Labor in Europe and America, 1900–1925* (Philadelphia: Temple University Press, 1983), pp. 197–220; and the important article by Craig Phelan, "William Green and the Ideal of Christian Cooperation," in Melvin Dubofsky and Warren Van Tine, eds., *Labor Leaders in America* (Urbana: University of Illinois Press, 1986), pp. 141–43.

103. For a revealing glimpse into the steadfast support for labor in the Federal Council of Churches, despite the soul-searching engendered by the "age of industrial violence," see Church and Social Service Department, "Minutes," 1910–1912, in National Council of Churches Records.

Chapter 7

1. John Reed, "Back of Billy Sunday," *Metropolitan Magazine*, May 1915, pp. 9–12, 66–72.

2. Donald Disbrow, "The Progressive Movement in Philadelphia, 1910–1916," unpub. Ph.D. diss., University of Rochester, 1956, pp. 209–10. For the boycott of the building trades on the Sunday tabernacle, see *Electrical Worker*, Jan. 1915, p. 25.

3. Johnson quoted in Reed, "Back of Billy Sunday," p. 10; William G. McLoughlin, Jr., *Billy Sunday Was His Real Name* (Chicago: University of Chicago Press, 1955), pp. 66–70.

4. *Electrical Worker*, Jan. 1915, p. 25; *Coopers' International Journal*, Feb. 1915, p. 88; *Trades' Union News*, Jan. 7, 14, 28, 1915.

5. W. J. McSorley to William Crawford, Mar. 27, 1915, in Lathers Union Local 58 Papers, Urban Archives Center, Temple University, Philadelphia, Pa. (hereafter UAC); Reed, "Back of Billy Sunday," p. 12.

6. Disbrow, "Progressive Movement," pp. 207–14. For the anti-

Catholic and anti-radical tide of nativism during the World War I era, see John Higham, *Strangers in the Land: Patterns of American Nativism, 1860–1925* (New York: Atheneum, 1977), pp. 183–86, 194–233.

7. George M. Marsden, *Fundamentalism and American Culture: The Shaping of Twentieth-Century Evangelicalism, 1870–1925* (New York: Oxford University Press, 1980), pp. 118–23. For Sunday's role in the schism in Philadelphia, see McLoughlin, *Billy Sunday*, pp. 223–30, 238–42.

8. Disbrow, "Progressive Movement," pp. 207–14; George H. Nash, III, "Charles Stelzle: Apostle to Labor," *Labor History* 11 (Spring 1970): 151–74; Reed, "Back of Billy Sunday," pp. 9–10. For earlier evidence of a liberal–conservative tension in the Presbyterian Church, see the attitudes expressed about the Men and Religion Forward Movement in *The Presbyterian*, Jan. 31, 1912.

9. Scott Nearing, *The Making of a Radical: A Political Autobiography* (New York: Harper and Row, 1972), pp. 77–92; McLoughlin, *Billy Sunday*, p. 240; *Trades' Union News*, Mar. 4, 1915. I am grateful to the late Fred Zimring for the details of Nearing's firing, which he painstakingly researched in the University of Pennsylvania Archives.

10. Central Labor Union, "Minutes," Nov. 23, 1914, microfilm in UAC (hereafter cited as CLU, "Minutes"); *Trades' Union News*, Mar. 4, 1915; J. Wesley Twelves, *A History of the Diocese of Pennsylvania of the Protestant Episcopal Church, 1784–1968* (Philadelphia: The Diocese, 1969), pp. 34–35.

11. Lawrence B. Davies, *Immigrants, Baptists, and the Protestant Mind in America* (Urbana: University of Illinois Press, 1973), pp. 139–43; also see ch. 5 above.

12. CLU, "Minutes," Nov. 23, 1914; *Trades' Union News*, Mar. 4, 11, 1915; Montgomery County Manufacturers' Association, "Minutes," Apr. 28, 1920, in Box 2, Montgomery County Manufacturers' Association Records, UAC.

13. See, for instance, Ronald W. Schatz, "American Labor and the Catholic Church, 1919–1950," *International Labor and Working Class History* no. 20 (Fall 1981): 46–53; Neil Betten, *Catholic Activism and the Industrial Worker* (Gainesville: University Presses of Florida, 1976); and Steve Fraser, "*Landslayt* and *Paesani*: Ethnic Conflict and Cooperation in the Amalgamated Clothing Workers of America," in Dirk Hoerder, ed., *"Struggle a Hard Battle": Essays on Working–Class Immigrants* (DeKalb: Northern Illinois University Press, 1986), pp. 280–303.

Conclusion

1. American Federation of Labor, *Proceedings*, 1908, p. 125; *Trades' Union News*, Sept. 3, Dec. 17, 1908, Jan. 21, Feb. 11, 1909.

2. John Buenker, *Urban Liberalism and Progressive Reform* (New

York: Norton & Co., 1973); Ken Fones-Wolf, "Religion and Trade Union Politics in the U.S., 1880–1920," *International Labor and Working Class History* no. 34 (Fall 1988): 39–55.

3. In particular, the suggestion that popular participation and commitment to an entire range of voluntary activities changed at this time comes from Stephen Yeo, *Religion and Voluntary Organizations in Crisis* (London: Croom Helm, 1976). He compares the apparent decline in religious sentiment to a similar drop-off in working-class participation in other activities, including trade unionism and socialism. Other works, such as those investigating working-class leisure, while not making the same point, lend support to the picture of the more limited emotional commitment of workers, but place the analysis within the context of the commercialization of leisure. See, for instance, Roy Rosenzweig, *Eight Hours for What We Will: Workers and Leisure in an Industrial City, 1870–1920* (New York: Cambridge University Press, 1983); and Francis G. Couvares, *The Remaking of Pittsburgh: Class and Culture in an Industrializing City, 1877–1919* (Albany: State University of New York Press, 1984).

4. Here, my conclusions parallel the analysis offered by Leon Fink in his article "The New Labor History and the Powers of Historical Pessimism: Consensus, Hegemony, and the Case of the Knights of Labor," *Journal of American History* 75 (June 1988): 115–36.

5. Neil Betten, *Catholic Activism and the Industrial Worker* (Gainesville: University Presses of Florida, 1976), pp. 3–10; Mel Piehl, *Breaking Bread: The Catholic Workers and the Origin of Catholic Radicalism in America* (Philadelphia: Temple University Press, 1982), pp. 29–41; Joseph M. McShane, S.J., *"Sufficiently Radical": Catholicism, Progressivism, and the Bishops' Program of 1919* (Washington, D.C.: Catholic University of America Press, 1986), ch. 1; Marc Karson, *American Labor Unions and Politics, 1900–1918* (Boston: Beacon Press, 1965), ch. 7.

6. See, especially, John Bodnar, *The Transplanted: A History of Immigrants in Urban America* (Bloomington: Indiana University Press, 1985), pp. 92–104, 169–83; Olivier Zunz, "The Synthesis of Social Change: Reflections in American Social History," in Olivier Zunz, ed., *Reliving the Past: The Worlds of Social History* (Chapel Hill: University of North Carolina Press, 1985), pp. 82–92.

A Note on Sources

THE decision to focus this study on Philadelphia was not based on an assumption of its representativeness. Instead, while still in the early stages of my research, I had the good fortune to work in the Urban Archives Center (UAC) at Temple University. It was through the serendipity of plumbing the range and depth of its collections that I discovered the importance of broadening the time frame of my original project while concentrating on a single city.

My initial intention was to examine the Labor Forward Movement by comparing the revivals in several regions, including the Philadelphia area. But that changed as I encountered other related and equally fascinating episodes documented in the UAC collections, such as the conflict in the YM and YWCAs, spanning 1890 to 1919, or the struggles over child labor and Sabbatarianism running from the 1870s to 1920. These instances helped me to see that I did not want to investigate an anachronism, but rather a relationship. The importance of explaining the specific incident —the trade-union revival—receded, and was replaced by more general questions linked to the social history of religion, class, politics, and organized labor. Yet if I was to gain any true insights about how workers competed for power within the American social order, and what role Christianity played in that contest, it seemed to me that a local study was necessary. The sources for exploring Philadelphia, which I already knew were available, made that choice a foregone conclusion.

Since my conclusion and my footnotes throughout discuss the historiographical context of this study and the secondary works most influential in shaping my thinking, this note will focus on the primary sources consulted. Anyone interested in a more or less complete bibliography should check my dissertation.

The largest collection of Philadelphia trade-union archives is in the UAC. While the records of American Federation of Musicians Local 77, Operative Plasterers International Association Local 8, United Brotherhood of Carpenters and Joiners of America Local 8, Tile Layers Local 6, and Wood, Wire, and Metal Lathers Local 58 were of marginal importance for examining how workers experienced religion, they were invaluable for obtaining insight into the cultural world of craft unionism and its relationship to churches. Also important in this respect were the records of Paperhangers Local 9, formerly at the Jewish Archives Center of Philadelphia (now at the Balch Institute), and the records of the Philadelphia Typographical Union Local 2 at the Historical Society of Pennsylvania. They helped chart the ebb and flow of Philadelphia labor and enabled me to make connections to what at times appeared to be the separate worlds of religion, politics, and social reform. These collections helped to revise my original picture of "pure and simple" craft unions along the lines suggested by Michael Kazin's *Barons of Labor* and Patricia Cooper's *Once a Cigarmaker*. Both of these books appeared after work on the manuscript was largely completed; however, their sophisticated analyses of craft-union culture and politics gave me more confidence in my own analysis.

More central to the study of labor–religion interaction were the minutebooks of the United Labor League (1892–1900) and the Central Labor Union (1908–1914). I first read through these at the headquarters of the Philadelphia Council, AFL–CIO, through the courtesy of its president, Edward Toohey. Since then, they have been microfilmed by the UAC and are available there. These books first alerted me to what became important dimensions of my study because of the time these city-wide labor federations devoted to discussion of political and social reform and because of the influence that Protestant clergy and lay activists exerted in those discussions. The total absence of Catholic priests, as well as the positions taken by Irish Catholic trade unionists in debates over social reform and political alliances with Protestants, surprised me and shattered many of my expectations. Together with the information contained in the records of the individual union locals cited above, future historians should find it difficult to ignore the political initiatives of organized labor or to make any easy generalizations about the Progressive-Era coalitions responsible for urban liberal reform.

The Terence V. Powderly Papers at Catholic University shed very little light on the Philadelphia scene during the period of the Knights of Labor. They were better, however, at uncovering the variety of rank-and-file attitudes toward churches. The Samuel Gompers *Letterbooks* at the Library of Congress and the American Federation of Labor Records at the State Historical Society of Wisconsin (SHSW) and the AFL–CIO headquarters were somewhat more useful for events in Philadelphia, particularly the files on the Philadelphia Labor Forward Movement in the AFL Convention files. The Thomas Phillips Papers and the International Workingmen's Association Records at the SHSW, as well as the minutebooks of the Social Democratic Workingmen's Party–Philadelphia Branch at the Library of Congress, provided a good understanding of late nineteenth-century labor radicalism. The debates in the Central Labor Union "Minutes" in the twentieth century revealed the strength of socialism in the local labor movement.

The contemporary labor press was perhaps the most important source for labor attitudes. Weekly labor newspapers in Philadelphia consulted for this study included *The Trades* (1878–1880), *The Workingman* (1882), *The Tocsin* (1883–1887), *Industrial Republic* (1891), *New Era* (1901–1903), *Eastern Laborer* (1907), and *Trades' Union News* (1904–1917). The short existence of many of these papers belies their lively character and the range of topics covered. Through the labor press, one begins to realize how the popular Christianity of the working class intersected with mainstream religious organizations. In addition, both the *Public Ledger* (a local daily), and *The Press* carried substantial reports on labor activities. The *North American* was important for covering middle-class reform and the *Catholic Standard* was the best source for understanding the Catholic Church and its shifting attitudes toward organized labor.

The monthly magazines of national trade unions often carried letters by workers in Philadelphia or reports on events in the city written by organizers or union officials. Especially useful for this study were the *Cigar Makers' Official Journal*, the *Electrical Worker*, the *Coopers' International Journal*, the *Garment Worker*, the *International Molder's Journal*, the *Machinists' Monthly Journal*, the *Typographical Journal*, and the *Weekly Bulletin of the Clothing Trades*.

Finally, government documents and Congressional investigations hold a wealth of information on the culture and ideology of workers. The published census volumes not only had information on population characteristics and occupations but also on religion. The reports of the Pennsylvania Secretary of Internal Affairs and the U.S. Commissioner of Labor contained invaluable material on changes in production methods, working-class standards of living, and strikes and lockouts. Even more important, the testimonies taken at three government investigations—the U.S. Senate Committee Upon the Relations Between Capital and Labor (4 vols., 1885), the U.S. Industrial Commission (19 vols., 1902), and the U.S. Commission on Industrial Relations (11 vols., 1916) provide a close reading of what was actually on the minds of workers and unionists. Philadelphia workers testified at all three investigations.

The activities of Social-Gospel Christians are well documented. The UAC provided access to the archives of Christian social service agencies and reform organizations unsurpassed by any other repository I know for documenting a single city. The records of settlements, social service exchanges, child-labor opponents, and urban and labor reformers contributed to my understanding of the broad sweep of organized labor's interaction with Christian-inspired political activism. In addition to the archives of the Housing Association, the Octavia Hill Association, University Settlements, the Philadelphia–Camden Social Service Exchange, and the Philadelphia Child Labor Association, among others, the UAC also holds an extensive collection of annual reports from an even larger number of Christian voluntary organizations. Particularly useful for my purposes were the reports from the Lighthouse, the Home Missionary Society, the College Settlement Association, the New Century Guild, the Philadelphia County Sabbath School Association, the Protestant Episcopal City Mission, the Philadelphia Society for Organizing Charity, the Workingman's Club of Germantown, and the City Mission Society of the Evangelical Lutheran Church.

The records of the YM and YWCAs at the UAC deserve special mention. The wonderful cache of records documenting the city-wide boards and the individual branches debunked the myth that the Ys were principally middle-class institutions. More importantly, the way that these records reveal how class tensions penetrated Christian voluntary organizations (explored in Chapter 5) really shaped the subsequent direction of this study. I should also, at this point, acknowledge my debt to Mrs. Belle Henderson of Philadelphia, a long-time YWCA activist. My first exposure to the complexity of the Ys came in discussions with her as I boxed up YWCA records for transfer to the UAC. As I uncovered some of the incidents mentioned in Chapter 5, she confirmed my hunches. She has an abiding commitment to both the flattering and unflattering chapters of Y history and is an important part of a progressive tradition in an organization far more important than I previously realized.

The Presbyterian Historical Society in Philadelphia held several important collections in addition to a fine library on religion. Central to this study were the records of the National Council of Churches and its predecessor the Federal Council of Churches of Christ in America. The minutes of the Social Service Department, the files on the Men and Religion Forward Movement, and the pamphlets contained in these records were instrumental in illuminating the local scene as well as the national context of the Protestant Social Gospel and the attitudes of reformers toward organized labor. Also useful were the records of the Labor Temple of New York, which shed light on Charles Stelzle, and the records of the North Philadelphia Presbytery. The Presbyterian Historical Society, as well as the Lutheran Seminary in Mount Airy, the UAC, the Philadelphia Free Library, and the Historical Society of Pennsylvania (HSP) also held valuable pamphlets detailing the activities of the Episcopal, Baptist, Methodist, Lutheran, and Presbyterian Churches in Philadelphia. Furthermore, I consulted *The Presbyterian*, *The Lutheran*, and *Lutheran Church Review* on either a weekly or monthly basis for a better understanding of two important denominations, as I did *Survey*, which is arguably the most important Social-Gospel reform magazine.

I was surprised and disappointed by the paucity of useful material in the records of individual congregations that I surveyed at the Presbyterian Historical Society and the HSP. Published reports, pamphlets, and the writings of clergymen active with labor organizations were more rewarding; in general, city-wide bodies discussed social issues more frequently than individual congregations, and voluntary organizations seemed to generate more conflict than churches. Since I was far more concerned with labor than with religious organizations, however, I probably missed much otherwise interesting material. A social history of the religious and voluntary organizations of Philadelphia, along the lines of Stephen Yeo's study of Reading, England, would be a fascinating contribution.

On the business community's connection with Protestanism, there was ample material. Of greatest use were pamphlets and reports of voluntary organizations in the UAC, the Free Library, the HSP, and the Presbyterian Historical Society. Also revealing were the records of the Metal Manufacturers Association of Philadelphia and of the YMCAs at the UAC; less important but still useful were the papers of Samuel M. Vauclain, the "Daybook" of John and James Gay, and the "Minutebook" of the Bricklayers' Company of Philadelphia, all held by the Manuscripts Department of the HSP. The papers of Russell Conwell at Temple University were a major disappointment in documenting the Gospel of Wealth in the city. However, employer testimony in the three government investigations mentioned earlier were especially enlightening as to the moral perceptions of Philadelphia's business community.

Index

AMERICAN CIVILIZATION

A series edited by Allen F. Davis

Gospel Hymns and Social Religion: The Rhetoric of Nineteenth-Century Revivalism, by Sandra S. Sizer

Social Darwinism: Science and Myth in Anglo-American Social Thought, by Robert C. Bannister

Twentieth Century Limited: Industrial Design in America, 1925–1939, by Jeffrey L. Meikle

Charlotte Perkins Gilman: The Making of a Radical Feminist, 1860–1896, by Mary A. Hill

Inventing the American Way of Death, 1830–1920, by James J. Farrell

Anarchist Women, 1870–1920, by Margaret S. Marsh

Woman and Temperance: The Quest for Power and Liberty, 1873–1900, by Ruth Bordin

Hearth and Home: Preserving a People's Culture, by George W. McDaniel

The Education of Mrs. Henry Adams, by Eugenia Kaledin

Class, Culture, and the Classroom: The Student Peace Movement of the 1930s, by Eileen Eagan

Fathers and Sons: The Bingham Family and the American Mission, by Char Miller

An American Odyssey: Elia Kazan and American Culture, by Thomas H. Pauly

Silver Cities: The Photography of American Urbanization, 1839–1915, by Peter B. Hales

Actors and American Culture, 1880–1920, by Benjamin McArthur

Saving the Waifs: Reformers and Dependent Children, 1890–1917, by LeRoy Ashby

A Woman's Ministry: Mary Collson's Search for Reform as a Unitarian Minister, a Hull House Social Worker, and a Christian Science Practitioner, by Cynthia Grant Tucker

Depression Winters: New York Social Workers and the New Deal, by William W. Bremer

Forever Wild: Environmental Aesthetics and the Adirondack Forest Preserve, by Philip G. Terrie

Art and Labor: Ruskin, Morris, and the Craftsman Ideal in America, by Eileen Boris

Paths into American Culture: Psychology, Medicine, and Morals, by John C. Burnham

Pastoral Inventions: Rural Life in Nineteenth-Century American Art and Culture, by Sarah Burns

Before It's Too Late: The Child Guidance Movement in the United States, 1922–1945, by Margo Horn

Mary Heaton Vorse: The Life of an American Insurgent, by Dee Garrison

Mind's Eye, Mind's Truth: FSA Photography Reconsidered, by James Curtis

Trade Union Gospel: Christianity and Labor in Industrial Philadelphia, 1865–1915, by Ken Fones-Wolf